The Character of
Theology

The Character of
Theology

*An Introduction to Its Nature,
Task, and Purpose*

John R. Franke

Baker Academic
Grand Rapids, Michigan

Published by Baker Academic
a division of Baker Publishing Group
P.O. Box 6287, Grand Rapids, MI 49516-6287
www.bakeracademic.com

Printed in the United States of America

Library of Congress Cataloging-in-Publication Data
Franke, John R.
    The character of theology : an introduction to its nature, task, and purpose /
John R. Franke.
        p.   cm.
    Includes bibliographical references and index.
    ISBN 0-8010-2641-5 (pbk.)
    1. Theology, Doctrinal. I. Title.
BT65.F68 2005
230—dc22   200500169

Material that appeared in previous form, as noted on page 10, is used by permission of the following: *Westminster Theological Journal*, P.O. Box 27009, Philadelphia, PA 19118; *Books & Culture*, 465 Gundersen Drive, Carol Stream, IL 60188; *Christian History*, 465 Gundersen Drive, Carol Stream, IL 60188; and Reformation & Revival Ministries, P.O. Box 88216, Carol Stream, IL 60811.

Contents

153082

Preface

It is better to be blatant than latent. Over the years I have spent in the classroom, I have discovered a great deal of wisdom in this simple phrase and have tried to conduct my teaching accordingly. It assumes that the long-standing notions of academic neutrality and objectivity are both overrated and unattainable. This does not mean that teachers do not have an obligation to maintain intellectual integrity to the best of their ability and to treat alternative and opposing points of view with fairness and charity. Nor can they come to their intellectual and pedagogical tasks with minds that are not open to the possibility of change. It does assume, however, that teachers, as well as students, come to their work from a particular context and vantage point, with particular opinions and outlooks, and that these shape not only their approach to teaching but its content as well. In light of this state of affairs, it seems that students have a right to know something about the assumptions and perspectives of their teachers at the outset of an intellectual endeavor and that teachers ought to be willing to provide some preliminary disclosure with respect to these matters. For this reason, I always start my courses with a brief account of my ecclesial and theological location and commitments as well as giving some indication as to how these have shaped my perspective on the matters we will be discussing. It would seem that readers are entitled to no less.

Three perspectives on the Christian faith have significantly shaped my Christian identity and my conception of theology: evangelical Protestantism, the Reformed tradition, and ecumenical orthodoxy. From the beginning of my Christian experience, throughout the entire course of my postsecondary educational career, including undergraduate, seminary, and doctoral studies, and over the past twelve years as a faculty member of an evangelical seminary, I have been nurtured and formed by evangelical communities and convictions with an emphasis on the importance of a personal relationship with Jesus Christ, sharing the faith through personal witness and evangelism, and the centrality of the Bible for Christian faith and life. Evangelical instincts and intuitions have deeply influenced my sense of what it means to be a Christian to the point that even where I dissent from aspects of North American evangelicalism, I do so for reasons that seem to me, at least, to be very evangelical.

By the time I graduated from Nyack College, I would also have called myself a Calvinist, and while in seminary and graduate school, this broad and fairly generic descriptor ripened into a full-bodied commitment to the ecclesial and confessional tradition of Reformed Protestantism. It was particularly from the Reformed tradition that I learned about the church and its significance for the mission of God in the world. This fueled a strong interest in the history of the church and theology, resulting in an extensive reading program and graduate work in historical theology. What particularly impressed me in this study was the rich diversity of Christian expression arising from the interpretation of Scripture. I also came to appreciate the presence of an ecumenical consensus on certain central matters of the faith that seemed to provide some important common ground in the midst of this diversity. I developed a conviction that ecumenical orthodoxy should inform the work of biblical interpretation and theological reflection as an ongoing conversation partner. These three traditions and perspectives shape and inform my thinking with regard to Christian faith and theology in one way or another and are in evidence throughout this book.

In addition to these theological perspectives, I have also come to use the term *postmodern* to identify myself. By this I do not mean that I endorse everything that claims to be postmodern, much of which I regard as incompatible with Christian faith. What I do mean is that insofar as a set of general philosophical beliefs, attitudes, and intellectual tendencies related to such matters as epistemology, language, and the nature of reality can be identified as postmodern rather than modern, I find much more affinity with the postmodern perspective and believe that it comports far better with Christian faith than does the modern. Some will object, particularly among evangelicals, that we should not adopt any such preferences, be they modern or postmodern, but instead maintain only a "biblical" outlook. As I hope to show in this book, such a view is simply untenable, and insistence on it will serve only to make us less willing to subject our own beliefs and practices, on the assumption that they are simply biblical, to the critical scrutiny that all views deserve if they are to be truly disciplined by the Word of God. What we do need to remember in the use of postmodern thought is that the intention of theology is never to be conformed to postmodern or any other type of reason but rather to bear faithful witness to the gospel of Jesus Christ.

This book attempts to provide an introduction to the character of theology—its nature, task, and purpose—which accounts for the diversity of the Christian faith, while maintaining a commitment to truth, the authority of Scripture, and ecumenical Christian orthodoxy. In so doing, it seeks to overcome the explicit and/or implicit assumption of much theology that its goal is to discover the right system or model of doctrine taught in Scripture and then to use this as a grid through which to interpret and apply Scripture. In this way of looking at things, all systems and models other than the chosen one are deemed defective and in need of correction. This work seeks to provide an alternative to this way of thinking about theology through the articulation of a nonfoundational and contextual approach that promotes an open and flexible construal of theology that is inherently self-critical and reforming. In light of my history and social location in conservative churches and institutions and to the extent that the approach offered here constitutes a genuine alternative to accepted and established norms for conservative theology, this work may be regarded as postconservative. As such, it seeks to make common cause with postliberal thinkers in the pursuit of the "generous orthodoxy" envisioned by the late Yale theologian Hans Frei, who coined the term to describe an understanding of Christianity that contains elements of both liberal and conservative thought while seeking to move beyond the views of knowledge and certainty that liberals and conservatives hold in common.

This book arises from two particular contexts. The first is the teaching of an introductory course in theology at Biblical Seminary for the past twelve years. Extensive formal and informal interaction with students and colleagues over the years, along with their critical and constructive responses and suggestions concerning the course, have shaped and honed every part of this project. I have learned a great deal from my students and am grateful for their attention, patience, curiosity, and inquisitiveness. The second is the attempt to write about the things I was learning in order to clarify and sharpen my thinking and as a means of extending the conversation through the wider dissemination of the ideas that were emerging in my mind through the process of teaching the class. The most significant of these efforts was my collaboration with Stanley Grenz in the writing of *Beyond Foundationalism: Shaping Theology in a Postmodern Context* (Louisville: Westminster John Knox, 2001). The present book is a sort of prequel to *Beyond Foundationalism* that introduces, recapitulates, refines, and anticipates its major themes by providing an exposition of the nature, task, and purpose of theology that gives rise to the methodological proposal developed in the earlier work. It is also intended to be more accessible to beginning theology students in college and seminary courses as well as to those in the church who are seeking alternative approaches to theology that will better serve the emerging church of the twenty-first century.

In addition, the book also draws on a number of essays I published in a variety of contexts that are related to its concerns in one way or another. These include the following: "Reforming Theology: Toward a Postmodern Reformed Dogmatics," *Westminster Theological Journal* 65, no. 1 (2003): 1–26; "Postmodern and Reformed? A Response to Professors Trueman and Gaffin," *Westminster Theological Journal* 65, no. 2 (2003): 331–43; "God Hidden and Wholly Revealed: Karl Barth, Postmodernity, and Evangelical Theology," *Books & Culture* 9, no. 5 (2003): 16–17, 40–42; "Origen: Friend or Foe?" *Christian History* 22, no. 4 (2003): 18–23; "Postmodern Reformed Dogmatics: Reformed Theology and the Postmodern Turn," *Reformation & Revival Journal* 13, no. 1 (2004): 117–32; "Postmodern Reformed Dogmatics: Indirect Revelation and the Knowledge of God," *Reformation & Revival Journal* 13, no. 2 (2004): 109–23; "Postmodern Reformed Dogmatics: Scripture, Culture, and the Local Character of Theology," *Reformation & Revival Journal* 13, no. 3 (2004): 129–43; and "Postmodern Reformed Dogmatics: Scripture, Tradition, and the Confessional Character of Theology," *Reformation & Revival Journal* 13, no. 4 (2004): 141–53. I extend my thanks to all of these publishers for granting permission to include previously published material in this volume.

In the course of working on this book, I have enjoyed the support and encouragement of the faculty, staff, and students of Biblical Theological Seminary. I am particularly grateful to my colleagues on the faculty for taking the time to listen patiently to the development of these ideas over the years and for their generosity and charity even in regard to those areas where we disagree. I have also had the opportunity to present and discuss portions of this project at various stages in its development in a number of academic settings, including Bible College of New Zealand, Westminster Theological Seminary, London Bible College, Prairie Bible College, Briercrest Biblical Seminary, and Canadian Theological Seminary. For the warm hospitality, stimulating conversation, and helpful criticism that I received at each of these schools, I express my sincere thanks to all those involved.

I would also like to express my particular thanks to the following individuals: David Dunbar, president of Biblical Seminary, for supporting my work over the years and providing a context in which to grow and develop theologically and professionally; Todd Mangum, my colleague in the theology department at Biblical, for being a generous and insightful conversation partner as well as a trusted friend; Robert N. Hosack, senior acquisitions editor for Baker Academic, for his support of this project from its inception and his constant encouragement while waiting patiently for its completion; and Stan Grenz for his generous investment in the development of my professional life and his ongoing support, encouragement, and friendship.

When I entered Biblical Seminary as a student in the fall of 1984, my first class was Old Testament history with Dr. Robert Vannoy, one of the founding faculty members of the school when it opened its doors in 1971. It quickly became my favorite class during that first semester. The combination of his exemplary and committed Christian scholarship, his charitable spirit, and an evident passion to teach the message of the Bible to his students left a lasting impression on me. Dr. Vannoy also served as my advisor over the course of my seminary career, and in that capacity I got to know him a bit better in the context of the advisor-advisee chapels that were then a staple of community life at the school. Here I saw a further, more personal manifestation of his confidence in the goodness of God and his devotion to Christ as well as his dedication and commitment to the young school he had helped to found. When I joined the faculty in 1993, Bob warmly welcomed me back as a colleague and a friend and has consistently encouraged me in my development as a teacher and a scholar. In gratitude for his faithful service to Christ, his example of committed Christian scholarship, and his sacrificial support of the ministry of Biblical Theological Seminary, I dedicate this volume to Professor J. Robert Vannoy.

Stanley Grenz died suddenly and unexpectedly of a brain aneurysm on March 12, 2005. His loss will be felt deeply by his family, friends, colleagues, and many others who were enriched by his life and ministry. He enthusiastically supported this project from its inception and through its various stages. He had a chance to see the page proofs when we were last together in San Diego in early February and looked forward to its publication later in the year. While his passing tinges the culmination of the project with sorrow for me, I also hope that it will help to expand the influence of his vision for the future of evangelical theology, particularly among emerging leaders and thinkers in whom he invested so much of his time, energy, and belief.

1

Doing Theology Today

Theology is disciplined consideration and exploration of the content of divine revelation. This succinct statement provides a fairly common and commendable way to define theology. It affirms that the work of theology involves careful and ordered thought and reflection and that it is dependent and focused on revelation. However, for all its strengths, such a definition, coupled with the etymology of the word *theology* (the study of God), can give the appearance that the knowledge of God is theology's only major concern. The sixteenth-century Reformer John Calvin, at the opening of his classic, seminal work in theology, *Institutes of the Christian Religion*, asserts that "nearly all the wisdom we possess, that is to say, true and sound wisdom, consists of two parts: the knowledge of God and of ourselves."[1] According to Calvin, the knowledge of God and the knowledge of ourselves are inextricably bound together and mutually dependent on each other in such a way that we cannot properly claim to possess an appropriate and adequate grasp of either apart from a knowledge of the other. As he puts it, "Without knowledge of self there is no knowledge of God" but also, "Without knowledge of God there is no knowledge of self."[2] To know ourselves as human be-

1. John Calvin, *Institutes of the Christian Religion*, ed. John T. McNeill, vol. 1 (Philadelphia: Westminster, 1960), 1.1.1.
2. Ibid., 1.1.1–2.

13

ings we must know God, and to know God we must know ourselves. A proper understanding of these interconnected and dialectical aspects of knowledge leads to "true and sound wisdom."

Calvin's observation continues to provide a helpful model for reflecting on the character of theology and suggests that we must always be attentive not only to the knowledge of God but also to the knowledge of ourselves as human beings if we hope to practice an approach to theology that leads to wisdom. We must also be attentive to the fact that the knowledge of God and the knowledge of ourselves are not available to us in the form of timeless and undisputed teaching. Instead, we learn from the history of Christian thought that doctrines and conceptions of God and the nature of the human condition, as well as many other significant matters, have been developed and formulated in the context of numerous social, historical, and cultural settings and have in turn been shaped by these settings. This suggests that in the discipline of theology we must take account of the particular social and intellectual settings in which we engage in theological reflection and exploration. This is part of the knowledge of ourselves that is crucial for theology. In the contemporary setting, our knowledge of self is intimately bound up with the postmodern condition and our awareness of the thoroughly situated nature of all human thought and activity. Doing theology that promotes true and sound wisdom means bearing faithful witness to the God revealed in Jesus Christ in ways that are appropriate to our status as finite creatures in the midst of ever-shifting contexts and circumstances. It also means being responsible to the church, the body of Christ, in its historical and global manifestations.

Thinking about theology in this way raises questions concerning the character of theology. What is theology? What is the nature and status of theological reflection as practiced by finite human beings? How can we talk responsibly about the infinite God? What does theology attempt to accomplish? What is its purpose? These questions are of considerable importance to the life and witness of the church. As J. Andrew Kirk maintains, in considering such questions, we are "investigating an operation on which hangs in large part the healthy life of the whole Christian community, for if we do not get the theological task right, every other task is likely to be out of kilter."[3] To reveal the opportunities and challenges facing the church as it seeks to do theology in the contemporary setting and to provide some background for a discussion of the character of theology, this chapter examines the contemporary situation in which the practice of theology takes place and the cur-

3. J. Andrew Kirk, *The Mission of Theology and Theology as Mission* (Valley Forge, PA: Trinity Press, 1997), 2.

rent state of the discipline, particularly as it relates to developments in liberal and conservative approaches to theology. It also provides a basic description of theology and a working definition. The next chapter focuses on the subject of theology, the Triune God revealed in Jesus Christ. The background provided by these two chapters will facilitate an introduction to the nature, task, and purpose of theology taken up in the final three chapters.

The Postmodern Situation

The current cultural context in North America, as well as in much of the world, can be generally and felicitously labeled and described as "postmodern." At the beginning of the twenty-first century, the intellectual milieu of Western thought and culture is in a state of transition precipitated by the perceived failure of the philosophical, societal, and ethical assumptions of the modern world spawned by the Enlightenment. This transition has been spurred on and marked by the emergence of postmodern theory and its thoroughgoing critique of the modern project, with its quest for certain, objective, and universal knowledge. It has also involved a series of disparate provisional attempts to engage in new forms of conversation and intellectual pursuit in the aftermath of modernity. One observer notes that when we survey "the panorama of contemporary thought it is evident in field after field, in discipline after discipline, that a significant critique of modernity has arisen along with a discussion of a paradigm change. The upshot is that the kind of change under discussion is not incremental or piecemeal, but structural and thoroughgoing."[4]

This state of affairs raises the question as to the proper conception of the postmodern situation. It is important to realize that a precise understanding of postmodernity is notoriously difficult to pin down. Yet in spite of the fact that there is no consensus concerning the meaning of the term, it has become almost a commonplace to refer to the contemporary cultural situation as "postmodern." The lack of clarity about the term has been magnified by the vast array of interpreters who have attempted to comprehend and appropriate postmodern thought. Paul Lakeland observes that there are "probably a thousand different self-appointed commentators on the postmodern phenomenon and bewildering discrepancies between the ways many of these authors understand the

4. Dan R. Stiver, "The Uneasy Alliance between Evangelicalism and Postmodernism: A Reply to Anthony Thiselton," in *The Challenge of Postmodernism: An Evangelical Engagement,* ed. David Dockery (Wheaton: BridgePoint, 1995), 243.

term *postmodern* and its cognates."[5] In the context of this lack of clarity about the postmodern phenomenon, the term has come to signify widely divergent hopes and concerns among those who are attempting to address the emerging cultural and intellectual shift it implies.

This situation has led David Tracy to assert that there is really "no such phenomenon as postmodernity."[6] Instead, there are only numerous and varied expressions of the postmodern condition. In this context, Kevin Vanhoozer speaks of the postmodern condition as "something that is at once intellectual/theoretical and cultural/practical, a condition that affects modes of thought as well as modes of embodiment." He points out that a condition should be differentiated from a position, a particular point of view on a certain idea, issue, or question, as something that is "altogether more diffuse, an environment in which one lives and moves and, in some sense, has one's being."[7] In this sense, the postmodern condition is not something we simply choose to affirm or deny. It is rather a descriptor of the social and intellectual context in which we function. Yet in spite of the numerous manifestations of the postmodern condition and the divergent opinions and struggles concerning the portrayal of postmodernity in various domains and situations, Steven Best and Douglas Kellner maintain "that there is a shared discourse of the postmodern, common perspectives, and defining features that coalesce into an emergent postmodern paradigm."[8] However, since this new postmodern paradigm is emerging but neither mature nor regnant, it continues to be hotly contested by both those who desire to embrace it for particular purposes and those who find reason to oppose it. Best and Kellner suggest that the representations of this emerging paradigm that take shape in the context of intellectual, social, and cultural activity constitute "a borderland between the modern and something new for which the term 'postmodern' has been coined."[9] Here we will focus on postmodern thought as it pertains to the practice of theology as part of the Christian witness to this borderland culture.

The intellectual and cultural transition from modernity to postmodernity is generating serious questions for the discipline of theology.

---

5. Paul Lakeland, *Postmodernity: Christian Identity in a Fragmented Age* (Minneapolis: Fortress, 1997), ix–x.

6. David Tracy, "Fragments: The Spiritual Situation of Our Times," in *God, the Gift, and Postmodernism*, ed. John D. Caputo and Michael J. Scanlon (Bloomington: Indiana University Press, 1999), 170.

7. Kevin J. Vanhoozer, ed., *The Cambridge Companion to Postmodern Theology* (Cambridge: Cambridge University Press, 2003), 4.

8. Steven Best and Douglas Kellner, *The Postmodern Turn* (New York: Guilford Press, 1997), xi.

9. Ibid., xiii.

However, while some have raised concerns about changes in the discipline due to shifting intellectual and cultural circumstances, it is important to remember that such challenges are not new for Christian faith, particularly given its missional impulse. The expression of Christianity and Christian teaching have taken shape and been revised and reformed in the context of numerous cultural and historical circumstances. Throughout this history, the discipline of theology has shown itself to be remarkably adaptable in its task of assisting the church in extending and establishing the message of the gospel in a wide variety of contexts. If we are to address faithfully and appropriately the opportunities and challenges presented by the contemporary setting, we must understand the nature of the cultural transition that is occurring as well as its significance for the theological discipline. In short, we must come to terms with the challenge of doing theology in a postmodern context.

One common response among Christian thinkers to the emergence of postmodern thought has been to view it primarily as a threat to Christian faith. Catholic theologian Richard John Neuhaus suggests that many have reacted to postmodernity by connecting it with relativism and subjectivism and calling it the enemy of basic thinking about moral truth.[10] This sort of response has been characteristic of thinkers across the theological spectrum. At the heart of this critique is the consistent identification of postmodern thought with relativism and nihilism. In this conception, postmodernism is viewed as fundamentally antithetical to Christian faith. Merold Westphal comments that at "varying degrees along a spectrum that runs from mildly allergic to wildly apoplectic," many Christian thinkers "are inclined to see postmodernism as nothing but warmed-over Nietzschean atheism, frequently on the short list of the most dangerous anti-Christian currents of thought as an epistemological relativism that leads ineluctably to moral nihilism. Anything goes."[11] This view has been especially common among conservative and evangelical Christian thinkers who have commonly tended to assume that postmodern thought is inherently opposed to the quest for truth, even the general notion of truth, and by extension the particular truth claims of the Christian faith.

One reason for this assumption has to do with a misunderstanding concerning the nature of metanarratives. Jean-François Lyotard famously summed up postmodernity in the following manner: "Simplifying to the

10. Richard John Neuhaus, "A Voice in the Relativistic Wilderness," *Christianity Today,* February 7, 1994, 34.

11. Merold Westphal, *Overcoming Onto-theology: Toward a Postmodern Christian Faith* (New York: Fordham University Press, 2001), ix.

extreme, I define *postmodern* as incredulity toward metanarratives."[12] This statement has led numerous Christian thinkers to conclude that, since Christianity is a metanarrative, postmodern thought must be incompatible with Christian faith. However, Lyotard's account of the postmodern condition as incredulity toward metanarratives need not be viewed as a critique of the Christian gospel. Westphal makes a distinction between the Christian *mega*narrative and a *meta*narrative, noting that in philosophical discourse the prefix "meta" signifies a difference of level rather than of size. "A metanarrative is a metadiscourse in the sense of being a second-level discourse not directly about the world but about first-level discourse."[13] As James K. A. Smith points out, for Lyotard, metanarratives are a distinctly modern phenomenon in that they not only attempt to articulate a meganarrative or grand story but also assert the ability to *legitimate* the story, along with its entailments, by an appeal to universal, autonomous reason.[14]

According to Westphal, the issue of legitimation is "absolutely central for Lyotard, the tight link between modernity and metanarrative in his mind."[15] Hence, Lyotard's incredulity refers to the suspicion and critique of the modern notion of a universal rationality without commitments as a basis for the legitimation of the narrative of modernity. As such, acceptance of this incredulity does not require the relinquishment of the meganarrative and message of Scripture. Therefore, this particular iteration of the postmodern project, with its thorough critique of autonomous human reason, is one in which orthodox Christians committed to the narratives and teachings of Scripture should find much of which to be supportive. In fact, Westphal concludes that Christians ought to share the skepticism and suspicion of Lyotard with respect to the metanarratives of modernity and their attempt at self-legitimation. "The Christian story legitimatizes only one kingdom, the Kingdom of God. In the process it delegitimizes every human kingdom, including democratic capitalism and the Christian church, just to the degree that they are not the full embodiment of God's Kingdom." The metanarratives and stories of modernity are established, told, and affirmed to legitimize their human raconteurs, while the Christian narrative places all human perception, effort, and accomplishment under scrutiny and judgment.

12. Jean-François Lyotard, *The Postmodern Condition: A Report on Knowledge*, trans. Geoff Bennington and Brian Massumi (Minneapolis: University of Minnesota Press, 1984), xxiv.

13. Westphal, *Overcoming Onto-theology*, xiii.

14. James K. A. Smith, "A Little Story about Metanarratives: Lyotard, Religion, and Postmodernism Revisited," in *Christianity and the Postmodern Turn*, ed. Myron Penner (Grand Rapids: Brazos, forthcoming).

15. Westphal, *Overcoming Onto-theology*, xiii.

While Christians may properly maintain that in one sense we know how the story ends, with the glorification of God in the exaltation of Jesus Christ, at whose name every knee will bow and every tongue will confess that he is Lord, in another important sense we do *not* know. For instance, while we may know how the story ends with respect to God and Jesus, "we do *not* know which aspects of our work will be burned as wood, hay, and stubble."[16]

Thus, while Christians may share the postmodern incredulity toward the metanarratives of modernity, this does not mean that Christians are therefore completely immune from this aspect of postmodern theory. As Westphal reminds us, "While the Christian *mega*narrative in not inherently a *meta*narrative in Lyotard's sense, it does not follow that it has not been and cannot be used as an instrument of epistemic, social, and ecclesiastical self-legitimation." Even a cursory reading of the history of Christianity provides numerous examples of such attempts at self-legitimation and the establishment of power that attends to it. "Whenever Christians tell the biblical story in such a way as to make their systems the repository of absolute truth or to claim divine sanction for institutions that are human, all too human, they become more modern than biblical." Knowing how the story of Jesus ends provides no assurances that our own theories and practices will not need to be cast aside or overthrown in the advent of God's reign.[17] Hence, while the postmodern suspicion of metanarratives need not be viewed as a critique of biblical Christian faith itself, it does pose an important challenge to all expressions of it that are connected with self-legitimation and empowerment.

Another reason for the Christian suspicion of postmodernity has to do with the atheistic assumptions and the character of the thought of many of the most recognizable claimants to the label *postmodern*. As Westphal points out, thinkers such as "Nietzsche, Heidegger, Derrida, Foucault, Lyotard, and Rorty are no friends of historic Christianity. Most are overtly atheistic, and even when this is not the case, God is conspicuously absent from the world as they present it to us."[18] This has led to the widespread assumption that the central themes and concerns of postmodern theory and orthodox Christian faith are mutually exclusive. Westphal maintains that while this may be true with respect to the antireligious or nonreligious character of the figures mentioned above, it does not necessarily follow that the central themes, arguments, and analyses that have been developed are of no value. He argues for the

16. Ibid., xv.
17. Ibid., xv–xvi.
18. Ibid., xi.

legitimacy of appropriating postmodern thought in the task of religious and moral thought in general and Christian theology in particular.[19]

In fact, this sort of appropriation has been going on for some time and should enable us to see that the wholesale identification of postmodern thought with a radical brand of nihilistic relativism is simply too narrow to do justice to the actual breadth of the phenomenon. It also fails to account for those postmodern thinkers who distance themselves from some of the more naturalistic implications and tendencies of poststructural and deconstructive thought. For instance, Nancey Murphy draws a distinction between Continental forms of postmodernism and those of Anglo-American postmodern thinkers. She employs the term *postmodern* to describe emerging patterns of thought in the Anglo-American context.[20] The Reformed epistemology of Alvin Plantinga and Nicholas Wolterstorff offers a vigorous defense and an affirmation of truth as well as a telling critique of modernity.[21] In ethics, the constructive communitarian approach of Alasdair MacIntyre may be viewed as postmodern.[22] In theology, the postliberalism associated with Hans Frei and George Lindbeck is indebted to postmodern theory and the later work of Wittgenstein.[23] Given the variety of intellectual endeavor that may be described as postmodern, we must conclude that postmodern thought cannot be narrowly associated with only a few select interpreters.

The breadth of postmodern thought raises the question as to what, if anything, gives unity and cohesion to postmodern thought. Dan Stiver points out that we should not expect postmodernism to be characterized by a tight conformity to particular categories and patterns of thought. He reminds us that we "use terms like analytic philosophy, existentialism, phenomenology, structuralism, process philosophy, and pragmatism with meaning but also with awareness that it is notoriously difficult to come up with demarcation criteria that will tell us in any and every

19. Ibid., 75–88. See also Merold Westphal, *Suspicion and Faith: The Religious Uses of Modern Atheism* (New York: Fordham University Press, 1998).

20. Nancey Murphy, *Anglo-American Postmodernity: Philosophical Perspectives on Science, Religion, and Ethics* (Boulder, CO: Westview Press, 1997), 1.

21. Alvin Plantinga and Nicholas Wolterstorff, eds., *Faith and Rationality: Reason and Belief in God* (Notre Dame: University of Notre Dame Press, 1983).

22. Alasdair MacIntyre, *Whose Justice? Which Rationality?* (Notre Dame: University of Notre Dame Press, 1988).

23. Hans W. Frei, *The Eclipse of Biblical Narrative: A Study in Eighteenth- and Nineteenth-Century Hermeneutics* (New Haven: Yale University Press, 1974); and George Lindbeck, *The Nature of Doctrine: Religion and Theology in a Postliberal Age* (Philadelphia: Westminster, 1984). On the implications for theology of Wittgenstein's later writings, see especially Fergus Kerr, *Theology after Wittgenstein*, 2nd ed. (London: SPCK, 1997).

case who is and is not in the pertinent group. Postmodernism is that kind of term."[24] This situation presses the question as to whether any similarity can be found within the diversity of postmodern thought so as to make sense of the movement while moving beyond the narrow understanding that sees it only as a synonym for deconstructive relativism. To address this circumstance, it is helpful to see postmodernism as a label that identifies an ongoing paradigm shift in Western culture. Almost without exception, those who are engaged in the pursuit of this paradigm shift use the term *postmodern*. Stiver suggests that this engagement generally involves three dimensions: first, the stringent criticism of modernity; second, the belief that "radical surgery" is required to address the ailments of modernity and that "a massive reconfiguration," or major paradigm shift, is unavoidable; and third, the presentation of a basic sketch as to the possible shape of an alternative paradigm.[25] From this description it is clear that the unity of the movement lies not in a tentative sketch of the details of a new paradigm but rather in the rejection of the program of modernity.

This observation enables us to suggest a basic, minimalist understanding of postmodernism as referring primarily to the rejection of the central features of modernity, such as its quest for certain, objective, and universal knowledge, along with its dualism and its assumption of the inherent goodness of knowledge. It is this critical agenda, rather than a proposed constructive paradigm to replace the modern vision, that unites postmodern thinkers. Nancey Murphy employs the term *postmodern* to describe emerging patterns of thought and to "indicate their radical break from the thought patterns of Enlightenment modernity."[26] As Diogenes Allen puts it, postmodern thought is simply discourse in the aftermath of modernity.[27] At this level, we find a remarkable congruence among those who adopt the label *postmodern* as a description of their work, a congruence that extends from Derrida to postliberals to postconservative evangelicals.

The postmodern quest for new paradigms has significantly shaped the discipline of theology in the past twenty years as theologians from various contexts and traditions have sought to fill the void left by the rejection of modernity. Terrence Tilley cites ten alternative postmodern theologies that he divides into four categories: constructive postmodernisms, postmodern dissolutions, postliberal theology, and theologies of

24. Stiver, "Uneasy Alliance between Evangelicalism and Postmodernism," 242.

25. Ibid., 243.

26. Murphy, *Anglo-American Postmodernity*, 1.

27. Diogenes Allen, "The End of the Modern World," *Christian Scholar's Review* 22, no. 4 (June 1993): 341.

communal praxis.[28] Kevin Vanhoozer identifies seven types of theology that he characterizes as postmodern: Anglo-American postmodernity, postliberal theology, postmetaphysical theology, deconstructive theology, reconstructive theology, feminist theology, and radical orthodoxy.[29] Each of these typologies indicates the presence today of a number of alternative constructive postmodern theological programs.

The Protestant Reformation provides an example of a similar situation. The sixteenth-century Protestants were in agreement that the medieval Roman Catholic tradition had corrupted the Christian faith and so made a reformation of the church necessary. Although they were united in what they were against, when it came to the task of setting forth a positive agenda, they were fragmented. Consequently, they struggled without success to achieve a unified movement. In a similar manner, postmodern thinkers are united, not by agreement about a particular constructive agenda but by their shared belief that the modern project is inadequate and by their shared commitment to the task of developing new paradigms for intellectual pursuit.

This construal of postmodern thought as a critique and a rejection of modernity leads to one central dimension of postmodern theory that is especially important. At the heart of the postmodern ethos is the attempt to rethink the nature of rationality in the wake of the modern project. Postmodern thought does not seek to do away with rationality, but it does raise questions about the assumptions that govern the understanding of rationality prevalent in modernity. This rethinking of the nature of rationality has resulted not in irrationality, as is often claimed by some opponents of postmodern thought, but rather in numerous redescriptions and proposals concerning appropriate construals of rationality and knowledge. In spite of their variety, these attempts can be broadly classified as producing a chastened, situated, and contextual rationality that is more inherently self-critical than the constructions of rationality commonly associated with the thought forms of modernity.[30] Two features that serve to distinguish this postmodern rationality from the modernist conceptions it seeks to critique and replace are of particular importance for the practice of theology in the contemporary setting: the linguistic turn and the nonfoundationalist turn.

28. Terrence W. Tilley, *Postmodern Theologies: The Challenge of Religious Diversity* (Maryknoll, NY: Orbis, 1995).

29. Vanhoozer, *Cambridge Companion to Postmodern Theology*, 26–145.

30. For a helpful discussion of this rethinking of rationality, see J. Wentzel van Huyssteen, *The Shaping of Rationality: Toward Interdisciplinarity in Theology and Science* (Grand Rapids: Eerdmans, 1999).

Postmodern Thought: The Linguistic Turn

One of the characteristics of postmodern thought is known as the linguistic turn and the corresponding transition from a realist to a constructionist view of the world.[31] Postmodern thinkers maintain that humans do not view the world from an objective or neutral vantage point but instead structure their world through the concepts they bring to it, particularly language. Human languages function as social conventions and symbol systems that attempt to engage and describe the world in a variety of ways that are shaped by the social and historical contexts and perceptions of various communities of discourse. No simple, one-to-one relationship exists between language and the world, and thus no single linguistic description can provide an objective conception of the "real" world. Language structures our perceptions of reality and as such constitutes the world in which we live.

In his frequently cited definition of culture as "an historically transmitted pattern of meanings embodied in symbols, a system of inherited conceptions expressed in symbolic forms,"[32] Clifford Geertz reminds us of the central importance of symbols to culture. We construct our world and communicate our understanding of it through a variety of symbols that together form elaborate systems. The primary purpose of these socially devised symbol systems is to convey meanings and facilitate the task of world construction. Hence, the value of symbols lies in their connection to meaning, which in turn resides in the mind rather than in the symbols themselves. As Paul Hiebert explains, symbols "link physical things with mental concepts, and these concepts can be distinguished from the form and immediate context of the symbols and can be combined in new contexts to create new ideas."[33] Despite the tendency to confuse symbols with their meanings, there is no necessary connection between a symbol and what it symbolizes; the assigning of meanings to symbols is arbitrary. At the same time, symbols are generally public rather than private. It is this public aspect of symbols that leads to their importance as purveyors of cultural meaning. The public dimension of symbols, in turn, fosters participation in social groups.

31. See, for example, Walter Truett Anderson, *Reality Isn't What It Used to Be: Theatrical Politics, Ready-to-Wear Religion, Global Myths, Primitive Chic, and Other Wonders of the Postmodern World* (San Francisco: Harper & Row, 1990).

32. Clifford Geertz, *The Interpretation of Cultures* (New York: Basic Books, 1973), 89.

33. Paul G. Hiebert, *Cultural Anthropology*, 2nd ed. (Grand Rapids: Baker, 1983), 115.

Inherent in the function of symbols is their representative character. Symbols represent something else. Through this representation, a symbol comes to be associated with the meaning of what it stands for.[34] Further, a symbol becomes a means to opening up a level of meaning for which nonsymbolic communication is inadequate.[35] According to Paul Tillich, symbols are able to disclose the deepest dimension of human existence: "We can call this the depth dimension of reality itself, the dimension of reality which is the ground of every other dimension and every other depth, and which therefore, is not one level beside the others but is the fundamental level, the level below all other levels, the level of being itself, or the ultimate power of being."[36] While numerous types of symbols are involved in the process of world construction, the most paradigmatic symbolic systems are linguistic. Indeed, language ranks as the central cultural form involved in the world-constructing and meaning-creating task.[37] Language provides the conceptual tools through which we construct the world we inhabit. As Hiebert asserts, "We cannot perceive nature or think or communicate about it without language, but language, to a great extent, also molds what we see and how we see it."[38] In addition, linguistic concepts serve as the vehicles through which we communicate and thereby share meaning with others.

The work of Ludwig Wittgenstein is of central importance in the development of the linguistic turn. Wittgenstein realized that rather than having only a single purpose, to make assertions or state facts, language has many functions. This conclusion led to Wittgenstein's concept of "language games." According to Wittgenstein, each use of language occurs within a separate and seemingly self-contained system complete with its own rules. Similar to playing a game, we require an awareness of the operative rules and significance of the terms within the context of the purpose for which we are using language. Each use of language, therefore, comprises a separate language game, and each game may have little to do with the other language games.[39] For Wittgenstein, meaning is not related, at least not directly or primarily, to an external world of facts waiting to be apprehended. Instead, meaning is an internal func-

---

34. Paul Tillich, *Theology of Culture*, ed. Robert C. Kimball (New York: Oxford University Press, 1959), 54.

35. Ibid., 56.

36. Ibid., 59.

37. Naomi Quinn and Dorothy Holland, "Culture and Cognition," in *Cultural Models in Language and Thought*, ed. Dorothy Holland and Naomi Quinn (Cambridge: Cambridge University Press, 1987), 9.

38. Hiebert, *Cultural Anthropology*, 119.

39. Ludwig Wittgenstein, *Philosophical Investigations*, trans. G. E. M. Anscombe (New York: Macmillan, 1953).

tion of language. Because the meaning of a statement is dependent on the context or the language game in which it appears, a sentence has as many meanings as contexts in which it is used.

Another key figure in the linguistic turn is the Swiss linguist Ferdinand de Saussure. In contrast to his predecessors who viewed language as a natural phenomenon that develops according to fixed and discoverable laws, Saussure proposed that a language is a social phenomenon and that a linguistic system is a product of social convention.[40] Others, such as anthropologist Claude Levi-Strauss and the proponents of what has come to be known as the sociology of knowledge, generated an awareness of the connection between language and culture and both personal identity formation and social cohesion.[41] Viewing language in this fashion presumes that it does not have its genesis in the individual mind grasping a truth or fact about the world and then expressing it in statements. Rather, language is a social phenomenon, and a statement acquires its meaning within the process of social interaction. From this perspective, language and culture generate a shared context in which people engage in the construction of meaning and in the task of making sense out of the world. In the words of Raymond Williams, culture functions as a "signifying system through which necessarily (though among other means) a social order is communicated, reproduced, experienced and explored."[42] In this process, language plays a crucial role. The language that we inherit from our social community, together with nonlinguistic modalities such as metaphorical images and symbols, provides the conceptual tools through which we construct the world we inhabit as well as the vehicles through which we communicate and thereby share meaning with others. In the words of Peter Berger and Thomas Luckmann, "Language objectivates the shared experiences and makes them available to all within the linguistic community, thus becoming both the basis and the instrument of the collective stock of knowledge."[43]

40. David Holdcroft, *Saussure: Signs, System, and Arbitrariness* (Cambridge: Cambridge University Press, 1991), 7–10.

41. See, for example, Peter L. Berger and Thomas Luckmann, *The Social Construction of Reality: A Treatise in the Sociology of Knowledge* (New York: Anchor Books, 1967), 99–104. For a fuller statement of Berger's views, see Peter L. Berger, *The Sacred Canopy: Elements of a Sociological Theory of Religion* (Garden City, NY: Doubleday, 1969), 3–51. For a summary and appraisal of Berger's contribution, see Robert Wuthnow, *Rediscovering the Sacred: Perspectives on Religion in Contemporary Society* (Grand Rapids: Eerdmans, 1992), 9–35.

42. Raymond Williams, *The Sociology of Culture* (New York: Schocken Books, 1982), 13.

43. Berger and Luckmann, *Social Construction of Reality*, 68.

In this social process of world construction and identity formation, language provides the structure of our particular and collective experience, perspective, and understanding. Our conceptions of what it means to be human, the formation and development of our moral, ethical, religious, and ideological convictions, and our understanding of our place and responsibilities in the world are shaped by our language and the discourse and practices of the particular communities in which we participate. We learn to use language and make sense of it in the context of our participation in a community of users that are bound together through common social conventions and rules of practice. Hence, the world we experience is mediated in and through our use of language, meaning that to some extent the limits of our language constitute the limits of our understanding of the world. Further, since language is a socially construed product of human construction forged in the context of ongoing interactions, conversations, and engagements, words and linguistic conventions do not have timeless and fixed meanings that are independent from their particular usages in human communities and traditions. In this sense, language does not represent reality as much as it constitutes reality.

Postmodern Thought: The Nonfoundationalist Turn

Postmodern thought is also characterized by a nonfoundationalist turn. The chastened rationality of postmodernity entails the rejection of epistemological foundationalism and the adoption of a nonfoundationalist and contextual conception of epistemology. In the modern era, the pursuit of knowledge was deeply influenced by Enlightenment foundationalism. In its broadest sense, foundationalism is merely the acknowledgment that not all beliefs are of equal significance in the structure of knowledge. Some beliefs are more basic or "foundational" and support other beliefs that are derived from them. Understood in this way, nearly every thinker is in some sense a foundationalist, rendering such a description unhelpful in grasping the range of opinion in epistemological theory found among contemporary thinkers. In philosophical circles, however, foundationalism refers to a much stronger epistemological stance than is entailed in this general observation about how beliefs intersect. At the heart of the foundationalist agenda is the desire to overcome the uncertainty generated by the tendency of fallible human beings to err and the inevitable disagreements and controversies that follow. Foundationalists are convinced that the only way to solve this problem is to find some universal and indubitable means of grounding the entire edifice of human knowledge.

The modern quest for epistemological certitude, often called "strong" or "classical" foundationalism, has its philosophical beginnings in the thought of the philosopher René Descartes. Descartes sought to reconstruct the nature of knowledge by rejecting traditional medieval or "premodern" notions of authority and replacing them with the modern conception of indubitable beliefs that are accessible to all individuals. The goal to be attained through the identification of indubitable foundations is a universal knowledge that transcends time and context. In keeping with this pursuit, the ideals of human knowledge since Descartes have tended to focus on the universal, the general, and the theoretical rather than on the local, the particular, and the practical. This conception of knowledge became one of the dominant assumptions of intellectual pursuit in the modern era and decisively shaped its cultural discourse and practices.

In the postmodern context, however, foundationalism is in dramatic retreat, as its assertions about the objectivity, certainty, and universality of knowledge have come under fierce criticism.[44] Merold Westphal observes, "That it is philosophically indefensible is so widely agreed that its demise is the closest thing to a philosophical consensus in decades."[45] J. Wentzel van Huyssteen agrees: "Whatever notion of postmodernity we eventually opt for, all postmodern thinkers see the modernist quest for certainty, and the accompanying program of laying foundations for our knowledge, as a dream for the impossible, a contemporary version of the quest for the Holy Grail."[46] And Nicholas Wolterstorff offers this stark conclusion: "On all fronts foundationalism is in bad shape. It seems to me there is nothing to do but give it up for mortally ill and learn to live in its absence."[47] The heart of the postmodern quest for a situated and contextual rationality lies in the rejection of the foundationalist approach to knowledge along with its intellectual tendencies.

Postmodern thought raises two related but distinct questions in regard to the modern foundationalist enterprise. First, is such an approach to knowledge *possible*? Second, is it *desirable*? These questions are connected with what may be viewed as the two major branches of postmodern hermeneutical philosophy: the hermeneutics of finitude and the hermeneutics of suspicion. The challenges to foundation-

44. John E. Thiel, *Nonfoundationalism* (Minneapolis: Fortress, 1994), 37.

45. Merold Westphal, "A Reader's Guide to 'Reformed Epistemology,'" *Perspectives* 7, no. 9 (November 1992): 10–11.

46. J. Wentzel van Huyssteen, "Tradition and the Task of Theology," *Theology Today* 55, no. 2 (July 1998): 216.

47. Nicholas Wolterstorff, *Reason within the Bounds of Religion* (Grand Rapids: Eerdmans, 1976), 52.

alism, however, are not only philosophical. They also emerge from the material content of Christian theology. Westphal suggests that postmodern theory, with respect to hermeneutical philosophy, may be properly appropriated for the task of explicitly Christian thought on theological grounds: "The hermeneutics of finitude is a meditation on the meaning of human createdness, and the hermeneutics of suspicion is a meditation on the meaning of human fallenness."[48] In other words, many of the concerns of postmodern theory can be appropriated and fruitfully developed in the context of the Christian doctrines of creation and sin.

Viewed from this perspective, the questions that are raised by postmodern thought concerning the possibility and the desirability of foundationalism are also questions that emerge from the material content of Christian theology. They both lead to similar conclusions. First, modern foundationalism, with its emphasis on the objectivity, universality, and certainty of knowledge, is an impossible dream for finite human beings, whose outlooks are always limited and shaped by the particular circumstances in which they emerge. Second, the modern foundationalist emphasis on the inherent goodness of knowledge is shattered by the fallen and sinful nature of human beings who desire to seize control of the epistemic process in order to empower themselves and further their own ends, often at the expense of others. The limitations of finitude and the flawed condition of human nature mean that epistemic foundationalism is neither possible nor desirable for created and sinful persons. This double critique of foundationalism, emerging as it does from the perspectives of both postmodern philosophy and Christian theology, suggests the appropriateness and suitability, given the current intellectual situation, of the language of nonfoundationalism as descriptive of an approach to the task of theology that is both postmodern and faithful to the Christian tradition. These aspects of the postmodern turn have played a significant role in the development and practice of theology over the course of the past twenty-five years and have contributed substantially to the current situation.

The Contemporary Theological Landscape

Commenting on the current state of theology, J. Wentzel van Huyssteen observes the following: "Even the briefest overview of our contemporary theological landscape reveals the startling fragmentation caused

---

48. Westphal, *Overcoming Onto-theology,* xx.

by what is often called 'the postmodern challenge' of our times."[49] This theological fragmentation extends beyond the traditional two-party division between liberal and conservative theology that typified much of the theological conversation that occurred over the course of the twentieth century. Today, we find important differences not only between these groups but also within them concerning basic questions about the nature of theology and the theological task. Hence, while it was once commonplace to view the main fissure in theology as a debate involving two sparring partners, the liberals and the conservatives, today we see significant divisions in both groups.

Among liberals this division is represented in the rift between revisionists and postliberals. On one side of this divide stands a group of thinkers who desire to maintain the theological trajectory that finds its roots in the program pioneered by nineteenth-century liberalism. David Tracy uses the term *revisionist* to describe this group of contemporary theologians who continue, in some sense, to pursue the goals and concerns of liberal theology.[50] These theologians continue to uphold the primacy of universal human experience as providing the foundation for the theological task.[51] For example, Tracy maintains that Christian theology "can best be described as philosophical reflection upon the meanings present in common human experience and language and upon the meanings present in the Christian fact."[52] Moreover, he asserts that scriptural claims must be scrutinized and critiqued according to the criteria of common human experience so as to correlate Christian faith with the common concerns and experiences shared by all people and the development of an objective and universally accessible approach to religion.[53] In short, according to Tracy, theology must speak in ways that are "disclosive and transformative for any intelligent, reasonable, responsible human being."[54] In the revisionist paradigm, it is of vital importance that theologians do not conceive of their task as that of speaking only to religious adherents, since this would serve to marginalize the contribution of theology to public discourse. Rather, the task of theology is to develop

---

49. Van Huyssteen, "Tradition and the Task of Theology," 213.

50. David Tracy, *Blessed Rage for Order: The New Pluralism in Theology* (New York: Seabury Press, 1975).

51. The most prominent voices associated with the revisionist paradigm include Paul Tillich, Karl Rahner, Hans Küng, Edward Schillebeeckx, Langdon Gilkey, Peter Hodgson, and Schubert Ogden. See Francis Schüssler Fiorenza, *Foundational Theology: Jesus and the Church* (New York: Crossroad, 1984), 276–77.

52. Tracy, *Blessed Rage for Order*, 43.

53. Ibid., 44.

54. David Tracy, "Defending the Public Character of Theology," *Christian Century* 98 (1981): 351–52.

appropriate patterns of discourse and argument that seek to persuade all people, Christian or not, of the truths they profess.

In recent years, the contemporary embodiment of the liberal program has come under sharp critique from another group of theologians who are often associated with the designation *postliberal*. From the standpoint of these theologians, Tracy's proposal is a classic example of allowing the world to "absorb the text." Postliberal theology is marked by two distinctive tendencies. The first is the rejection of philosophical foundationalism, the tendency to resist any attempt to find a neutral and ultimate vantage point from which to assess the truth and coherence of theological statements. This nonfoundational approach to theology leads to a second tendency, that of understanding Christian theology primarily as an act of communal self-description. One of the two most significant figures in the development of the nonfoundational perspective in theology is Hans Frei. His book *The Eclipse of Biblical Narrative* (1974) established him as one of the leading thinkers in the development of what has come to be known as postliberalism. In another significant work, *Types of Christian Theology* (1992), an edited and fragmentary book based on his lectures and published after his untimely death, we are able to glimpse Frei's conception of the developments in theology during the twentieth century.

In this work, Frei attempts to sort out the approaches of various modern theological alternatives to the perennial question of the relationship of theology to philosophy. He achieves this by posing a spectrum of opinion ranging from strong foundationalism, the belief that Christian theology is subordinate to the discipline of philosophy, which sets forth the rules of correct discourse for all fields of knowledge, to strong nonfoundationalism, the belief that Christian theology is an internal, contextual exercise in self-description that rejects in principle the notion of general, universally valid theories of knowledge that apply to all intellectual disciplines. The question that Frei seeks to address concerns the very nature of the discipline: Is Christian theology primarily a philosophical discipline that is open to *external* description (that is, explication from outside the believing community), or is it primarily an *internal* act of Christian self-description (i.e., faith seeking understanding)? In the former, theology is subject to the current canons of reason in philosophy and is therefore best done in the context of the academy, while the latter account suggests that theology is subject only to explicitly Christian discourse and is thus best pursued in the context of the church.

Frei identifies three representatives of positions that seek to navigate between these extremes: revisionist (or liberal) David Tracy, nineteenth-century liberal Friedrich Schleiermacher, and Karl Barth. Tracy is on the foundationalist end of the spectrum but allows, at least in theory, for a serious accounting of the explicitly Christian religion that is to be correlated with common human experience. The result of his procedure, however, given his assumptions concerning the nature of human experience as universal and therefore its priority in the task of correlation, leads inevitably to the eclipse of *distinctively* Christian theology. This is because the specifically Christian content of theology is thoroughly subsumed by philosophy on the basis of a general and supposedly universal theory of integration, in this case that of philosophical anthropology.

The main difference between Schleiermacher and Tracy, in Frei's reckoning, is that Schleiermacher attempts to correlate the external, philosophical description of theology, which is subject to accepted criteria of universal validity, with Christian self-description apart from any general theory that would predetermine the outcome of the process. The two are seen as bearing equal weight in the task of theological correlation. In this sense, Schleiermacher is technically not, contrary to the standard portrait, a foundationalist. However, in his definitive theological work, *The Christian Faith*, his application of the formal principles of his theological method can often give the appearance of foundationalism. This is due to the significant alterations he makes to the historical content of Christian theology on the basis of his conception of the "essence" of Christianity as a particular communal expression of the universal human condition (the feeling of absolute dependence). Given the material content of his teaching and the way it has been appropriated by those who have sought to follow his theological program, it is hardly surprising that he has come to be viewed as one of the chief advocates of liberal foundationalism.

In his presentation, Frei maintains that Barth agrees with Schleiermacher's conception of Christian theology as a nonsystematic correlation of Christian self-description and general philosophical method but does not regard them as equals. Barth places greater priority on Christian self-description than does Schleiermacher and reverses the procedure of Tracy by arguing that self-description governs and limits the use of philosophy in theology rather than vice versa. According to Frei, Barth affirms that "absolute priority be given to Christian theology as Christian self-description within the religious community called the Church, or the Christian community," and thus conceives of theology as "normed Christian self-description or critical self-examination by the Church of her language concerning God, in God's presence."[55] In this understanding, Christian theology can be viewed as being primarily concerned with

---

55. Hans W. Frei, *Types of Christian Theology*, ed. George Hunsinger and William C. Placher (New Haven: Yale University Press, 1992), 41–42.

teaching the particular language and concepts that shape the beliefs and practices of the community.

Building on the pioneering work of Frei, postliberal theologians advocate a move beyond the latent liberal program they find within much of the theology of the twentieth century. In addition to Frei, the other formative influence on the shape and development of postliberal theology is fellow Yale theologian George Lindbeck. Lindbeck's work *The Nature of Doctrine* is one of the seminal texts for postliberal thought and has made Lindbeck the other standard-bearer of the movement. He offers a program for theology that reverses the direction of conformity he thinks characterizes the revisionist paradigm.[56] Instead of seeking to contextualize the biblical message in such a way that conforms it to the conceptualities of the modern world, as in the revisionist program, Lindbeck calls for an approach to theology that seeks to redescribe and contextualize the modern world using the stories, symbols, and categories of the Bible. From his perspective, this allows Christian Scripture rather than the secular world, whose thought forms are alien to those of the Bible, to play the lead role in the process of Christian culture formation. He calls this program "intratextual theology" and defines its task as follows: "Intratextual theology redescribes reality within the scriptural framework rather than translating Scripture into extrascriptural categories. It is the text, so to speak, which absorbs the world, rather than the world the text."[57]

Postliberal theology takes as its starting point the shared language and practices of a particular religious community and understands its primary task as that of self-description rather than of correlation with universal human experience and reason. It is concerned with reflection on the intrasystemic relationship of beliefs within the Christian faith and the constructive and coherent articulation of these beliefs or doctrines. As William Placher puts it, this approach to theology attempts to provide a coherent explanation of "how the world looks from a Christian perspective, with whatever persuasive force that account musters and whatever connections it may happen to make with other perspectives, but it does not systematically ground or defend or explicate that picture in terms or universal criteria of meaningfulness or truth."[58] However, as

56. Nicholas Wolterstorff has suggested that this reversal of conformity constitutes the deepest "guiding metaphor" for Lindbeck and postliberal theologians. Nicholas Wolterstorff, *What New Haven and Grand Rapids Have to Say to Each Other* (Grand Rapids: Calvin College, 1993), 2.

57. George Lindbeck, *The Nature of Doctrine: Religion and Theology in a Postliberal Age* (Philadelphia: Westminster, 1984), 118.

58. William Placher, *Unapologetic Theology: A Christian Voice in a Pluralistic Conversation* (Louisville: Westminster John Knox, 1989), 19.

Lindbeck notes, postliberalism does not advocate "abandoning modern developments and returning to some form of preliberal orthodoxy."[59] Nevertheless, from the perspective of those who work from the revisionist paradigm, such an approach to theology amounts to a retreat into a sort of Christian ghetto that insulates Christianity, or for that matter any other religion, from critical scrutiny and cuts off any relevance for theology in the arena of public discourse.[60] Revisionist theologian James Gustafson has attacked Lindbeck's position as a destructive "sectarian" inducement that legitimates the withdrawal of Christianity from its cultural surroundings. He asserts that if theology follows such a "perilous" path its voice will be silenced and its message eclipsed.[61]

In the debate between postliberals and liberals concerning theology, it is important to remember that, like liberal theology, postliberal theology constitutes a diverse set of theological outlooks and positions. George Hunsinger has noted that in spite of the common concerns shared by Hans Frei and George Lindbeck, some important but often overlooked differences are also critical in the development of their respective positions. Hunsinger points out that while Frei was oriented toward Barth, Lindbeck tended to follow the directions of Aquinas and Luther. He summarizes that the direction of Frei's theology "tended to move from the particular to the general, from the ecclesial to the secular, and from the confessional to the methodological; while the logic of Lindbeck's theology moved more or less in the opposite direction, from the general to the particular, from the secular to the ecclesial, and from the methodological to the confessional."[62] He concludes that while both were nonfoundationalists sympathetic to the linguistic turn found in the later Wittgenstein, they manifested these commitments in quite different ways. In Hunsinger's view, Frei is more directly postliberal than Lindbeck, while Lindbeck is better understood as moving in a slightly more "neoliberal" direction. Thus, according to Hunsinger, the postliberalism of Frei "bids for a paradigm shift in which liberalism and evangelicalism are overlapped, dismantled, and reconstituted on a new and different plane." On the other hand, the postliberalism of Lindbeck, which Hunsinger refers to as neoliberalism, "would be more

59. Lindbeck, *Nature of Doctrine*, 7.

60. David Kelsey, "Church Discourse and Public Realm," in *Theology and Dialogue: Essays in Conversation with George Lindbeck,* 7–34, ed. Bruce D. Marshall (Notre Dame: University of Notre Dame Press, 1990).

61. James M. Gustafson, "The Sectarian Temptation: Reflections on Theology, the Church, and the University," *Proceedings of the Catholic Theological Society* 40 (1985): 93–94.

62. George Hunsinger, "Postliberal Theology," in *Cambridge Companion to Postmodern Theology,* 43.

nearly a revisionist extension within the established liberal program. It does not so much depart from as perpetuate the liberal/evangelical split characteristic of modernity itself."[63] The point to take note of here is not so much the differences between Frei and Lindbeck but rather that postliberal theology is a diverse enterprise and that its theological conclusions cannot be predetermined simply on the basis of its core assumptions and commitments.

While the advent of postliberal thought has been the subject of intense interest in the mainline theological community, similar developments have been evident on the conservative side of the traditional theological divide. In fact, in recent years an increasing number of commentators have sounded warnings concerning the division in conservative thought, particularly in the context of evangelical theology. In attempting to describe this division, these commentators have devised a variety of taxonomies. Millard Erickson has identified what he sees as the dangerous tendencies of a group of thinkers he lumps together as "the evangelical left."[64] While Erickson suggests that evangelicals are fragmenting over whether they should appropriate a reigning theological outlook of a past generation, Timothy Phillips and Dennis Okholm maintain that the emergence of postliberalism accounts for the tension within evangelical theology. They identify three distinct groups. On the right are those who follow Carl Henry's earlier wholesale rejection of the new movement. On the left are the postconservatives who "have linked their proposals with the postliberals." In between is a group of moderates, with whom they identify, who purportedly establish a common cause with the postliberals while sharply questioning the postliberal agenda.[65]

In another construal of the fragmentation in evangelical theology, Roger Olson sees the emergence of two loose coalitions among evangelical theologians.[66] On one side are the traditionalists, who uphold "traditional interpretations and formulations as binding and normative" and tend "to look with suspicion upon any doctrinal revisions and new proposals arising out of theological reflection." On the other side are the reformists, who value "the continuing process of constructive theology

63. Ibid., 44.

64. Millard J. Erickson, *The Evangelical Left: Encountering Postconservative Evangelical Theology* (Grand Rapids: Baker, 1997); and idem, *Postmodernizing the Faith: Evangelical Responses to the Challenge of Postmodernism* (Grand Rapids: Baker, 1998).

65. Timothy R. Phillips and Dennis L. Okholm, "The Nature of Confession: Evangelicals and Postliberals," in *The Nature of Confession: Evangelicals and Postliberals in Conversation*, ed. Timothy R. Phillips and Dennis L. Okholm (Downers Grove, IL: InterVarsity, 1996), 14–15.

66. Roger E. Olson, "The Future of Evangelical Theology," *Christianity Today*, February 9, 1998, 40–48.

seeking new light breaking forth from God's word."[67] Olson provides a perceptive description of the attitudes of these two constituencies toward three significant issues: theological boundaries, the nature and progress of doctrine, and interaction with nonevangelical theologies and culture in general.

Olson describes evangelical traditionalists as responding to the question of theological boundaries by viewing evangelicalism as a "bounded set" category and seeking to determine those who are inside the community and those who are on the outside. They believe that the only way to "avoid the slide into debilitating relativism and pluralism" is to develop firm boundaries. One way of achieving this is to "look to the past and acknowledge some outstanding signposts and landmarks in the history of theology as irreversible and unquestionable achievements in interpreting Scripture." As an example, many evangelical traditionalists turn to the writings and confessions of the sixteenth-century magisterial Reformation as providing the "touchstone of doctrinal truth for authentic evangelicalism."[68]

As to the nature and progress of doctrine, according to Olson's characterization, traditionalists emphasize the close identification of central doctrinal affirmations with what is "directly taught in Scripture." Therefore, they tend to see doctrine as lying at the heart of the enduring essence of Christianity. For traditionalists, it is not "experience or liturgy or forms of community but belief in a set of doctrinal affirmations that can be translated without substantial loss across cultures and languages throughout the centuries and across continents." In this way, doctrine is the "enduring essence" of Christianity, and thus traditionally accepted doctrinal formulations constitute a first-order language of revelation. Given this understanding of doctrine as a first-order language of revelation, traditionalists view doctrinal progress as "digging deeper into the historic sources and translating them for contemporary people." Thus, progress is viewed as the "effective spelling out of past achievements in theology."[69]

Because evangelical traditionalists believe the doctrinal products of their theologizing communicate the essence of Christianity and are normative for Christian faith, they tend to view the theology produced by those who do not share their particular evangelical convictions as being of little positive value in the development and formulation of theology. Rather, such theologies must be exposed as false, heretical, and dangerous in order to safeguard the theological boundaries of the

---

67. Ibid., 41.
68. Ibid.
69. Ibid., 44.

church. Likewise, traditionalists tend to be resistant to the incorpora-
tion of culture as an integral part of the theological enterprise, believing
that doing so will lead to the sort of cultural accommodation they see
in various forms of liberal theology.

Evangelical reformists differ strongly with traditionalists on these
issues. Reformists understand evangelicalism as a "centered set" category rather than as the "bounded set" of the traditionalists. They insist
that the boundaries remain "open and relatively undefined" and look
to the broad, central evangelical commitments as providing coherence
for their approach to theology.[70] While nurturing a respect for the rich
theological tradition of the past, reformists "recognize the fallibility of
every human tradition and the need for ongoing reformulation of human
perceptions of truth." Therefore, reformists look to the future and seek
legitimate change within the continuity of the past as the basis for the
continuing vitality of evangelical theology.[71]

In contrast to traditionalists, reformists draw a sharp distinction
between doctrinal and theological formulations and the language of the
biblical text. They view theological constructions as the church's later
interpretations of the stories and teachings of canonical Scripture. As
such, these are continually subject to the judgment of Scripture and
must therefore be "held more lightly than the first-order language of
the Bible and worship." The enduring essence of Christianity is not to
be found in the fallible doctrines of the church but rather in the work
of God in the lives of human beings. Doctrinal and theological progress
for the reformist involves the discovery of "new light" and better comprehension of the Christian faith through the careful study of the biblical narratives and their witness to the gospel in the context of various
social and historical contexts and circumstances. Reformists maintain
that by reflecting on the meanings of revelation "in the light of contemporary problems, theology can discover new solutions that may have
even seemed heretical to earlier generations steeped in philosophies
and cultures alien to the biblical thought world."[72]

This conception of the provisional, ongoing nature of theology means
that reformist evangelicals tend to view nonevangelical theologies as
"ambiguous and flawed quests for truth" from which they can learn.

---

70. Olson defines this central evangelical core as a commitment to the Bible as the
supreme norm of truth for Christian belief and practice; a supernatural worldview that
is centered in a transcendent, personal God; a focus on the forgiving and transforming
grace of God through Jesus Christ in the experience of conversion; and the notion that
the primary task of theology is to serve the church in its mission to make the grace of
God known to the entire world (ibid., 40).

71. Ibid., 42.

72. Ibid., 44.

Such belief systems can raise appropriate theological questions over-looked by more conservative theologians and stimulate fresh thinking on the part of evangelicals. In the same way, reformists believe that they can learn from the study and examination of the thought forms and insights of contemporary culture. "Reformists live by the motto that 'all truth is God's truth—wherever it is found' and attempt to remain open to the contributions of any and all serious thinkers who seek honestly after truth." Reformists emphasize dialogue as the proper approach to the ideas of the broader theological community and contemporary culture.[73]

Robert Webber offers another perspective on the differences in evangelical thought. Webber examines the evangelical movement from the perspective of the church as well as theology and identifies three types that he labels traditional evangelicals, pragmatic evangelicals, and younger evangelicals.[74] In Webber's account, traditional evangelicals represent the movement that emerged in the aftermath of World War II and the culture of modernity. Their theological commitments and agenda were built around an understanding of Christianity primarily as a rational worldview. Webber identifies Billy Graham as the quintessential leader of this group. Pragmatic evangelicals are those shaped by the social and cultural tumult and upheaval of the 1960s whose theological commitments involve an understanding of Christianity as therapy that provides answers to particular needs and forms the basis for a meaningful and fulfilled life. Bill Hybels is identified as the paradigmatic leader of this group. Younger evangelicals are those who have grown up in the context of postmodern culture and whose theological commitments are shaped by an understanding of Christianity as a community of faith. They seek to embrace and learn from the ancient Christian tradition and have strong ecumenical instincts. Webber identifies Brian McLaren as the representative leader of this group.[75]

A variety of labels have been used to describe the shift occurring in the evangelical theological community among some thinkers who are seeking reform without abandoning their evangelical heritage. These labels include reformist evangelicals, the evangelical left, the younger evangelicals, postmodern evangelicals, postconservatives, and even post-evangelicals. One of the common features among the typologies that gives rise to these labels is the identification of postmodernity as one of the decisive factors in accounting for the changes described and sought.

---

73. Ibid., 47.

74. Robert E. Webber, *The Younger Evangelicals: Facing the Challenges of the New World* (Grand Rapids: Baker, 2002).

75. Ibid., 13–20.

Hence the significance of postmodern thought for understanding contemporary developments in conservative as well as liberal theology.

While the label *postconservative* is, like that of *postliberal*, not without its own difficulties, it is to be preferred for our purposes for at least two reasons. First, it highlights the fact that conservative theology has not been the sole province of evangelicals. Many confessional traditions have remained firm in their conservative commitments while resisting the outlook and tendencies that have characterized evangelical thought and practice for a variety of sociological and theological reasons. Yet these communities are also grappling with the challenges of postmodernity and are adopting approaches to theology that may be described as postconservative without being evangelical. Second, the use of the term *postconservative* highlights the similarity between developments in liberal theology and the advent of postliberalism and those in the conservative community and is thus suggestive of the opportunities for fruitful conversation and the possibilities for genuine convergence in the effort to move beyond the liberal/conservative impasse that shaped and distorted theology over the course of the twentieth century.

It should also be noted that, like postliberal theology, postconservative theology is a diverse enterprise that is characterized by some common perspectives on the discipline of theology and not by a particular set of theological conclusions. For instance, while the so-called open view of God is a position held by some who have been viewed as postconservative, it does not follow that all postconservatives hold to this view of divine interaction with the created order. In fact, a wide spectrum of theological opinion is present among postconservative thinkers who are shaped not only by their conviction concerning the character of theology but also by their various ecclesial, communal, and confessional commitments.

Reflecting on the state of the discipline more than twenty years ago, Jeffrey Stout quipped that contemporary theology, "like an empty pile in solitaire, is waiting for a new king to come along and get things started again."[76] While Stout's observation was astute, Nancey Murphy perceptively comments that he failed to consider the possibility that rules of the game may have changed.[77] The advent of the postmodern situation brings to light the realization that although conservative and liberal theologians have seemingly been going their separate ways, both

76. Jeffrey Stout, *Flight from Authority: Religion, Morality, and the Quest for Autonomy* (Notre Dame: University of Notre Dame Press, 1981), 148.
77. Nancey Murphy, *Beyond Liberalism and Fundamentalism: How Modern and Postmodern Philosophy Set the Theological Agenda* (Valley Forge, PA: Trinity Press International, 1996), 85.

have actually been responding, albeit in different ways, to the same agenda, the agenda of modernity.[78] Therefore, rather than evidencing a progression from preliberal to liberal to postliberal, as George Lindbeck proposes,[79] recent theological history suggests a different trajectory. Modernity, not liberalism, was the focal point of the theological conversation from Schleiermacher to the present. In this conversation, the liberal and conservative theological traditions offered their own particular responses to the challenges raised by the modernist cultural milieu they both shared.

However, the rules of this modern theological discourse have been challenged and, for some, have been found to be defective. Theology, which earlier moved from the premodern to the modern and in the process spawned both liberalism and conservatism, now finds itself confronted with the postmodern situation. The current fragmentation of theological discourse, which has emerged even within traditionally liberal and conservative circles, is in part the fallout from this change in the rules for theological discourse. Given the long-standing entrenchment of modernist assumptions, we should not be surprised to find that the postmodern challenge engenders suspicion and hostility among persons on both sides of the theological divide. Commenting on the significance of this cultural transition, Murphy states that although the relationship between liberals and conservatives has generally been acrimonious, the differences between the two "are less significant than those between modern thinkers of all sorts and those who have adopted the standpoint of a new intellectual world in the making."[80]

From this perspective, it is likely that the current tensions between liberals and postliberals and between conservatives and postconservatives will continue to intensify as those in the liberal and conservative constituencies feel that long-standing commitments are being compromised by postliberals and postconservatives. Ironically, one of the general critiques of postliberals by liberals will be that they have become too conservative, while conservatives will accuse postconservatives of being too liberal. In the midst of this, some of the most fruitful conversation in contemporary theology has been and will continue to be between postliberals and postconservatives who share aspects of postmodern thought, particularly the linguistic and nonfoundational turns. George Hunsinger's words with respect to postliberals apply equally well to postconservatives:

78. For a detailed comparison of the ways in which both the conservative agenda and the liberal theological agenda have been shaped by modernity, see ibid., 11–82.

79. Lindbeck, *Nature of Doctrine*, 15–19.

80. Murphy, *Beyond Liberalism and Fundamentalism*, x.

They can be recognized by a common set of goals, interests, and commitments, especially their ecumenical interests and their desire to move
beyond modernity's liberal/evangelical impasse. As made newly possible
in our culture by the rise of nonfoundationalism they have begun to think
through old questions like the truth of theological language, interdisciplin-
ary relations, and religious pluralism.[81]

Together, postliberals and postconservatives make common cause in the
pursuit of what Hans Frei describes as a "generous orthodoxy."[82]

With this background concerning the postmodern situation, the linguistic and nonfoundationalist turns in postmodern thought, and the
current state of theology, we now turn our attention to a basic description of some of the salient features of theology and a working definition
that takes into account the context in which we do theology and our
responsibility to the historical and global church.

What Is Theology?

The word *theology* has been used in a variety of ways over the course
of Christian history with a significant number of meanings and nuances.
For our purposes here, pending a fuller discussion of the term, theology
is understood as the orderly study and investigation of the truths of the
Christian faith. Among the many designations that have been used to
describe this activity, the term *dogmatics* has been used to accent the
importance of anchoring such study and investigation in the normative, ecumenically received teachings of the Christian church. In other
words, for reasons that will be explored later, dogmatics involves not
only the careful study of Scripture but also the task of engaging in that
study in ways that are responsible to the entire church, historically and
globally. Dogmatics, then, refers to the attempt to define and clarify the
distinctive content of the Christian faith for the church to enable the
Christian community to be clear about what it believes in its witness
to the gospel in the midst of the world. It is also an investigation of the
content of Christian theology for the practical purpose of considering
how that content is to be most properly and effectively conveyed and
communicated in each new social, linguistic, and cultural setting. In
this sense, as Karl Barth remarks, "Dogmatics as such does not ask what

81. Hunsinger, "Postliberal Theology," 57.
82. Hans Frei, "Response to 'Narrative Theology: An Evangelical Appraisal,'" *Trinity
Journal* 8 (Spring 1987): 21.

the apostles and prophets said but what we must say on the basis of the apostles and prophets."[83]

In this attempt to be clear about what we must say today on the basis of the prophets and apostles, it has become common to speak of doing a particular kind of dogmatics, such as Reformed dogmatics, Lutheran dogmatics, or Roman Catholic dogmatics. In one sense, this is perfectly correct, since all attempts to offer a coherent account of the Christian faith emerge from a particular tradition or location. It is important to remember, however, that, strictly speaking, there is no such thing as Reformed, Lutheran, or Roman Catholic dogmatics but only Christian dogmatics pursued from the perspective of a particular ecclesial tradition. It is not the goal of dogmatics to promote a sectarian spirit in the church. Rather, the various traditions within the Christian church, united by consensual ecumenical orthodoxy, offer their distinctive witness to the Christian faith through the act of dogmatics as an ecumenical enterprise for the purpose of contributing to the common task of the entire church, in its various confessional and ecclesial expressions, to clarify the teaching of the one faith.

Likewise, there is technically no such thing as premodern, modern, or postmodern dogmatics. There is only Christian dogmatics pursued in the context of particular social and intellectual situations. In these local settings, contemporary challenges and concerns are addressed and critical theological use is made of the conceptual tools and concepts of a specific time and place for the purpose of clarifying, explaining, and illuminating the universal truth of the Christian faith in the midst of numerous historical and cultural locations. Hence, the adjective *postmodern* in a phrase descriptor such as "postmodern Christian dogmatics" signifies the importance of attending to the social and historical location of the church and should be understood as providing explicit identification of the particular cultural context in which a particular proposal for Christian dogmatics is situated, pursued, and developed. This does not mean that dogmatics simply conforms to the intellectual milieu in which it is situated. Rather, it must address and engage with the social and cultural challenges particular to its specific context. The subject of Christian dogmatics signifies the importance of attending to the historical tradition of the church and should be understood as a commitment to pursuing the task of dogmatics in conversation and continuity with the church throughout the ages.

In spite of the advantages of the language of dogmatics as a descriptor for theology, its connotations have come to be closely associated

83. Karl Barth, *Church Dogmatics*, ed. G. W. Bromiley and T. F. Torrance, 2nd ed. (Edinburgh: T & T Clark, 1975), 1/1.

with a narrowness of vision and an inflexibility of mind not proper to the task of theology. Therefore, it may not be the most helpful term for the contemporary situation. Be that as it may, the principles and commitments implied by dogmatics as sketched above are crucial for the health and vitality of the church. However, to avoid the confusion and the misunderstanding that often accompany the use of the word *dogmatics*, we will employ *theology* as a synonymous term while attempting to remain faithful to the commitments inherent in the practice of theology as dogmatics.

In addition to this general description, it should also be noted that the discipline of theology, particularly in the Protestant tradition, is a reforming enterprise. This assertion arises from the commitment to the ongoing reformation of the faith and practice of the church according to the Word of God in the context of ever-changing circumstances and situations. The Latin slogan *ecclesia reformata et semper reformanda* (the reformed church is always reforming) captures this Protestant concern for the continual reformation of the church and suggests a corresponding principle with respect to an approach to theology that would seek to serve the church. In keeping with the premise that the church is always reforming, it is also true that theology is always reforming according to the Word of God in order to bear witness to the eternal truth of the gospel in the context of an ever-changing world characterized by a variety of cultural settings: *theologia reformata et semper reformanda*, reformed theology is always reforming. Among the most central intellectual commitments that inform this approach to reformation and theology are the primacy and freedom of God in the governance and guidance of the church and the world along with the contextual and corrupted nature of human knowledge. Accordingly, the process of reformation is not, and never can be, something completed once and for all and appealed to in perpetuity. In the words of Jürgen Moltmann, reformation is not "a one time act to which a confessionalist could appeal and upon whose events a traditionalist could rest."[84] Rather, an approach to the reformation of church and theology that acknowledges and seeks to live out the implications of the primacy and freedom of God in all creaturely relations along with the limited and distorted conceptions of human knowledge will be an ongoing process that is "always reforming."

However, while this reforming principle preserves the primacy of the Word of God in the church and properly acknowledges the contextual nature of all human confession, Michael Welker observes that it has

---

84. Jürgen Moltmann, *"Theologia Reformata et Semper Reformanda,"* in *Toward the Future of Reformed Theology: Tasks, Topics, Traditions,* ed. David Willis and Michael Welker (Grand Rapids: Eerdmans, 1999), 121.

also raised significant questions and challenges for theology. Speaking particularly of theology in the Reformed tradition but with implications for the practice of theology in all reformist traditions, Welker observes that commitment to the reforming principle has brought theology into a "profound crisis" at the beginning of the new millennium. He notes that the speed, diversity, and complexity of social and cultural change in Western industrialized settings have taxed theological traditions that are open to contemporary cultural developments. Thus, the practice of a reformist theology can sometimes appear "to be at the mercy of the shifting Zeitgeist," in which it falls "victim to the cultural stress of innovation." He concludes that this reformist approach to theology faces a double challenge. When it enters into the cultural stress of various social and historical situations, it can risk compromising or losing important and defining commitments. Yet when it opposes that stress, it can betray its affirmation of the necessity of continual reformation and run the danger of becoming anachronistic and inconsequential in the contemporary setting.[85]

These observations point to two distortions to which Protestant theology has been susceptible and that must be avoided if the vitality and faithfulness of its particular witness to the gospel are to be maintained. One is the conservative distortion of so closely equating theology with the events, creeds, and confessions of the sixteenth and seventeenth centuries as to virtually eliminate, in practice if not in theory, the reforming principle, thus betraying the formal character of theology. The other is the revisionist distortion of becoming so taken with the opportunities and possibilities for innovation that theology loses its profile as a distinctively Christian enterprise, thus betraying its material concerns. Good theology must avoid these distortions if it is to be faithful in its calling before God as a proper and faithful witness to the gospel of Jesus Christ and a servant of the church.

In light of these concerns, we now turn our attention to the definition of theology. Much is at stake in the question of definition. Indeed, the way in which theology is defined plays a significant and often decisive role in the development of the material content of theology and the way in which that content is related to the life and work of the church. Yet the way in which theology is defined is itself a matter of theological construction that emerges and takes shape only in the context of particular theological commitments and convictions. Defining theology is a matter of theological construction that has implications for the

---

85. Michael Welker, "Travail and Mission: Theology Reformed according to God's Word at the Beginning of the Third Millennium," in *Toward the Future of Reformed Theology*, 137.

whole of the theological enterprise, and the whole enterprise bears on the question of definition. In the same way that there are no neutral starting points from which to engage in the work of theology, neither are there any neutral definitions of theology's nature, task, and purpose. No theological tradition has a privileged position with respect to the definition of theology, and yet numerous theological commitments and convictions are at stake in any attempt at defining theology. Thus, in the very act of defining theology, we find ourselves engaged in the process of theologizing. Simply stated, the act of defining theology is part of the process of doing theology.

From this perspective, the following working definition of theology is provided as a guide for a discussion of the character of theology: Christian theology is an ongoing, second-order, contextual discipline that engages in the task of critical and constructive reflection on the beliefs and practices of the Christian church for the purpose of assisting the community of Christ's followers in their missional vocation to live as the people of God in the particular social-historical context in which they are situated.

This definition can be broken down into three distinct yet overlapping components: the nature of theology (an ongoing, second-order, contextual discipline), the task of theology (critical and constructive reflection on the beliefs and practices of the Christian church), and the purpose of theology (assisting the community of Christ's followers in their missional vocation to live as the people of God in the particular social-historical context in which they are situated). Each of these aspects of the character of theology will be introduced and examined in chapters 3, 4, and 5. Before launching into a consideration of this material, however, we must first take account of the subject of theology to orient properly our conception of the discipline to the one to whom it seeks to bear faithful witness, the Triune God revealed in Jesus Christ.

2

The Subject of Theology

The etymology of the word *theology,* the study of God, suggests that its central concern is with the nature, character, and actions of God. The chief inquiry for any theology, therefore, is the question of the identity of God. For Christians, the subject of theology is the God revealed in Jesus Christ. Accordingly, the Christian answer to the question of God's identity ultimately leads to the doctrine of the Trinity. Christians maintain that the one God is triune, Father, Son, and Spirit, to cite the traditional designations for the trinitarian persons. Consequently, the confession of the Triune God has been the sine qua non of the Christian faith. In keeping with this particularly Christian confession, both the Apostles' Creed and the Nicene Creed, the ancient and ecumenical symbols of the church, are ordered around and divided into three articles that correspond to the three persons of the Triune God: the Father and creation; the Son and reconciliation; and the Spirit, the church, and redemption. For much of the history of the church, this creedal pattern gave rise to a trinitarian construal of the exposition of Christian faith. This creedal and confessional pattern reflects the reasoning of the Christian community that since Christian faith is committed to finding its basis in the being and actions of God, Christian theology should be ordered in such a way as to reflect the primacy of the Christian confession about the nature of God. In keeping with this ecumenical commitment, this discussion concerning the subject of theology focuses on the doctrine of the Trinity and considers some of its implications for the development and explication of Christian faith.

God as Triune

The word *Trinity* is not found in the Bible, nor is the theological concept developed or fully delineated in Scripture. The absence of any explicit reference to God as triune in the Bible led Swiss theologian Emil Brunner to conclude, "The ecclesiastical doctrine of the Trinity, established by the dogma of the ancient Church, is not a Biblical *kerygma*, therefore it is not the *kerygma* of the Church, but it is a theological doctrine which defends the central faith of the Bible and the Church."[1] In this terse statement, Brunner calls attention to the fact that the doctrine of the Trinity was not formulated in Scripture but by the church during the patristic era. Nevertheless, by the fourth century, the Christian community had come to the conclusion that understanding God as triune was a nonnegotiable aspect of the gospel because it encapsulated the Christian conception of God. The doctrine of the Trinity that unfolded in the patristic era was a natural—and perhaps even necessary—outworking of the faith of the New Testament community. Above all, it was based on the concrete witness of the biblical narrative. It emerged as the fundamental theological conclusion arising from and embodying that narrative. In fact, the trinitarian conception of God is so closely tied to the biblical narrative that it serves as a shorthand way of speaking not only about the God of the narrative but also about the narrative itself as the act of the God of the Bible.

The doctrine of the Trinity is often portrayed as a highly abstract teaching that emerged from the philosophical concerns and speculations of third- and fourth-century theologians rather than from the content of the biblical witness. In truth, however, the doctrine arose as a response to the concrete historical situation encountered by the early Christian community. The early Christians faced a grave theological problem, namely, how to reconcile the inherited commitment to the confession of one God with the lordship of Jesus Christ and the experience of the Spirit. Far from a philosophical abstraction, therefore, the doctrine of the Trinity was the culmination of an attempt on the part of the church to address the central theological question regarding the content of the Christian faith, a question that arose out of the experience of the earliest followers of Jesus.

1. Emil Brunner, *The Christian Doctrine of God*, trans. Olive Wyon (Philadelphia: Westminster, 1950), 206.

The early Christians, following their Jewish heritage, vigorously maintained belief in one God and the attendant rejection of the polytheistic practices of other nations. This commitment was rooted in their claim that the Christian faith was a continuation of what God had initiated in the covenant with Abraham. The Hebrew community that had been shaped by the promises contained in the Abrahamic covenant asserted unequivocally that there was only one God and that this God alone was to be the object of their loyalty and worship (e.g., Deut. 6:4). The early Christians viewed themselves as the continuation of the one people of the one God, and consequently, they steadfastly continued in the Old Testament tradition of monotheism. The followers of Jesus asserted that the God they worshiped was none other than the God of the patriarchs, the one and only true God. This commitment to one God provided the Christian community with an indispensable framework in which to reflect on its experience of the living God in the person of Jesus Christ.

Although the early Christians continued the Jewish practice of worshiping only one God, they also believed that this God had been revealed preeminently in the person of Jesus of Nazareth. They confessed that this Jesus was the head of the church and the Lord of all creation. This confession resulted in a second core belief. In addition to the commitment to one God, the early church asserted the deity and lordship of Jesus (John 1:1; 20:28; Rom. 9:5; Titus 2:13). At the same time, the followers of Jesus made a clear distinction, following the pattern of Jesus himself, between Jesus as the Son of God and the God of Israel, the Creator of the world, whom he addressed as "Father." In short, the church asserted that while Jesus was divine, he was nevertheless distinct from the Father.

In addition to God the Father and Jesus the Son, the early Christian community also experienced the living God present among them through one who was neither Jesus nor his heavenly Father. Through the ministry of the Holy Spirit, the early Christian believers enjoyed an intimate fellowship with the living God. They equated the Spirit's work with the presence of God among and within them. The community believed that through the presence of the Spirit, Christians, individually and corporately, comprised the true temple of God (Rom. 8:9; 1 Cor. 3:16; 2 Cor. 3).

This assertion is particularly striking in light of the significance of the temple in first-century Judaism. As the focal point of all aspects of Jewish national life, the temple was regarded as the place where God lived and ruled. Thus, the fact that the presence of the Spirit in the life of the Christian community constituted that community as the temple of God intimately linked the Spirit with God. In addition, the early Christians closely connected the Holy Spirit with the risen Lord (2 Cor. 3:17;

Phil. 1:19), while also making a clear and definite distinction between the Spirit and both the Father and the Son. This distinction among the trinitarian members is evident in the trinitarian formulations found in the New Testament canon (e.g., 2 Cor. 13:14).

The early Christians were faced with the task of integrating into a coherent, composite understanding these three commitments born out of their experience of God. More particularly, they were faced with the challenge of maintaining both the unity and the differentiated plurality of God. They did not want to posit three Gods, yet the three experiences of God were far too concrete to be seen as simply different "modes" of the one God. As a result, trinitarian theology is rooted in the practical, concrete concern to provide a Christian account of God that is in accord with the experience and witness of the community. Of course, subsequent attempts to provide such an account drew from the philosophical terminology and thought forms of the Greek culture in which the patristic church was embedded. Yet this does not mean that the doctrine itself is merely the product of philosophical speculation. As David Cunningham points out, when Christian theologians engaged in the attempt to make sense of the God of the Bible, "they (quite naturally and appropriately) turned to the philosophical categories that were available to them. But this fact should not be allowed to eclipse the concrete reality of the particular narratives that gave rise to trinitarian thought."[2]

The biblical narratives speak of three historical encounters with God—with the one God of Israel, with Jesus the incarnate Son, and with the Spirit as the manifestation of the ongoing presence and guidance of God in the community and in the world. While the constitutive narratives of the Christian tradition bear witness to the engagement of God with the world, they also point beyond this encounter to the eternal divine life. In addition to acting in the history of the world, the biblical materials view God as having a "history." In this history, creation is not the beginning point but an event in the continuing story of God's existence, which stretches from the eternal past into the eternal future. Catherine LaCugna notes that although the acts of God in history were the original subject matter of the doctrine of the Trinity, theologians have come to understand that "God's relations to us in history are taken to be what is characteristic of the very being of God."[3] In other words, God has an internal "history" (the inner divine life) as well as an external history (God's actions and engagement with the world). The narratives

2. David S. Cunningham, *These Three Are One: The Practice of Trinitarian Theology* (Malden, MA: Blackwell, 1998), 22.

3. Catherine Mowrey LaCugna, "Philosophers and Theologians on the Trinity," *Modern Theology* 2 (1986): 173.

of Scripture invite theologians to take account of both the internal and the external aspects of God's life and to think through the details and the implications of this history.

The significance of God's internal and external history was taken for granted throughout much of the history of theology, and numerous systems of speculative theology were produced based in no small part on this distinction, arising out of the biblical narrative.[4] In the aftermath of the Enlightenment, however, the biblical narratives began to suffer neglect due to the incredulity toward the veracity of the narratives displayed in the Age of Reason and the corresponding rise of biblical criticism.[5] As a result of this suspicion toward the biblical narratives, there was a shift away from the belief that Scripture provides the basis for Christian belief, which led in turn to a rejection of Christian doctrines such as the Trinity, which was seen as a product of abstract, philosophical speculation.

In the twentieth century, however, proponents of trinitarian theology sought once again to link the doctrine of the Trinity with the biblical narratives. Karl Barth's *Church Dogmatics* stands out as a monumental attempt to reassert the centrality of the Trinity in the task of theology by grounding the doctrine in the narratives of God's relationship with Israel and the church. For Barth, trinitarian theology is the story of God and God's action in the world, which finds its ultimate center in Christ.[6] Like Barth, Robert Jenson is committed to showing that the doctrine is grounded in the concrete narratives of the Christian faith, which witness to the life, death, and resurrection of Christ, and therefore that the Trinity is not the product of mere abstract, philosophical speculation.[7] To this end, he seeks to free the doctrine of God in particular and Christian theology in general from their excessive dependence on the categories of Hellenistic philosophy, such as divine timelessness, simplicity, and impassibility. Although agreeing that the communities of ancient Israel and the church experienced God as eternal, Jenson argues that they did not understand this eternity as timelessness but as faithfulness through time. The God of the biblical narratives does not transcend time by being immune to it but by maintaining faithful continuity through it, a continuity that Jenson describes as "personal." The eternity of the Christian

---

4. Cunningham, *These Three Are One*, 22.

5. On the history of this development, see Hans W. Frei, *The Eclipse of Biblical Narrative: A Study in Eighteenth- and Nineteenth-Century Hermeneutics* (New Haven: Yale University Press, 1974).

6. David Ford, *Barth and God's Story* (Frankfurt: Lang, 1985).

7. Robert W. Jenson, *The Triune Identity: God according to the Gospel* (Philadelphia: Fortress, 1982).

God, he concludes, is intrinsically a matter of relationship with God's creatures. By working from the biblical texts in this manner rather than drawing from Greek philosophical categories, Jenson seeks to ensure that trinitarian theology remains firmly grounded in the narrative of the experience of Israel and the church with the God of the Bible.

Jürgen Moltmann and Wolfhart Pannenberg have also made significant attempts to link trinitarian theology with the biblical narratives. Although they differ at a number of important points, both seek to liberate the doctrine of the Trinity from abstract speculation about a distant being and to connect the Triune God with the historical process. To this end, both thinkers have followed Barth in linking the doctrine of the Trinity with the doctrine of revelation through the assertion that God is revealed in history. This emphasis on revelation has served to reconnect the doctrine of God in general and the understanding of the Trinity in particular with the biblical story. Some scholars find in the separation of the doctrine of God from the biblical narratives the genesis of modern atheism, which emerged in the wake of Enlightenment theology, with its propensity to develop generic conceptions of God believed to be demonstrable by reason.[8] In the estimation of these observers, the rationalist approach of the Enlightenment led to the belief that the existence of God could be "proved" rationally, an assumption that, when it was subsequently undermined, led to the undermining of the conception of God as well.[9] This historical appraisal implies that modern atheism emerged in part as the result of the neglect of the biblical narratives in theology, as theologians discarded the biblical witness to the active presence of God in the world in favor of speculation about a generic, completely transcendent deity.

The renewed emphasis on the narratives of the Christian faith as the narratives of God's history has reinvigorated trinitarian theology by asserting that its claims are not grounded in abstract, philosophical speculation but in the intellectual challenges about God and God's relationship to creation raised by these narratives. Moreover, as David Cunningham notes, the biblical narrative is properly read and interpreted, "not according to the supposedly context-independent assumptions of rationalism, but in the context of Christian participation in concrete practices of worship, education, and discipleship."[10] The doctrine of the Trinity is not the product of philosophically speculative theology gone awry but the outworking of communal Christian reflection on the con-

---

8. The most detailed account of this development is Michael J. Buckley, S.J., *At the Origins of Modern Atheism* (New Haven: Yale University Press, 1987).

9. Cunningham, *These Three Are One*, 24.

10. Ibid., 25.

crete narratives of Scripture, which call for coherent explanation. For this reason, the centrality of the Trinity in giving shape to theology is likewise demanded by these narratives, which witness to the revelation of God in Christ. The biblical narratives lead to the conclusion that the affirmation of God as triune lies at the very heart of the Christian faith and comprises its distinctive conception of God. Therefore, insofar as the theological enterprise is embedded in the biblical narratives, Christian theology is characterized by its confession of God as triune.

Trinitarian Theology in the Tradition of the Church

The doctrine of the Trinity has stood at the heart of theology throughout church history, providing the impetus for the theological task and giving shape to the theological deposit that has continually arisen from that enterprise. In fact, in one sense, the history of theology is the history of the genesis and development of the doctrine of the Trinity, the engagement with the trinitarian conception of God, and the quest to set forth a theology that is truly trinitarian. As noted earlier, the early Christians faced the challenge of coming to grips with the theological situation spawned by their confession of the lordship of Jesus, their experience of the Holy Spirit, and their commitment to the one God of the Old Testament. The preoccupation with the unity of God thrust upon the second-century church by its struggle with paganism and Gnosticism initially left the theologians of the day with little interest in exploring the eternal relations of the Trinity or in devising a conceptual and linguistic apparatus capable of expressing these relations.[11] The situation soon changed as the church became embroiled in a theological controversy that eventually ensured that all subsequent theology was trinitarian in nature.

Since Hellenism was the chief audience to which Christian thought was directed by the latter half of the second century, the early Christian apologists busied themselves with the task of finding common ground between the Christian message and the Greek philosophical tradition. For this reason, the attempt to articulate the relationship between Jesus and God took on a decidedly Greek philosophical flavor. The Greek intellectual setting produced and framed emerging theological controversy about the person of Christ.

The particular formulation of Christology that eventually climaxed in the formal development of the doctrine of the Trinity arose in the

---

11. J. N. D. Kelly, *Early Christian Doctrines*, rev. ed. (San Francisco: Harper & Row, 1978), 109.

context of the Arian controversy. In his desire to protect the absolute uniqueness and transcendence of God, Arius, who agreed with Origen that the Father begets or generates the Son, argued that rather than an eternal movement within the divine life, this begetting occurred at a temporal point. The Father made the Son, he asserted, and this meant that the Son is a creature who must have had a beginning. In concluding that there was a time when the Son was not, Arius in effect made the trinitarian distinctions external to God and claimed that in the divine eternal nature God is one, not three. The church, however, disagreed with Arius, unequivocally affirming the full deity of Christ at the Council of Nicea in 325. The creed issued by the council asserted that the Son is "begotten of the Father as only begotten, that is, from the essence of the Father, God from God, Light from Light, True God from True God, begotten not created, of the same essence as the Father."[12]

At Nicea, the church set the christological basis for a trinitarian theology. A second theological debate occurring in the aftermath of Nicea provided the corresponding pneumatological basis. The dispute about the Holy Sprit had its roots in Arius's teaching about the Son, for his followers, including Macedonius, the bishop of Constantinople for whom the controversy is often named, asserted not only that the Son was the first creature of the Father but also that the Holy Spirit was the first creature of the Son.[13] The church father Athanasius countered this claim by showing that the full deity of the Spirit, like that of the Son, was a necessary component of Christian faith, especially the Christian teaching about salvation. He asserted that if the Spirit who enters the hearts and lives of the faithful is not fully divine, then believers do not enjoy true community with God. The Council of Constantinople (AD 381) agreed with Athanasius and stated in the Nicene Creed that the Holy Spirit is "worshiped and glorified together with the Father and the Son."[14]

The decisions of the ecumenical councils at Nicea and Constantinople provided the framework for the future development of trinitarian theology. Yet although the councils affirmed the full deity of the Son and the Spirit along with the Father, the creeds that articulated the results of the conciliar deliberations did not address the question as to how the three comprise one God or the implications of this doctrine for the Christian message. The task of providing a formulation of the relation-

12. "The Creed of Nicaea," in *Creeds of the Churches: A Reader in Christian Doctrine from the Bible to the Present*, ed. John Leith, 3rd ed. (Atlanta: John Knox, 1982), 30–31.

13. Kelly, *Early Christian Doctrines*, 256.

14. "The Constantinopolitan Creed," in *Creeds of the Churches*, 33. This creed is popularly known as the Nicene Creed.

ship among Father, Son, and Spirit fell to the Cappadocian fathers: Basil the Great, Gregory of Nyssa, and Gregory of Nazianzus.[15] In developing their conception of the Triune God, the Cappadocians appropriated two Greek terms, *ousia* and *hypostasis*, theorizing that God is one *ousia* (essence) but three *hypostaseis* (independent realities) who share the one essence. The Cappadocian formulation of the Trinity provided the church with a fixed reference point, but it did not bring the discussions of the doctrine to an end. On the contrary, it opened the door for an ensuing debate as to the exact way of construing the threeness and the oneness of God, a debate that eventually led to a theological parting of the ways between the Eastern and Western churches.

The theologians of the East sought to draw out the implications of the distinction between the words *ousia* and *hypostasis*. Colin Gunton notes that by the time of the Cappadocians the Greek term *hypostasis* referred to the concrete particularity of Father, Son, and Spirit.[16] In this rendering, the three are not viewed simply as individuals but rather as persons whose reality can be understood only in terms of their relations to one another. By virtue of these relations, they together constitute the being, or *ousia*, of the one God. The persons are therefore not relations but concrete particulars who are in relation to one another.[17] Gunton notes that this conceptual development not only provided a way to understand the threeness of the Christian God without loss to the divine unity but also established a new relational ontology: For God to be, God must be in communion. This theological conclusion arose out of the linguistic connection between the terms *hypostasis* and *ousia*. Although conceptually distinct, because of their mutual involvement with each other, they are inseparable in thought.[18] The Eastern understanding was also characterized by the tendency to focus on the three individual members of the Trinity rather than on the divine unity. Although not denying that Father, Son, and Spirit possess one divine essence, the Eastern thinkers tended to highlight the specific operations of the Father, the Son, and the Spirit in the divine acts of creation, reconciliation, and consummation.

The linguistic differences between Latin and Greek as well as the differing cultural and theological temperaments of East and West led the Western theologians to travel a somewhat different path. Their use of Latin meant that they were not fully cognizant of the nuances of the

---

15. Ibid., 258.
16. Colin Gunton, *The Promise of Trinitarian Theology*, 2nd ed. (Edinburgh: T & T Clark, 1997), 39.
17. Ibid.
18. Ibid.

linguistic formulations emerging in the East. Instead, they drew on the work of Tertullian, whose formula *tres personae, una substantia* became a staple of the Latin conception. Tertullian's formula served to complicate the discussion with Eastern thinkers, however, in that the term *substantia* was the usual Latin translation of *hypostasis*, not *ousia*. The linguistic difficulties were compounded by the continuing influence of Athanasius, who had understood *ousia* and *hypostasis* as synonyms.[19] Use of the formula *tres personae, una substantia* led Western theologians to emphasize the one divine essence or substance rather than the plurality or threeness of the Trinity characteristic of the East.

The classic statement of the Western understanding of the Trinity came in Augustine's influential work *De Trinitate*. Augustine appealed to the nature of human beings, who, because they are created in the image of God, display "vestiges" of the Trinity, an approach that led him to look for analogies of the Trinity in the nature of the human person.[20] In his estimation, the key to understanding the Trinity is found in the concept of love. According to Augustine, the human mind knows love in itself and as a consequence knows God, for God is love. This leads to a knowledge of the Trinity in that love implies a Trinity: "he that loves, and that which is loved, and love."[21] Actually, Augustine offered a long series of analogies based on humans as the *imago Dei*, the most central of which is the triad of being, knowing, and willing. Augustine's psychological analogy of the Trinity, with its focus on the oneness of God in contrast to the Eastern emphasis on the divine threeness and with its starting point in the divine essence rather than the saving act of God in Christ, set the stage for the trinitarian theologizing prominent in the West.[22] In the case of both East and West, however, although the concept of God as triune was definitely not the only topic of discussion, it clearly framed the dominant theological agenda and structured the theologizing of the great minds of the day.

The linguistic and cultural differences between the Eastern and Western churches contributed to the Great Schism, which came in the wake of the *filioque* controversy.[23] Yet the ecclesiastical breach did not terminate discussions of the doctrine or move the Trinity from the center

19. Edmund Fortman, *The Triune God: A Historical Study of the Doctrine of the Trinity* (Philadelphia: Westminster, 1972), 72–83.

20. Cyril C. Richardson, "The Enigma of the Trinity," in *A Companion to the Study of St. Augustine*, ed. Roy Battenhouse (Oxford: Oxford University Press, 1955), 248–55.

21. Augustine, *On the Trinity* 8.10.14, trans. Arthur West Haddon, in *The Nicene and Post-Nicene Fathers*, vol. 3, first series (Grand Rapids: Eerdmans, 1980), 124.

22. Fortman, *Triune God*, 141.

23. Jaroslav Pelikan, *The Melody of Theology: A Philosophical Dictionary* (Cambridge: Harvard University Press, 1988), 90.

of Christian theology, especially in the West. Throughout the history of the medieval church, the doctrine of the Trinity continued to receive considerable attention from both scholastic and mystical theologians who viewed God's triune nature as a central concern for Christian faith and who attempted to systematize and explicate trinitarian doctrine. During the twelfth century, a number of significant works on the Trinity served to codify and standardize the insights of the early fathers and thereby provided a basis in tradition for the speculations of the following century. Leading thinkers such as Anselm of Canterbury and Peter Abelard developed a dialectical approach to theology that attempted to demonstrate the coherence between revealed and rational truth. Perhaps the most significant twelfth-century contribution to trinitarian theology, however, was that of Richard of St. Victor, whose treatise *De Trinitate* stands as one of the most learned expositions of the Trinity from the Middle Ages.

In keeping with the classical understanding of theology as faith seeking understanding, Richard attempted to provide a rational demonstration of the Trinity and to discover "necessary reasons" for God's unity and triunity[24] that could be coupled with faith and experience.[25] Hence, he maintained that while the Trinity is beyond independent, rational proof, human reason is able to provide lines of thinking that support and explicate what faith declares. Of particular interest is Richard's discussion of the necessary plurality of persons in the Godhead. To develop this point, he turned to the concept of divine goodness and observed that supreme goodness must involve love. Richard argued that because self-love cannot be true charity, supreme love requires another, equal to the lover, who is the recipient of that love. In addition, because supreme love is received as well as given, such love must be a shared love, one in which each person loves and is loved by the other. Cognizant that the witness of Christian faith declares that the one God is three, not merely two, persons, Richard claimed that further analysis of supreme love demonstrates that indeed three persons are required. He argued that for love to be supreme it must desire that the love it experiences through giving and receiving be one that is shared with another.[26] Consequently, perfect love is not merely mutual love between two but is fully shared among three and only three.[27]

24. Fortman, *Triune God*, 193.

25. Ewert Cousins, "A Theology of Interpersonal Relations," *Thought* 45 (1970): 59.

26. For an English translation of book 3 of Richard's *De Trinitate*, see Grover Zinn, ed., *Richard of St. Victor* (New York: Paulist Press, 1979), 373–97.

27. Fortman, *Triune God*, 194.

Richard's work is significant in that it provides a relationally based alternative to Augustine's psychological approach to the Trinity. As Gunton notes regarding Richard, "Unlike Augustine, the fountainhead of most Western theology of the Trinity, he looks not at the inner soul for his clues to the nature of God, but at persons in relation."[28] Moreover, Richard's conception of the interior life of God demands a fully personal Trinity. By extension, the relationality within the divine life captured in Richard's theological model carries implications for a theological understanding of humans as the *imago Dei* as well. As Grover Zinn explains, "The reflection of this life should lead to a renewed appreciation of charity as a love lived in community with others, involving interpersonal sharing of the deepest kind."[29] In short, whereas Augustine's conception of the individual soul as an image of the Trinity provided the basis for an interior approach to spirituality that emphasizes the ascent of the individual to union with God, Richard's approach suggests the possibility of spirituality based on interpersonal community.[30] Although it would be misleading to say that Richard developed a fully relational view of the person in his thought, he provided, as Gunton points out, "an approach to the doctrine of the Trinity that contains possibilities for the development of a relational view of the person."[31]

During the thirteenth century, the theologians of the Dominican and Franciscan orders produced what one historian calls "the greatest contribution to trinitarian systematization that the Western Church ever had seen or would see."[32] Clearly, the most significant figure of this period is Thomas Aquinas. The comprehensive detail and philosophical precision of his trinitarian theology have won for him the admiration of many who would affirm with Fortman that there can be "little doubt that Aquinas produced the finest metaphysical synthesis of trinitarian doctrine that had thus far appeared in West or East."[33] The work of Aquinas provides an outstanding example of a comprehensive understanding of the Christian faith and the created order developed into a coherent whole through the doctrine of the Triune God, "to which everything was made tributary and in the light of which all things were viewed."[34]

However, the approach of the medieval theologians to the doctrine of the Trinity has recently come under scrutiny, largely because of its

28. Gunton, *Promise of Trinitarian Theology*, 89.
29. Zinn, *Richard of St. Victor*, 46.
30. Cousins, "Theology of Interpersonal Relations," 59.
31. Gunton, *Promise of Trinitarian Theology*, 91.
32. Fortman, *Triune God*, 233.
33. Ibid., 234.
34. Arthur C. McGiffert, *A History of Christian Thought*, vol. 2 (New York: Scribner's, 1933), 293.

focus on the unity of God. Aquinas has been the particular recipient of much of the criticism. Karl Rahner, for example, suggests that by turning first to the doctrine of the one God and only later developing an understanding of God as triune, Aquinas contributed to the decline of robust trinitarian theology in the life of the church.[35] Critiques such as Rahner's often leave the impression that Aquinas was not genuinely interested in the doctrine of the Trinity and that his relative lack of concern was symptomatic of the decline of the doctrine over the course of the Middle Ages. This is, however, manifestly not the case. Medieval theology is marked by extensive trinitarian discourse motivated by a robust concern for a proper understanding of the nature of God as triune. To the criticism that Aquinas's method of beginning with the doctrine of the one God effectively marginalized the doctrine of the Trinity, Cunningham replies that Aquinas could not even have imagined that his readers would think of God "in anything *other* than trinitarian categories." He adds that today "audiences may no longer operate with this assumption; we need to take this into account, but it can hardly be blamed on Thomas."[36] Evident in the thought of the medieval theologians in general and Aquinas in particular is a deep commitment to the trinitarian faith and witness of the early church coupled with an earnest desire to provide a compelling account of that confession as an integral component of the faith of the Christian community.

In many ways, the medieval period was the high-water mark of trinitarian discourse in the history of the church, at least until the twentieth century. As the cultural ethos of the medieval world gave way to the Renaissance and the emergence of the modern world, the theological concerns of the church shifted. The most significant development in the Western church was, of course, the Protestant Reformation with its focus on the nature of authority and the doctrine of individual salvation. The advent of the Reformation and the emergence of the modern world inaugurated a period of decreased theological interest in the Trinity and the waning of trinitarian discourse in the church.

The doctrine of the Trinity was not central in the theological debates of the Reformation. The magisterial Reformers essentially affirmed the trinitarian doctrine of the ancient creeds as expressing the teaching of Scripture on the doctrine while doing little to advance trinitarian theology itself. Although the Reformers were committed to the confession of the Trinity, they had little interest in the speculative reflection

---

35. Karl Rahner, *The Trinity* (New York: Herder & Herder, 1970), 16–17. For a similar critique, see Catherine Mowry LaCugna, *God for Us: The Trinity and the Christian Life* (San Francisco: HarperCollins, 1991), 145.
36. Cunningham, *These Three Are One*, 33.

of medieval theology as a result of their desire not to move beyond the testimony of the biblical writings. The magisterial Reformers were content merely to affirm the classical Western position. Some leaders in the radical tradition of the Reformation, however, transformed the general reticence to engage in speculative matters into an actual rejection of the doctrine of the Trinity. A few went so far as to claim that the doctrine is an unbiblical human construction and therefore ought to be dropped from the Christian confession.

Perhaps the most well-known antitrinitarian is Faustus Socinus. Socinus accepted Scripture as the supreme authority in matters of faith, but he insisted that it be interpreted in accordance with reason and not in the context of the traditional creeds. On this basis, he argued that God was one in both essence and person. According to Socinus, if the divine essence is one, it cannot include several divine persons, since a person is nothing else than an intelligent, indivisible essence. Thus, although orthodox theology had always carefully distinguished between essence and person, Socinus equated the two and as a consequence asserted that God is a single person. The Socinian understanding later provided the theological basis for Unitarianism in England and America.

During the Enlightenment, the doctrine of the Trinity came under widespread attack as the benign neglect of earlier years turned into outright hostility. The thinkers of the Age of Reason eschewed revealed religion in favor of a religion based solely on reason. Because the basis for the traditional understanding of the Trinity lay in divine revelation and church tradition rather than in universal reason, the doctrine was cast aside as a relic of a superstitious and uninformed past. Enlightenment thinkers called into question the possibility of structuring an entire theology around the Trinity by challenging the very possibility of asserting such a concept about God. The hegemony of Enlightenment thought came to an apex in the work of Immanuel Kant, who represented both the culmination and the destruction of the rationalist mind-set.[37] Kant opened the way for the modern theological situation through the rejection of both the classical orthodox and the purely rationalist understanding of theology. His abnegation of any special revelation as the source for religious truth or any church authority as the interpreter of theological truth undermined the classical understanding of the Trinity. His claim that "scientific" knowledge must be limited to the realm of experience shaped by the rational structures of the mind meant that claims to knowledge of God through pure reason were impossible. Although Kant provided a telling critique of many of

---

37. Jaroslav Pelikan, *From Luther to Kierkegaard* (St. Louis: Concordia, 1950), 97.

the claims of the Enlightenment, he also sealed off the possibility of a rational knowledge of God and thereby made traditional trinitarian discourse both impractical and superfluous.

In the wake of Kant, nineteenth-century theologians followed three basic trajectories, each of which continued to play a major role in the twentieth-century discussion. One approach, that of the conservatives who sought to maintain traditional, confessional orthodoxy, simply held fast to the classical position on the basis of Scripture or tradition. Despite their commitment to orthodox doctrine, however, conservatives gave little place to the Trinity or to a trinitarian structure in their constructive theological work. As a result, in conservative circles, the doctrine of the Trinity increasingly came to be viewed as a mystery to be confessed on the basis of Scripture and tradition, not as a motif that can provide content and structure for the theological enterprise.

A second approach, pioneered by Friedrich Schleiermacher, denied that the doctrine of the Trinity is an essential component of Christian faith. In his major theological work, *The Christian Faith*, he provides only a brief treatment of the Trinity at the conclusion of the work. In this short discussion, Schleiermacher confesses that he is unable to provide an adequate construction of the doctrine,[38] largely because the Trinity is "not an immediate utterance concerning the Christian self-consciousness but only a combination of several such utterances."[39] For Schleiermacher, trinitarian theology is the product of synthetic construction based on a variety of faith utterances that led to the doctrine of the Trinity only after the fact. He works on the assumption that the primary Christian experience, and therefore the primary Christian symbols, are bound up with the concept of the one God, the God of monotheism. In this understanding, the threeness of God is not a part of the primary witness of Christian faith but merely the product of the attempt to pull together the various elements of early Christian experience. As Ted Peters points out, the assumption that trinitarian doctrine is "a synthesis of otherwise random convictions regarding a more fundamental monotheism renders the Trinity systematically superfluous." In this way, Schleiermacher shifted the triunity of God to the margins of Christian faith, effectively "relegating it to the status of a second-rank doctrine."[40]

G. W. F. Hegel stands at the headwaters of the third nineteenth-century approach to the Trinity. Hegel understood God as the Absolute

---

38. Friedrich Scheiermacher, *The Christian Faith*, ed. H. R. MacKintosh and J. S. Stewart (Edinburgh: T & T Clark, 1999), 751.

39. Ibid., 738.

40. Ted Peters, *God as Trinity: Relationality and Temporality in Divine Life* (Louisville: Westminster John Knox, 1993), 83–85.

Spirit and developed a speculative trinitarianism in which God seeks differentiation and determination through a dialectical process that develops under three determinations, which correspond to the three members of the Trinity.[41] However, Hegel's model of trinitarianism falls short of the classical conception. For example, his model suggests that the reality of God is fully manifest only in the third mode, the Spirit, thereby effectively denying the traditional doctrine with its clear assertion that all three persons participate equally in the deity. In addition, Hegel reduces the Christian theological conception of God as Trinity to a symbolic illustration of a philosophical truth accessible through human reason apart from Christian revelation or experience. In short, as Peters concludes, Hegel and his followers affirm a philosophical trinitarianism in which the Trinity "is the equivalent of a metaphysical truth that can be established more or less independently of the Christian revelation."[42] In spite of these shortcomings, Hegel is important in that he broke with his Enlightenment philosophical predecessors and many of his contemporaries who saw the concept of the Trinity as an embarrassing relic from the ancient Christian past. Going against the philosophical grain, he reestablished the concept of the Trinity as a crucial component in both philosophy and theology. As a consequence, Hegel's reaffirmation of the importance of the trinitarian conception of God opened the way for the revival of trinitarian theology in the twentieth century. In this sense, his understanding of the Trinity marked the first stage in the contemporary recovery of the doctrine.

Christian theology must be trinitarian because the understanding of God as triune reflects the biblical narrative and, apart from a hiatus generated by the Enlightenment, has informed and shaped the theological conversation throughout the history of the church. Modern theology did mark a momentary move away from this approach to theology, leading to the marginalization of the Trinity, as both liberal and conservative theologians pursued the agenda of the Enlightenment, even if in differing ways. Yet the twentieth century launched a renewal of trinitarian theology characterized by a return to the classical supposition that the Trinity ought to be a central concern for Christian faith and life and that the content and exposition of theology should be ordered around the trinitarian conception of God. The renewed commitment to the centrality of the Trinity that typifies the contemporary theological environment is in keeping with the historical trajectory of the Christian community's reflection on the content of theology. The one God is Father, Son, and

41. G. W. F. Hegel, *The Phenomenology of Mind*, trans. J. B. Ballie (New York: Harper & Row, 1967), 766–85.
42. Peters, *God as Trinity*, 83.

Spirit. This confession reflects the Christian experience of God and stands as the chief hallmark of the Christian faith. The ecumenical symbols of the Christian tradition are ordered around this confession, and the history of Christian theological reflection has been decisively shaped by it. Hence, Christian theology is properly trinitarian in keeping with the position of the ecumenical Christian community, which has been committed to finding its basis in the being and action of the Triune God. Theological reflection that seeks to be particularly and distinctively Christian must continue in this tradition if it is to make any claim of continuity with the past.

Trinitarian Theology in the Twentieth Century

The biblical witness and the theological tradition of the church converge to indicate that Christian theology is trinitarian. We now turn our attention to a consideration of the character of such a theology beginning with the resurgence of trinitarian theology in the twentieth century. Although several theologians at the turn of the century were busily unfolding the implications of Hegelian trinitarianism, arguably the most significant thinker responsible for launching theology on a new path was Karl Barth. A central aspect of Barth's agenda was clearly to reestablish the significance of the Trinity for theology. In his *Church Dogmatics*, the doctrine functions both as a type of prolegomenon and as the structural motif for his presentation of Christian theology.

At the heart of Barth's program is his assertion that the revelation of God that provides the basis for theology is a trinitarian event in which the divine self-disclosure involves three moments: Revealer, Revelation, and Revealedness. He maintains that these correspond to Father, Son, and Spirit.[43] Departing from Schleiermacher's model of synthesis, Barth engages in an analysis of the biblical witness that leads him to the conclusion that the doctrine of the Trinity emerges as a logical necessity. Actually, for Barth it is the Christocentric focus of the biblical witness that necessitates a trinitarian revelational theology. He is convinced that the biblical affirmation that through the mission of Jesus Christ God has reconciled the world to himself leads to a trinitarian conception of God. Moreover, the scriptural witness to the life and mission of Jesus and the New Testament confession that this Jesus is Lord entail the corresponding belief that God is triune. Hence, for Barth, the threefoldness indicated by Father, Son, and Spirit is "a threefoldness in the structure or pattern

43. Karl Barth, *Church Dogmatics*, trans. G. W. Bromiley, 2nd ed. (Edinburgh: T & T Clark, 1975), 1/1, 295.

of the one act of God in Christ and therefore the structure of all divine activity and of the being of God."[44] In short, the doctrine of the Trinity is deeply embedded in the biblical witness and therefore is, in fact, contrary to Schleiermacher, a primary Christian symbol.

Barth's Christocentric, revelational trinitarianism emerges as well from his conviction that the Christian conception of God does not begin with a generic monotheism to which Christology is added at a later point. Instead, the Christian understanding of God begins with the Son, through whom God is revealed as Father. It is through the revelation of the Son that God is known as the triune one. Thus, for Barth, the Christian understanding of God as triune is distinct from all other conceptions of the divine reality. In Barth's estimation, then, the doctrine of the Trinity follows directly from the Christian confession that God has revealed himself to the world in Jesus Christ. Claude Welch praises Barth's Christocentric revelational approach in that in it the Trinity is "an immediate consequence of the gospel" due to the fact that the revelation "on which everything depends" cannot be developed or stated except in a trinitarian fashion. Welch then adds, "The doctrine of the Trinity is of all-embracing importance because it is the objective expression, the crystallization of the gospel itself. It is not just one part of the doctrine of God, but is integral to every aspect of the doctrine of God and to every other doctrine as well."[45]

Barth's great accomplishment, therefore, was to argue conclusively that the Christian community's primary experience of revelation is trinitarian in nature and, as a consequence, that the doctrine of the Trinity is a logically necessary component of the early Christian experience and confession of Jesus Christ as Lord and revealer of God. In so doing, Barth avoided splitting up elements of the Christian experience that had in fact been received by the early community as a whole. Ted Peters summarizes the far-reaching theological implications of this innovation: "It not only prevents us from identifying God simply with a Creator-God of nature and natural theology, thus falling into a 'unitarianism of the Father,' but it also makes impossible a Christology that is not wholly theocentric or a pneumatology that is not genuinely Christocentric and theocentric."[46] These implications are evident in the *Church Dogmatics* itself, as the renewed emphasis on the threefold nature of God as a primary component of Christian faith provides structure for everything that follows.

---

44. Claude Welch, *In This Name: The Doctrine of the Trinity in Contemporary Theology* (New York: Scribner's, 1952), 234.
45. Ibid., 238.
46. Peters, *God as Trinity*, 88.

We noted earlier Hegel's importance in opening the way for a revival of trinitarian theology. Despite its shortcomings, Hegel's work leads to an important insight for theological method. Insofar as the Triune God is connected to the historical process (even if not in the manner Hegel himself proposed), the doctrine of the Trinity is not merely a subtheme of theology proper but rather the topic of the entire systematic theological construction, which views all the theological loci as in some sense participants in the central topic of theology, namely, the Triune God. Barth's renewal of the doctrine of the Trinity took this Hegelian implication a step further. In his estimation, all theology is the explication of the being and action of God in Christ. As a consequence of this Barthian insight, a truly trinitarian theology is one that is structured around the self-disclosure of the Triune God as centered in Christ and given through Scripture to the believing community. In this context, a trinitarian theology is one in which all the theological loci are both informed by and, in turn, inform the explication of the Trinity.

Following the trail blazed by Barth, many theologians have risen to the challenge of placing the doctrine of the Trinity back into the center of constructive theology. Often ranked with Hegel and Barth in setting the theological agenda is Karl Rahner. Rahner articulated the important thesis that the economic Trinity is the immanent Trinity and that the immanent Trinity is the economic Trinity.[47] This thesis, known as Rahner's rule, marks the new phase that trinitarian discourse has entered, as this basic principle has engendered a broad consensus of opinion among theologians of various traditions.[48] Rahner's rule indicates that God's ongoing interaction with creation always comes as the work of one or another of the three divine persons. God does not relate to the world in the unity of the divine being. Because the Christian experience of God occurs through the economy of salvation, that is, through God's redemptive activity in history, knowledge of God is never simply knowledge of God in general but always knowledge of God in God's triune being. At the same time, Rahner argues that the experience of God that arises in the economy of salvation remains a genuine experience of the eternal God, for through the process of salvation, the eternal God reveals his own true self to humans. Thus, Rahner declares that the internal life of God is the way we experience the divine in relation to ourselves, namely, as Father, Son, and Spirit. Although theologians such as Jürgen Moltmann and Robert Jenson subsequently developed the idea that God finds his identity in the temporal events of the economy of salvation,

47. Rahner, *Trinity*, 22.
48. Walter Kasper, *The God of Jesus Christ*, trans. Matthew J. O'Connell (London: SCM, 1983), 274.

Rahner himself did not move in this direction. He retains the classical belief that God's eternal being is independent of historical events. His rule simply affirms that the way in which God relates to the world must be understood with reference to each of the three persons and not as emerging from a prior understanding of God as a unity.[49]

Hegel, through his connection of the Trinity and the unfolding historical process; Barth, through his insistence on the connection between the Trinity and revelation as the basis for all theological assertions; and Rahner, through his connection of the immanent Trinity and the economic Trinity as one identical reality, set the context for the discussion of trinitarian theology in the twentieth century. Eberhard Jüngel, Moltmann, Jenson, and Wolfhart Pannenberg, in turn, attempted to develop a trinitarian theology within the context of the framework and the insights provided by the three pioneers. All of these theologians are committed to a relational interpretation of the Trinity and to the methodological premise that the revelation of God as Trinity, along with the corresponding trinitarian theology, must be grounded solely in the historical person of Jesus, not based on alien philosophical categories and structures. Their work launched a relatively new emphasis that bases the doctrine of the Trinity on relationality and, as such, represents, at least to some degree, an extension and development of ancient trinitarian thought.[50]

Pannenberg's work reflects a carefully developed statement of the doctrine and its interrelatedness to the whole of theology. He asserts that rather than relegating the Trinity to the status of a footnote, we ought to place God's triune nature at the very heart of theology. In a manner reminiscent of Barth, Pannenberg asserts that all systematic theology is in some sense the explication of this central doctrine. At the same time, Pannenberg is also critical of the theological tradition from Augustine to Barth. He claims that by viewing the trinitarian members as the internal relations within the one God theologians have made God into a fourth person above the three members of the Trinity. Rather than speaking of the one God who is above the three, Pannenberg argues that the one God is the three and that there is no God other than the Father, Son, and Spirit.

These insights are significant in that they seek to maintain that the explication of the Triune God in God's self-disclosure in and to creation is at the same time the explication of the Triune God in the divine reality. This assertion takes us back to our earlier discussion of the history of

49. Peters, *God as Trinity,* 97.

50. Catherine Mowry LaCugna, "Current Trends in Trinitarian Theology," *Religious Studies Review* 13, no. 2 (April 1987): 141–47.

God. As noted, throughout much of church history, theologians assumed that God's internal history corresponded to God's external history. This assumption, however, eventually led to a focus on God's internal history, which elevated a kind of speculative trinitarian theology separated from the concrete historical narratives of the Bible. This "theology from above" no longer had much interest in the "theology from below" to which it was in fact necessarily linked and on which it was dependent. In the aftermath of the attendant loss of trinitarian theology, Rahner and Pannenberg have reunited God's internal and external histories and in so doing have brought together theology "from above" and "from below."

Methodologically, this means that trinitarian theological explication runs in two directions. On the one hand, it moves *from* the self-disclosure of God in and to creation, centered on the coming of Christ and the ongoing work of the Spirit, *to* the eternal life of the Triune God. Viewed from this perspective, theology (proper) is dependent on Christology and pneumatology. On the other hand, theological construction moves as well *from* the eternal reality of the Triune God, which is confessed by the ecumenical church of all ages, *to* an understanding of the trinitarian persons in the creative and redemptive work of the one God. In this sense, Christology and pneumatology can be ventured only in light of theology (proper).

The Social God

The insights drawn from the renewal of trinitarian theology suggest that in a trinitarian understanding of the doctrine of God, the traditional loci of theology proper, Christology, and pneumatology must be inter-related. However, perhaps the single most significant development in the contemporary renaissance of trinitarian theology has been the emphasis on relationality. The category of relationality enjoys a considerable degree of consensus among recent interpreters of trinitarian theology who see it as providing an alternative to the metaphysics of substance that dominated theological reflection on the Trinity throughout much of church history. The traditional emphasis on an abstract property of substance, or a divine essence, has come under scrutiny in recent trinitarian studies. Theologians today routinely critique the concept as implying that God is an isolated, solitary individual.

The question of the nature of a substance was initially placed on the theological table by the early church father Tertullian through his famous formula *tres personae, una substantia*. Theologians, especially in the West, subsequently took up the challenge of devising an understanding of the nature of a substance when used with reference to God. Hence, Augustine spoke of God as a substance that was eternal and unchangeable. Later, Thomas Aquinas defined God as pure act, thereby excluding such ideas as "becoming" or "potency" in reference to God insofar as they implied change in the immutable God. The definitional link these theologians forged between substance and unchangeability meant that they viewed God as eternal and unchanging, in contrast to creation, which is temporal and in a constant state of change in its relation to God.

The substantialist conception carried within itself the distinction between absolute essence and relational attributes. According to this understanding, essence is absolute, and therefore it must remain unchanged in order to preserve its identity. If change occurs in the essence of an entity, its identity is lost. Relationality, in turn, belongs to the dimension of attributes, not substance. Consequently, substantialist theologians suggested that God is absolute and immutable in his essential nature, whereas he maintains relationality to creation through the divine attributes. As Ted Peters notes regarding the classical position, "What could not be countenanced is the notion that the divine essence is contingent upon the relational dimensions of its being."[51] The result, however, has been the obscuring of God's internal relationality and of God's loving relationship to creation in much of the classical literature on the nature of God. In recent years, the classical commitment to a substantialist conception of God's nature has been critiqued. At the heart of this critique is the apparent incompatibility of an eternal, essentially immutable God with the portrait in the biblical narratives of a God who has entered into loving relationship with creation. Although the debate continues as to the degree to which the category of substance ought to be abandoned, theologians voice considerable agreement that the primary accent should be placed on the category of relationality.

Catherine LaCugna, to cite one example, asserts that person rather than substance is the primary ontological category, noting that the ultimate source of reality is not a "by-itself" or an "in-itself" but a person, a "toward-another." She concludes that the Triune God is "self-communicating" and exists from all eternity "in relation to another."[52] Likewise, Robert Jenson writes, "The original point of trinitarian dogma and analysis was that God's relations to us are internal to him, and it is in carrying out this insight that the 'relation' concept was introduced to define the distinction of identities."[53] In a similar manner, Elizabeth

51. Peters, *God as Trinity*, 31.
52. LaCugna, *God for Us*, 14–15.
53. Jenson, *Triune Identity*, 120.

Johnson claims that the priority of relation in the Triune God challenges and critiques the concentration of classical theism on "singleness" in God. Because the persons are "constituted by their relationships to each other, each is unintelligible except as connected with the others."[54] The assertion that each of the persons in the triune life is constituted only in relationship to the others leads Johnson to the conclusion that the "very principle of their being" is to be found in the category of relation.[55]

David Cunningham notes that the breadth of the current consensus about the priority of relationality in trinitarian discourse is evidenced by the fact that both Jenson and Johnson may be cited in support of it, even though the two thinkers "are not usually noted for being in close agreement with one another."[56] This theological consensus encompasses a variety of thinkers, including Jürgen Moltmann, Wolfhart Pannenberg, Leonardo Boff, Colin Gunton, and Alan Torrance, although these theologians may differ on the precise construction of relationality.

At the heart of the contemporary consensus concerning the divine relationality is the apostolic witness that God is love (e.g., 1 John 4:8, 16). Developing the doctrine of the Trinity in accordance with the category of relationality indicates how this biblical assertion is to be understood. Throughout all eternity, the divine life of the Triune God is aptly characterized by the word *love*, which, when viewed in light of relationality, signifies the reciprocal self-dedication of the trinitarian members to one another. Indeed, there is no God other than the Father, Son, and Spirit bound together in love throughout eternity. The term *love*, in turn, provides a profound conception of the reality of God as understood by the Christian tradition. Love expressed and received by the trinitarian persons among themselves provides a description of the inner life of God throughout eternity apart from any reference to creation. In addition to enjoying the support of the biblical witness, *love* is an especially fruitful term as an explication of the divine life because it is a relational concept. Love requires both subject and object. Because God is triune—that is, multiplicity within unity—the divine reality comprehends both love's subject and love's object. For this reason, when viewed theologically, the statement "God is love" refers primarily to the eternal, relational, intratrinitarian fellowship among Father, Son, and Holy Spirit, who together are the one God. In this way, God is love within the divine reality, and in this sense, through all eternity, God is the social Trinity, the community of love.

---

54. Elizabeth A. Johnson, *She Who Is: The Mystery of God in Feminist Theological Discourse* (New York: Crossroad, 1992), 216.

55. Ibid., 216.

56. Cunningham, *These Three Are One*, 26.

The Missional God

The social and relational character of the Triune God as an eternal community of love is further developed by the concept of mission. This idea of mission as a central aspect of the character of God is captured by the term *missio Dei* (mission of God). It suggests that God has a particular concern in engagement with the world. The idea of mission is at the heart of the biblical narratives concerning the work of God in human history. It begins with the call to Israel to be God's covenant people and the recipient of God's covenant blessings for the purpose of blessing the nations. The mission of God is at the heart of the covenant with Israel and is continuously unfolded over the course of the centuries in the life of God's people recorded in the narratives of canonical Scripture. This missional covenant reaches its revelatory climax in the life, death, and resurrection of Jesus Christ and continues through the sending of the Spirit as the one who calls, guides, and empowers the community of Christ's followers, the church, as the socially, historically, and culturally embodied witness to the gospel of Jesus Christ and the tangible expression of the mission of God. This mission continues today in the global ministry and witness to the gospel of churches in every culture around the world and, guided by the Spirit, moves toward the promised consummation of reconciliation and redemption in the eschaton.

This missional pattern is captured in the words of Jesus recorded in the Gospel of John: "As the Father has sent me, so I send you" (John 20:21). God is missional by nature. The love of God lived out and expressed in the context of the eternal community of love gives rise to the missional character of God, who seeks to extend the love shared by Father, Son, and Holy Spirit into the created order. According to David Bosch, mission is derived from the very nature of God and must be situated in the context of the doctrine of the Trinity rather than in ecclesiology or soteriology. In this context, the logic of the classical doctrine of *missio Dei* expressed as God the Father sending the Son, and the Father and the Son sending the Spirit, may be expanded to include yet another movement: "Father, Son, and Spirit sending the church into the world."[57] In this context, the church is seen as the instrument of God's mission, and its various historical, global, and contemporary embodiments may be viewed as a series of local iterations of God's universal mission to all creation.

This understanding of God as missional, arising from the very character of God's triune life, has significant implications for the conception of the church and mission as it has been understood in the West. In

---

57. David Bosch, *Transforming Mission: Paradigm Shifts in Theology of Mission* (Maryknoll, NY: Orbis, 1991), 390.

reflecting on the missionary expansion of the church over the last two centuries, many missiologists began to be concerned about the particular shape of this enterprise. It has become increasingly clear that Western mission was traditionally very much a European-church-centered enterprise and that the gospel was passed on in the cultural shape of the Western church. "The subtle assumption of much Western mission was that the church's missionary mandate lay not only in forming the church of Jesus Christ, but in shaping the Christian communities that it birthed in the image of the church of western European culture." This understanding of mission, rooted in ecclesiology, has given way to a "profoundly theocentric reconceptualization of Christian mission." In the words of the authors of *Missional Church*, "We have come to see that mission is not merely an activity of the church. Rather, mission is the result of God's initiative, rooted in God's purposes to restore and heal creation. 'Mission' means 'sending,' and it is the central biblical theme describing the purpose of God in human history."[58]

This perspective has led to greater recognition of how the Western church has tended to construe and articulate the gospel in ways that are more reflective of its particular cultural context and has made the extension and survival of the institutional church its priority. It leads to the conclusion that "the church of Jesus Christ is not the goal of the gospel, but rather its instrument and witness. God's mission embraces all of creation."[59] The extension of God's mission is in calling and sending the church to be a missionary church in the cultures and societies in which it participates. This presents a challenge, however, in that the formation and the structures of the Western church are not missional. The structures have been shaped in the context of a historical and social setting that for centuries considered itself formally and officially Christian. In this context, the church was intimately involved in the shaping of the religious and cultural life of Western society. This situation led to what is known as Christendom, a system of church-state partnership and cultural hegemony in which the Christian religion maintains a unique, privileged, and protected place in society and the Christian church is its legally and socially established institutional form. This model of the church, and the outlooks and intuitions that attend to it, are so deeply pervasive that even when the formal and legal structures of Christendom are removed, as in the case of North America, its legacy is perpetuated in the traditions, patterns, structures, and attitudes that are its entailments. The continuance of these intuitions and entailments

---

58. Darrell L. Guder, ed., *Missional Church: A Vision for the Sending of the Church in North America* (Grand Rapids: Eerdmans, 1998), 4.

59. Ibid., 5.

of Christendom, even in the aftermath of its formal demise, can be described as "functional Christendom."

In the ecclesiocentric approach to mission that characterized the church of Western culture and Christendom, "mission became only one of the many programs of the church. Mission boards emerged in Western churches to do the work of foreign mission. Yet even here the Western churches understood themselves as sending churches, and they assumed the destination of their sending to be the pagan reaches of the world"[60] that would benefit from the influence of Western culture as well as the gospel. In a similar manner, many churches developed home mission programs and strategies to confront and attempt to hold at bay the emerging secularism of society that threatened to undermine Christian culture. These programs often involved significant political activism as an important part of preserving the ethos of a Christian society. In spite of all this mission-oriented activity, however, the church has been slow to comprehend that mission is not simply one of the programs of the church. Instead, mission is at the very core of the church's reason and purpose for being and should shape all that the church is and does. "It defines the church as God's sent people. Either we are defined by mission, or we reduce the scope of the gospel and the mandate of the church. Thus our challenge today is to move from church with mission to missional church."[61]

The move from church with a mission to missional church has significant implications for the character of theology. Like the church, the impulses and assumptions that have shaped the discipline of theology in the West are those of Christendom rather than the mission of God. All the loci of theology are still often taught and discussed from the vantage point of early modern debates and concerns with little reference to the missional character of God and the corresponding missional vocation of the church. Courses in missions or missiology are generally taught only in the practical theology department and, apart from a generic introductory course, are often thought to be primarily for those heading overseas. Rarely are such courses taught in the systematics department, and the two disciplines, missiology and systematic theology, have generally evidenced little significant overlap and cross-fertilization. Some signs exist that this is beginning to change, but progress is slow. Generally speaking, most of the teaching and research in universities and schools of theology in the West remain in thrall to traditional academic models that stress detached objectivity in the study of any discipline, including theology.

60. Ibid., 6.
61. Ibid.

Such an outlook is antithetical to the practice of Christian theology, particularly in light of its missional dimension. As J. Andrew Kirk remarks, theology that seeks to bear faithful witness to the living God "must have a personal dimension oriented to the present: that is, to personal, openly declared preferences involving engagement and commitment, including a solid identification with the Christian community." He notes that the reason for this is that the subject of theology, the living God, calls us to obedience, makes demands, and sets tasks. In this context, the study of theology cannot remain detached and uncommitted.[62] If theology is to serve the life and witness of the church to the gospel, and if we assume that "the church can only exist as truly itself only when dedicated to the mission of God, a burning question ensues: How should one reinvent theology and theological education so that they flow naturally for an integral perspective on God's consistent will and activity in the world?"[63] Just as the church must move from church with a mission to missional church, so the discipline of theology, if it is to serve the church and be faithful to its subject, must move from theology with a mission component to a truly missional conception of theology.[64]

In speaking of the social and missional aspects of God's character, we implicitly raise the question of the knowledge of God. How are we finite and fallen human beings able to speak knowingly concerning the character of the infinite God? The Christian answer to this question is that God has been made known through revelation. The notion of revelation is consistent with the social and missional character of God, who desires to be known and to draw all creation into participation in the eternal community of love that is Father, Son, and Holy Spirit. In this context, revelation can be understood as an outworking of the mission of God in the accomplishment of this creative intention. The concept of revelation points to the character of theology as a responsive discipline that is dependent on the self-revelation of God for the knowledge of its subject. One of the issues arising from the linguistic and nonfoundationalist turns in postmodern thought that is of considerable importance for Christian faith and the work of theology concerns the nature of revelation. If all thought is situated and contextual, what does this mean for the knowledge of God and the Christian belief in the ultimate authority of divine self-revelation? How should these concerns be accounted for in an understanding and articulation of revelation and

62. J. Andrew Kirk, *The Mission of Theology and Theology as Mission* (Valley Forge, PA: Trinity Press, 1997), 9–10.

63. Ibid., 2.

64. Darrell Likens Guder, "From Mission and Theology to Missional Theology," *Princeton Seminary Bulletin* 24, no. 1 (2003): 36–54.

theology? In seeking to address these questions, we must first turn our attention to Christology, since the revelation of God in the person of Jesus Christ is the particular paradigm by which all Christian conceptions of revelation must be measured.

Christology

The classical construction of ecumenical and orthodox Christology is the definition provided by the Council of Chalcedon. The guiding purpose behind the Chalcedonian formulation is soteriological, meaning that the saving work of Christ shapes its articulation of Christ's person. In the same way, its definition of the person of Christ serves as the indispensable premise of Christ's saving work. The person and work of Christ are inextricably related. A high view of Christ's person hardly seems necessary apart from an equally high view of his work, while a high view of his work is incoherent and difficult to sustain apart from an appropriately high view of his person.

The soteriological concern also shapes the way in which the aspects of Christ's nature, the divine and the human, are defined and related. On this point, George Hunsinger notes that the minimalism of the Chalcedonian formulation has often not been fully appreciated. "Chalcedonian Christology does not isolate a point on a line that one either occupies or not. It demarcates a region in which there is more than one place to take up residence."[65] This region is circumscribed by certain distinct boundaries. Jesus Christ is understood as one person in two natures, meaning that both his deity and his humanity are viewed as internal to his person. Jesus is not simply a human being with a special relationship with God or a divine being who is not really human. Rather, he is a single person who is complete and perfect in both deity and humanity.[66] The Chalcedonian formulation does not provide a definition of either Christ's deity or his humanity except to say that they are present in a way that is unabridged, perfect, and complete. Thus, while additional and further construals and articulations of Christ's deity and humanity are not excluded by the formulation, they are not supplied. From the perspective of Chalcedon, any conception of the two natures of Christ that does not meet this basic and minimal standard is inadequate because it does not provide a sufficient understanding of the saving work of Christ.

65. George Hunsinger, *Disruptive Grace: Studies in the Theology of Karl Barth* (Grand Rapids: Eerdmans, 2000), 132.
66. Leith, *Creeds of the Churches*, 34–36.

Hunsinger observes that the minimalism of the Chalcedonian formulation also points to its significance as a hermeneutical construct. "It attempts to articulate the deep structure of the New Testament in its witness to the person of Christ. It arises from an ecclesial reading of the New Testament, taken as a whole, and then leads back to it again. It offers a framework for reading to guide the church as it interprets the multifaceted depiction of Jesus Christ contained in the New Testament." Thus, the minimalism of Chalcedon is both constitutive and regulative. It is constitutive with respect to Christ's person in the work of salvation and regulative for the church with respect to its interpretation of Scripture. As a hermeneutical construct, the Chalcedonian formulation provides "no more and no less than a set of spectacles for bringing the central witness of the New Testament into focus" through the assertion that the truth of Christ's full deity does not negate the reality that he was also fully human and vice versa. "When the New Testament depicts Jesus in his divine power, status, and authority, it presupposes his humanity; and when it depicts him in his human finitude, weakness, and mortality, it presupposes his deity. No interpretation will be adequate which asserts the one at the expense of the other."[67]

This Chalcedonian interpretation is guided not only by a definition of Christ's two natures in themselves but also by a particular construal of the way in which they are related in one and the same person. Chalcedon maintains that Christ's two natures relate without "confusion" or "change" and without "division" or "separation," meaning that neither the deity nor the humanity of Jesus surrendered its defining characteristics in the convergence to form an indissoluble unity in the person of Christ.[68] As with the definition of the two natures themselves, the Chalcedonian formulation is minimalist and open-ended in regard to the relationship of the two natures. The formulation is negatively rather than positively phrased such that any definition that affirms or implies confusion, change, division, or separation is deemed unacceptable. At the same time, space is allowed for positive constructions within the framework of the definition. Nothing more is affirmed concerning the way in which Christ's two natures are related to each other except to rule out options that are not consistent with an orthodox confession of Christ's person.

As Hunsinger concludes, each nature retains "its integrity while engaging the other in the closest of communions. The relation of Christ's two natures, as stated by Chalcedon, suggests an abiding mystery of their

---

67. Hunsinger, *Disruptive Grace*, 133.
68. Leith, *Creeds of the Churches*, 36.

unity-in-distinction and distinction-in-unity."[69] Therefore, Christology that is faithful to the Chalcedonian formulation views Jesus Christ as one person in two natures who is at one and the same time complete and perfect in deity as well as in humanity in such a way that these two natures relate without confusion or change and also without division or separation. With this brief sketch of Chalcedonian Christology in mind, we now turn our attention to the Christian teaching concerning revelation. The following section seeks to provide a theological construction of the doctrine that is in continuity with ecumenically orthodox Christian faith while at the same time addressing the particular challenges posed by postmodern thought.

Indirect Revelation

In seeking to articulate a construal of revelation in the context of postmodern thought and orthodox faith, we must return to our previous discussion of the linguistic turn and the assertion that rather than inhabiting a prefabricated, given world, we live in a linguistically construed social-cultural world of our own creation.[70] This notion of the linguistically and socially constructed nature of the world raises a concern for Christian theology and the doctrine of revelation because of the corresponding conclusion of the inadequacy of human language to provide immediate access to ultimate reality. This "crisis of representation" raises the question of God and the very possibility of theology for many postmodern thinkers. It poses a challenge for Christian thought to provide a theological account of the meaningfulness of language in general and to address specifically the question concerning the way in which the Word of God comes to expression in human words. If we are immersed and embedded in language, how can we speak of truth beyond our linguistic contexts? Some have suggested that the Christian position on revelation simply negates postmodern thought in that revelation must entail the notion that God "breaks through" language in order to provide access to "ultimate reality."[71] Others, in seeking to affirm and extend the potential implications of postmodern thought concerning the linguistic turn, have maintained that the only things finite human beings can really "know" about God are his fundamental

69. Hunsinger, *Disruptive Grace*, 133.

70. Peter L. Berger, *The Sacred Canopy: Elements of a Sociological Theory of Religion* (Garden City, NY: Doubleday, 1969), 3–13.

71. R. Scott Smith, "Christian Postmodernism and the Linguistic Turn," in *Christianity and the Postmodern Turn*, ed. Myron Penner (Grand Rapids: Brazos, forthcoming).

hiddenness and his incomprehensibility.[72] How might we address the challenge posed by the linguistic turn within the framework of orthodox Christian faith?

We begin by asserting that God does not break through language and situatedness. Rather, he enters into the linguistic setting and uses language in the act of revelation as a means of accommodation to the situation and situatedness of human beings. This position arises out of theological commitments that are Christian and Reformed. The church has long maintained the distinction between finite human knowledge and divine knowledge. Even revelation does not provide human beings with a knowledge that corresponds to that of God. The infinite qualitative distinction between God and human beings suggests the accommodated character of all human knowledge of God. For John Calvin, this means that in the process of revelation God "adjusts" and "descends" to the capacities of human beings in order to reveal the infinite mysteries of divine reality, which by their very nature are beyond the capabilities of human creatures to grasp.[73] These observations give rise to the theological adage *finitum non capax infiniti*, the finite cannot comprehend the infinite.

The natural limitations of human beings with respect to knowledge of God made known in the process of revelation extend not only to the cognitive and imaginative faculties but also to the creaturely mediums by which revelation is communicated. In other words, the very means used by God in revelation, the mediums of human nature, language, and speech, bear the inherent limitations of their creaturely character in spite of the use God makes of them as the bearers of revelation. In Chalcedonian Christology, the divine and human natures of Christ remain distinct and unimpaired even after their union in Jesus of Nazareth. Reformed theological formulations of Christology have consistently maintained that one of the implications of the Chalcedonian definition is the denial of the "divinization" of the human nature of Christ. With respect to the revelation of God in Christ, this means that the creaturely medium of revelation, in this case the human nature of Christ, is not divinized through union with the divine nature. Instead, it remains subject to the limitations and contingencies of its creaturely character. Yet in spite of these limitations, God is truly revealed through the appointed creaturely medium.

---

72. Graham Ward, *Barth, Derrida, and the Language of Theology* (Cambridge: Cambridge University Press, 1995).

73. On Calvin's understanding of the accommodated character of all human knowledge of God, see Edward A. Dowey Jr., *The Knowledge of God in Calvin's Theology*, 3rd ed. (Grand Rapids: Eerdmans, 1994), 3–24.

This dynamic is captured in the dialectic of veiling and unveiling that animates the theology of Karl Barth and his notion of "indirect identity" with respect to the doctrine of revelation. In his self-revelation, God makes himself indirectly identical to the creaturely medium of that revelation. Such revelation is *indirect* because God's use of the creaturely medium entails no divinization of the medium. Yet at the same time, God is indirectly *identical* to the creaturely medium in that God chooses to truly reveal himself through such mediums. This is the dialectic of veiling and unveiling, which maintains that God unveils (reveals) himself in and through creaturely veils and that these veils, although they may be used by God for the purposes of unveiling himself, remain veils. Further, the self-revelation of God means that the whole of God, complete and entire, not simply a part, is made known in revelation but nevertheless remains hidden within the veil of the creaturely medium through which he chooses to unveil himself. Hence, nothing of God is known directly by natural human perception.

In christological terms, as Bruce McCormack observes, this means that the process by which God takes on human nature and becomes the subject of a human life in human history entails no impartation or communication of divine attributes and perfections to that human nature. This in turn means that "revelation is not made a predicate of the human nature of Jesus; revelation may not be read directly 'off the face of Jesus.' And yet, it remains true that God (complete, whole, and entire) is the Subject of this human life. God, without ceasing to be God, becomes human and lives a human life, suffers and dies."[74] The consequence of this notion of indirect revelation is that the revelation remains hidden to outward, normal, or "natural" human perception and requires that human beings be given "the eyes and ears of faith" in order to perceive the unveiling of God, which remains hidden in the creaturely veil. In this conception, revelation has both an objective moment, when God reveals himself through the veil of a creaturely medium, and a subjective moment, when God gives human beings the faith to understand what is hidden in the veil. In this instance, the objective moment is christological, while the subjective moment is pneumatological.

Another entailment of this position is its affirmation of the contextual character of revelation. Since the creaturely mediums God employs in revelation are not divinized, they remain subject to their historically and culturally conditioned character. What is true of the human nature of Jesus Christ with respect to divinization is also true of the words of the

---

74. Bruce L. McCormack, "Beyond Nonfoundational and Postmodern Readings of Barth: Critically Realistic Dialectical Theology," *Zeitschrift für dialektische Theologie* 13, no. 1 (1997): 68.

prophets and apostles in canonical Scripture. The use that God makes of the creaturely medium of human language in the inspiration and witness of Scripture does not entail its divinization. Language, like the human nature of Jesus, remains subject to the historical, social, and cultural limitations and contingencies inherent in its creaturely character. Yet this does not in any way negate the reality of biblical inspiration as a gracious act of the Holy Spirit or detract from the authority of Scripture. It simply means that in approaching the text of Scripture, we do so with an understanding of the infinite wisdom and majesty of God, the limitations of our finite and fallen nature, the economy of God in revelation, and an awareness of our complete and ongoing epistemic dependence on God for knowledge of God.

In the framework of indirect identity, we are able to affirm God's use of language in the act of revelation without denying our theological and existential awareness of its inherent limitations and contingencies as a contextually situated creaturely medium. It should be added that Barth secures the divine primacy in God's epistemic relations with human beings by maintaining the "actualistic" character of revelation. In other words, revelation is not simply a past event that requires nothing further from God. This would imply that God had ceased to act and had become directly identical to the medium of revelation. If this were the case, the epistemic relationship between God and human beings would be static rather than dynamic, with the result that human beings would be able to move from a position of epistemic dependency to one of epistemic mastery. Instead, God always remains indirectly identical to the creaturely mediums of revelation, thus requiring continual divine action in the knowing process and securing the ongoing epistemic dependency of human beings with respect to knowledge of God.[75]

Nonfoundational Theology

This epistemic dependency, which is the natural outworking of indirect revelation, points to the nonfoundational character of theological epistemology. For Barth, theology is, humanly speaking, an impossibility. It nevertheless becomes possible as a divine possibility. An approach to theology that accepts these insights finds its ongoing basis in the dialectic of the divine veiling and unveiling in revelation. For Barth, this construal of revelation demands a theology that takes seriously the ongoing reality of divine action not only on the level of the theological epistemology it presupposes but also on the level of the theological

75. Ibid., 69.

method it employs. Apart from this, theology is reduced to something that is humanly achievable and subject to human manipulation and control, a point at which it becomes "a regular, bourgeois science alongside all the other sciences."[76]

According to William Stacy Johnson, nonfoundationalist approaches to theology "share a common goal of putting aside all appeals to presumed self-evident, non-inferential, or incorrigible grounds for their intellectual claims."[77] They reject the notion that among the many beliefs that make up a particular theology there must be a single irrefutable foundation that is immune to criticism and provides the certain basis on which all other assertions are founded. In nonfoundationalist theology, all beliefs are open to criticism and reconstruction. This does not mean, as is sometimes alleged, that nonfoundationalists cannot make assertions or maintain strong convictions that may be vigorously defended. As Francis Schüssler Fiorenza says, to engage in nonfoundationalist theology is to accept that it is a "self-correcting enterprise" that examines all claims and relevant background theories without demanding that they be completely abandoned all at once.[78] Nonfoundationalist theology does not eschew convictions and commitments; it simply maintains that all such convictions and commitments, even the most long-standing and dear, remain subject to ongoing critical scrutiny and the possibility of revision, reconstruction, or even rejection.

The adoption of a nonfoundationalist approach to theology has raised concerns for many in the theological community who see the abandonment of foundationalism as little more than a potential (or actual) slide down the proverbial slippery slope into nihilistic relativism.[79] Doesn't such an approach really amount to a theological relativism that allows for anything? We might first respond that no epistemological approach or method can secure truth and that all are subject to distortion in the hands of finite and fallen human beings. A nonfoundationalist approach to theology seeks to respond positively and appropriately to the situatedness of all human thought and therefore to embrace a principled theological pluralism. It also attempts to affirm that the ultimate authority in the church is not a particular source, be it Scripture, tradition, reason, or experience, but only the living God. Therefore, if we must speak of

76. Ibid., 70.

77. William Stacy Johnson, *The Mystery of God: Karl Barth and the Postmodern Foundations of Theology* (Louisville: Westminster John Knox, 1997), 3.

78. Francis Schüssler Fiorenza, *Foundational Theology: Jesus and the Church* (New York: Crossroad, 1986), 287.

79. See, for example, Douglas Groothuis, *Truth Decay: Defending Christianity against the Challenges of Postmodernism* (Downers Grove, IL: InterVarsity, 2000).

"foundations" for the Christian faith and its theological enterprise, then we must speak only of the Triune God, who is disclosed in polyphonic fashion through Scripture, the church, and the world, albeit always in accordance with the normative witness to divine self-disclosure in Jesus Christ.

While the concern of relativism remains one of the major challenges for nonfoundationalist theology, let us here note one of its potentially significant benefits. It promotes a theology with an inherent commitment to the reforming principle and maintains without reservation that no single human perspective, be it that of an individual or a particular community or a theological tradition, is adequate to do full justice to the truth of God's revelation in Christ. Richard Mouw points to this issue as one of his own motivations for reflecting seriously on postmodern themes: "As many Christians from other parts of the world challenge our 'North Atlantic' theologies, they too ask us to think critically about our own cultural location, as well as about how we have sometimes blurred the boundaries between what is essential to the Christian message and the doctrine and frameworks we have borrowed from various Western philosophical traditions."[80] The adoption of a nonfoundationalist approach to theology accents an awareness of the contextual nature of human knowledge and mandates a critical awareness of the role of culture and social location in the process of theological interpretation and construction.

A nonfoundationalist conception envisions theology as an ongoing conversation between Scripture, tradition, and culture through which the Spirit speaks in order to create a distinctively Christian "world" centered on Jesus Christ in a variety of local settings. In this way, theology is both one, in that all truly Christian theology seeks to hear and respond to the speaking of the one Spirit, and many, in that all theology emerges from particular social and historical situations. Such a theology is the product of the reflection of the Christian community in its local expressions. Despite its local character, such a theology is still in a certain sense global in that it seeks to explicate the Christian faith in accordance with the ecumenical tradition of the church throughout its history and on behalf of the church throughout the world.

Further, despite its particularity as specifically Christian theology, such a theology is also public and carries an implicit claim to be articulating a set of beliefs and practices that are "universal" in the only way that any claim to universality can be made, as the faith of a particular believing community. In this way, such a theology calls for a response

80. Richard Mouw, "Delete the 'Post' from 'Postconservative,'" *Books & Culture* 7, no. 3 (May/June 2001): 22.

beyond the confines of the particular community from which it emerges. It is also set forth as a contribution to the wider public conversation about the nature of ultimate reality, meaning, and truth. As Kathryn Tanner explains, there is no reason to think that a specifically Christian context rules out theological claims that are universal in scope or that a Christian context means that theologians are discussing matters that concern only Christians. Instead, theologians seek to "proclaim truths with profound ramifications for the whole of human existence; that they do so from within a Christian cultural context simply means that the claims they make are shaped by that context and are put forward from a Christian point of view. Indeed, if, as an anthropologist would insist, assertions always show the influence of some cultural context or other, following a procedure like that is the only way that universal claims are ever made."[81] This perspective seeks to nurture an open and flexible theology that is in keeping with the local and contextual character of human knowledge while remaining thoroughly and distinctly Christian. It also provides a conceptual theological framework for the maintenance of the reforming principle.

Some fear that this nonfoundationalist approach to theology presupposes a denial of truth. The assumption is that the affirmation of finitude and the denial of foundationalism imply a corresponding denial of truth. This is another of the ways in which postmodern thought is viewed as wholly antithetical to, and therefore incompatible with, Christian faith. It is certainly correct that some postmodern theorists move in this direction and express their commitment to the finitude of human knowledge in a statement such as truth does not exist. Thus, the assertion is made that postmodern thought denies the reality of truth per se. However, Merold Westphal maintains that such a claim "stems not from analyzing the interpretive character of human thought but from placing that analysis in an atheistic context. If our thinking never merits the triumphalist title of Truth *and* there is no other knower whose knowledge is the Truth, then the truth is that there is no Truth. But if the first premise is combined with a theistic premise, the result will be: The truth is that there is truth, but not for us, only for God."[82] In employing the metaphorical language of foundations, an important distinction is made between epistemological and ontological foundations. While nonfoundationalist theology means the end of foundationalism, it does not signal the denial of foundations or truth.

81. Kathryn Tanner, *Theories of Culture: A New Agenda for Theology* (Minneapolis: Augsburg Fortress, 1997), 69.

82. Merold Westphal, *Overcoming Onto-theology: Toward a Postmodern Christian Faith* (New York: Fordham University Press, 2001), xvii.

However, these foundations are not a "given" to human beings. As Bruce McCormack notes, they "always elude the grasp of the human attempt to know and to establish them from the human side," and they cannot be demonstrated or secured "philosophically or in any other way."[83] Hence, human beings are always in a position of dependence and in need of grace with respect to epistemic relations with God. Attempts on the part of humans to seize control of these relations are all too common throughout the history of the church and, no matter how well intentioned, inevitably lead to forms of oppression and conceptual idolatry. Nonfoundationalist theology seeks to oppose such seizure through the promotion of a form of theology and a theological ethos that humbly acknowledge the human condition of finitude and fallenness and that, by grace if at all, do not belie the subject of theology to which theology seeks to bear faithful witness. On this basis, Karl Barth concludes that the focal point and foundation of Christian faith, the God revealed in Jesus Christ, determines that in the work and practice of theology "there are no comprehensive views, no final conclusions and results. There is only the investigation and teaching which take place in the act of dogmatic work and which, strictly speaking, must continually begin again at the beginning in every point. The best and most significant thing that is done in this matter is that again and again we are directed to look back to the center and foundation of it all."[84]

This chapter sketched some of the central convictions concerning the knowledge of God that will shape an understanding of the character of theology. These beliefs are brought into dialogical conversation with convictions concerning the knowledge of ourselves and the human condition that arise from an awareness of the postmodern situation discussed in chapter 1. The following chapters consider the nature, task, and purpose of theology as it arises from the relationship of these convictions through an explanation and exposition of our working definition of theology: Christian theology is an ongoing, second-order, contextual discipline that engages in the task of critical and constructive reflection on the beliefs and practices of the Christian church for the purpose of assisting the community of Christ's followers in their missional vocation to live as the people of God in the particular social-historical context in which they are situated. We will begin with a consideration of the nature of theology as an ongoing, second-order, contextual discipline.

---

83. Bruce L. McCormack, "What Has Basel to Do with Berlin? The Return of 'Church Dogmatics' in the Schleiermacherian Tradition," *Princeton Seminary Bulletin* 23, no. 2 (2002): 172.
84. Barth, *Church Dogmatics,* 1/2, 868.

3

The Nature of Theology

Following Calvin's maxim, we have maintained that good theology grows out of the knowledge of God and of ourselves. Based on the first two chapters, we can conclude that a reforming and nonfoundational approach to theology is both appropriate and necessary for finite and fallen human beings and is required by the nature of the subject of theology, the Triune God revealed in Jesus Christ. According to Karl Barth, the work of theology must always begin again at the beginning, and final conclusions or comprehensive views are not possible for an enterprise that seeks to be faithful to this particular subject. Based on this perspective, a working definition assists in the production of a theology whose forms and content are able to bear faithful witness to its subject while reflecting the situation of its human interpreters. Implicit in this account is a dialectical tension between doing theology "from above" and "from below." Each perspective offers important contributions to the work of theology, yet each can exercise a distorting influence when allowed to function in a reductionistic fashion at the expense of the other. Theology done "from above" is a reminder of the responsive nature of theology and its dependence on the self-revelation of God, but it can also lead to the assumption of one right, unchanging, timeless theology. Theology done "from below" is a reminder of the situated and contextual nature of all thought, but it can also lead to the development of sectarian theologies that work against the unity of the church. With the challenges of this tension in mind, this chapter examines the nature of theology as an ongoing, second-order, contextual discipline. It considers these aspects of theology in reverse order, since the conceptions of theology as a second-order and ongoing enterprise easily flow from the understanding of theology as an inherently contextual discipline.

The Contextual Nature of Theology

The sociology of knowledge declares that all forms of thought are embedded in social conditions. While this does not mean that those conditions unilaterally determine forms of thought, it does point to their fundamental situatedness. All human knowledge is situated. It is influenced and shaped by the social, cultural, and historical settings from which it emerges. As a human endeavor bound up with the task of interpretation, the discipline of Christian theology, like all other intellectual pursuits, bears the marks of the particular contexts in which it is produced. It is not the intent of theology simply to set forth, amplify, refine, and defend a timelessly fixed orthodoxy. As Karl Barth remarks, theology, or dogmatics, "is not a thing which has fallen from Heaven to earth. And if someone were to say that it would be wonderful if there were such an absolute dogmatics fallen from Heaven, the only possible answer would be: 'Yes, if we were angels.' But since by God's will we are not, it will be good for us to have just a human and earthly dogmatics."[1] Instead, theology is formulated in the context of the community of faith and seeks to bear witness to the God to whom faith is directed and to the implications of the Christian faith commitment in the context of the specific historical and cultural setting in which it is lived. Because theology draws from contemporary thought forms in theological reflection, the categories it uses are culturally and historically conditioned.

This is evident from the history of Christian thought, in which the expression of theology has taken shape and has been revised in the context of numerous social and historical settings. It has also developed in the process of navigating a number of significant cultural transitions: from an initially Hebraic setting to the Hellenistic world; from the thought forms of Greco-Roman culture to those of Franco-Germanic culture; from the world of medieval feudalism to the Renaissance; from the Renaissance to the Enlightenment; and from the developed world to the third world. Throughout this history, theology has been shaped by the thought forms and conceptual tools of numerous cultural settings

---

1. Karl Barth, *Dogmatics in Outline* (New York: Harper & Row, 1959), 10.

and has shown itself to be remarkably adaptable in its task of assisting the church in extending and establishing the message of the gospel in a variety of contexts. At the same time, theological history also provides numerous examples of the inappropriate accommodation of Christian faith to various ideologies and cultural norms to the detriment of its proclamation of the gospel. This checkered past confirms the vitality of Christian theology while warning of the dangers of too closely associating it with a particular form of cultural expression. It also implicitly raises the question of a proper construal of the contextual nature of theology. How do we take adequate account of the situatedness of theology without succumbing to the danger of cultural accommodation?

The significance of this question in the contemporary setting makes it clear that theology must take its context seriously. Colin Gunton states the point succinctly: "We must acknowledge the fact that all theologies belong in a particular context, and so are, to a degree, limited by the constraints of that context. To that extent, the context is one of the authorities to which the theologian must listen."[2] This raises the question as to the proper form this listening should take in the development of an approach to theology. Throughout the twentieth century, the issues of theological method were dominated by the presuppositions and assumptions of foundationalism. These intellectual tendencies had a significant effect on the accounts of the relationship between theology and its context in the work of liberal and conservative theologians. What follows briefly summarizes these accounts to provide a background for properly understanding the contextual nature of theology.

The attempt to construct theology on the basis of a universal human religious experience became a specific concern of classical Protestant liberalism. This experiential foundationalism provided a paradigm for the approach to liberal theology into the twentieth century and led to the task of reconstructing Christian belief in light of modern knowledge. Liberals believed that theology could not ignore the new scientific and philosophical understandings that had arisen in Western society since the Enlightenment and that the future survival of Christianity depended on its ability to adapt to the new thinking. Liberal theology, therefore, has been characterized, in the words of Claude Welch, by a "maximum acknowledgment of the claims of modern thought."[3] In keeping with this concern, liberal thinkers sought to give place to culture in their

2. Colin Gunton, "Using and Being Used: Scripture and Systematic Theology," *Theology Today* 47, no. 3 (October 1990): 253.

3. Claude Welch, *Protestant Thought in the Nineteenth Century*, vol. 1, *1799–1870* (New Haven: Yale University Press, 1972), 142.

theological reflections to the degree that they are commonly charged with linking theology too closely with the culture of the day.

For example, Shailer Mathews, professor of theology at the University of Chicago, emphasized the priority of religious experience over statements of doctrine. He maintained that Christian doctrine consisted of verbal expressions of the religious life that employed the patterns and thought forms current in the various periods of Christian history. These doctrines were not to be evaluated on the basis of their supposed objective truth content but on the basis of the degree to which they were effective in promoting and inspiring religious faith and conviction. Mathews spoke of the Bible as a historical record of the progressive religious experience of human beings. He was convinced that when the Bible was properly interpreted on the basis of appropriate historical-critical methods it provided "a trustworthy record of human experience of God."[4] Yet the Bible's importance did not lie in the past experience, he argued, but in the continuation of that experience into the present context. Mathews asserted that living Christian faith is not about the "acceptance of a literature but a reproduction of attitudes and faith, a fellowship with those ancient men of imperfect morals whose hearts found God, whose lives were strengthened by the divine spirit, whose words point out the way of life, and who determined the inner character of the Christian religion." In his estimation, the other components of the faith that have been passed down through the generations are "secondary accretions," and they are to be properly "separated from the religion of Jesus Christ."[5]

The well-known Baptist preacher Harry Emerson Fosdick popularized the liberal viewpoint that all doctrines spring from the experiences of life. Fosdick argued that human beings have experiences involving their own souls, other individuals, and God. The chief value of these experiences is found in their practical value for life. Fosdick admitted that there was something typically human about the construction of doctrine, for human beings quite naturally attempt to "explain, unify, organize, and rationalize. They make systematized doctrines out of their experiences. And when the formula has been constructed, they love it because the experience for which it stands is precious." But he quickly added that over the course of history these doctrines often become unintelligible in the face of new thinking. Here Fosdick asserted that the liberal approach to doctrine provides the way forward. In his estimation, liberals had done the church a great service by discovering that religion does not consist in the formula but in the experience to which

4. Shailer Mathews, *The Faith of Modernism* (New York: Macmillan, 1924), 47.
5. Ibid., 49–50.

the formula points. The liberal approach, he asserted, retreats from the formula "into the experience behind it, by translating the formula back into the life out of which it came."[6]

Although propounded in an increasingly subtle and complex fashion, the experienced-based approach to theology characteristic of liberalism continued to dominate mainline theology throughout the twentieth century. The work of Harvard theologian Gordon Kaufman provides a case in point. In his *Essay on Theological Method*, Kaufman notes at the outset his dissatisfaction with current options in foundationalist theology and his desire to think through afresh the task of theology and "to search for new and more adequate foundations."[7] At first glance, Kaufman appears to break with the liberal program. He avers that the difficulty of determining what in fact counts as religious experience means that theology cannot be based on such experience. He opts instead to ground theology in broader cultural experience as captured in a common language, thereby shifting the focus from experience to language. Hence, Kaufman declares, it would be more accurate "to say the language we speak provides a principal foundation for our religious experience, than to hold that some preconceptual, prelinguistic raw experience is the principal foundation of our theological language and thought."[8]

Philosopher Nancey Murphy provides a telling critique of the methodological proposal put forward by Kaufman. In her estimation, for Kaufman, theology becomes a "conceptual clarification of the religious terms found in ordinary language." She states, "Kaufman's particular concern is with the concept *God*, which, following Kant, he understands as a regulative concept, constructed to make sense of a set of concepts drawn from experience."[9] Hence, despite his attempts to go beyond the liberal program, Kaufman continues to emphasize experience as providing the foundation for theology, albeit in the modified form of an appeal to linguistic expressions, which arise out of cultural experience. As Murphy notes, although Kaufman has replaced the earlier foundationalist focus on certitude with a new concern for the public nature of criteria for judging theology, his quest for public consensus "is the same as that which drove the seventeenth-century development of the foundationalist epistemological theory in the first place."[10] The assumption of a universal

6. Harry Emerson Fosdick, *The Modern Use of the Bible* (London: SCM, 1924), 185–86.

7. Gordon Kaufman, *An Essay on Theological Method*, rev. ed. (Missoula, MT: Scholars Press, 1979), x.

8. Ibid., 6.

9. Nancey Murphy, *Beyond Liberalism and Fundamentalism: How Modern and Postmodern Philosophy Set the Theological Agenda* (Valley Forge, PA: Trinity Press, 1996), 26.

10. Ibid.

human experience that is able to serve as the foundation for theology inevitably leads to an overly accommodated approach to the relationship between theology and culture in which the prioritization of this universal experience results in the eclipse of distinctively Christian theology.

On the other hand, evangelical theology has tended to bypass questions raised by theological method and has moved directly to the task of making theological assertions and constructing theological systems, as though the process of moving from ancient texts to the contemporary affirmation of doctrine and theology was largely self-evident. Such an approach has led evangelical theologian Richard Lints to comment that the evangelical theological tradition "has not been nurtured to think methodologically."[11] A recent example of this long-standing tendency can be found in the best-selling work of Wayne Grudem, who defines systematic theology simply as any study that attempts to explain what the entire Bible teaches us today about any given topic. He explains that this definition suggests that an appropriate procedure in the task of doing theology "involves collecting and understanding all the relevant passages in the Bible on various topics and then summarizing their teachings clearly so that we know what to believe about each topic."[12] Earlier, Carl F. H. Henry asserted that the task of theology is "to exhibit the content of biblical revelation as an orderly whole."[13] This approach is based on the presupposition that the Bible, as the entirely truthful self-disclosure of God presented in propositional form, is the sole foundation for theology.[14]

This approach has typified evangelical theology and is characterized by a commitment to the Bible as a source of information for systematic theology. As such, it is viewed as a rather loose and relatively disorganized collection of factual, propositional statements. The task of theology, in turn, becomes that of collecting and arranging these varied statements in such a way as to bring their underlying unity into relief and to reveal the eternal system of timeless truths to which they point. This "concordance" conception of theology looks back to Charles Hodge, arguably the most influential American theologian for evangelicals, and his view that the task of theology "is to systematize the facts of the Bible, and ascertain the principles or general truths which those facts involve."[15] Hodge's own understanding of theology is generally derived from the scholasticism

11. Richard Lints, *The Fabric of Theology: A Prolegomenon to Evangelical Theology* (Grand Rapids: Eerdmans, 1993), 259.

12. Wayne Grudem, *Systematic Theology: An Introduction to Biblical Doctrine* (Grand Rapids: Zondervan, 1994), 21.

13. Carl F. H. Henry, *God, Revelation, and Authority,* vol. 1 (Waco: Word, 1976), 244.

14. For Henry's exposition of this thesis, see ibid., 181–409.

15. Charles Hodge, *Systematic Theology,* vol. 1 (New York: Scribner, Armstrong, & Co., 1872), 18.

characteristic of post-Reformation Protestant orthodoxy. Evangelicals in the twentieth century, buoyed by the assumptions of modernity, have continued, with some modifications, to follow the theological paradigm of scholasticism as exemplified in the work of Charles Hodge and others from the "old" Princeton tradition such as B. B. Warfield and J. Gresham Machen. By limiting the scope of theological reflection to the exposition of the biblical text, evangelicals have been able to avoid the thorny issues surrounding the role of culture in theology. Without sensing the need to deal with this concern, as a result of their exclusive focus on the text of Scripture, evangelicals have generally seen little reason to participate in the contemporary methodological discussion that has so captivated the rest of the theological community. It is worth noting that this lack of reflection on and engagement with contemporary methodological/theological issues has not been because of the lack of an approach to method. It is due to the particular understanding of method that evangelicals have generally followed.

Although this approach to theology is clearly still the dominant paradigm in traditional evangelical circles, there are signs that the situation is beginning to change. Recently, a number of theologians from within evangelicalism have called this paradigm into question. John Jefferson Davis, for example, critiques the concordance model of theology with the observation that it "does not take adequate account of the social context of the theological task and the historicity of all theological reflection. The method tends to promote a repetition of traditional formulations of biblical doctrine, rather than appropriate recontextualizations of the doctrines in response to changing cultural and historical conditions."[16] Similarly, Stanley Gundry raises the question as to whether evangelicals "really recognize that all theology represents a contextualization," including evangelical theology.[17]

Both Davis and Gundry urge evangelicals to adopt a contextual approach to theology that takes seriously the role of culture in theological formulation. This concern is evident in the work of leading evangelical theologian Millard Erickson, who defines theology as "that discipline which strives to give a coherent statement of the doctrines of the Christian faith, based primarily upon the Scriptures, placed in the context of culture in general, worded in contemporary idiom, and related to issues of life."[18] Although this concern for contextualization is welcome, the

16. John Jefferson Davis, *Foundations of Evangelical Theology* (Grand Rapids: Baker, 1984), 67.

17. Stanley N. Gundry, "Evangelical Theology: Where Should We Be Going?" *Journal of the Evangelical Theological Society* 22 (1979): 11.

18. Millard Erickson, *Christian Theology*, vol. 1 (Grand Rapids: Baker, 1983), 21.

traditional evangelical commitment to objectivism and propositional-
ism has worked against an adequate understanding of the relationship
between theology and culture, even among those who have called for
contextualization as a part of the theological process. Thus, while some
showed increasing awareness of the relationship between context and
theology, the ongoing concern about the risks of the cultural accommodation they perceived in liberalism led many conservatives to maintain that
careful attention to Scripture would lead to the discovery and expression
of transcultural theology. Hence, many evangelical and conservative
theologians have continued to be suspicious of claims concerning a
significant role for culture in the practice of theology, fearing that they,
at least implicitly, dilute the authority of Scripture and give rise to a
cultural relativity that is inappropriate for the discipline. Consequently,
they have tended to give little, if any, attention to culture and its role in
shaping human thought.

While the dangers involved in accommodating Christian faith to
particular cultural contexts are real, the quest to construct theology free
from the influence of culture is misguided. We simply cannot escape
from our particular setting and gain access to an objective, transcultural
vantage point. All views emerge from a particular location. Hence, all
theology is, by its very nature as a human enterprise, influenced by its
cultural context. The quest for a transcultural theology is also theologically and biblically unwarranted. As shown in the previous chapter, even
divine revelation is always embedded in culture. As Lesslie Newbigin
points out, this is the case with the gospel itself: "We must start with
the basic fact that there is no such thing as a pure gospel if by that is
meant something which is not embodied in a culture." He points out
that even the meaning of the most simple verbal statement of the gospel, "Jesus is Lord," is dependent on the content that culture gives to
the word *Lord.* How is "lordship" understood in the particular culture
in which this idea is proclaimed? "The gospel always comes as the testimony of a community which, if it is faithful, is trying to live out the
meaning of the gospel in a certain style of life, certain ways of holding
property, of maintaining law and order, of carrying on production and
consumption, and so on. Every interpretation of the gospel is embodied
in some cultural form."[19]

Justo González also makes this point. "The knowledge of Christ never
comes to us apart from culture, or devoid of cultural baggage," since
from its very beginning it was proclaimed and taught within the setting of a particular culture. The ministry of Jesus took place within the

19. Lesslie Newbigin, *The Gospel in a Pluralist Society* (Grand Rapids: Eerdmans, 1989), 144.

circumstances of the Jewish culture of his time and place, and it was concretely as Jews, and even more concretely as Galilean Jews, that his first disciples received him. "Ever since, in the passage to the various forms of Hellenistic culture, in the conversion of the Germanic peoples, and in every other missionary enterprise and conversion experience, people have met Christ mediated through cultures—both theirs and the culture of those who communicated the gospel to them."[20] As this statement suggests, the culture-specific nature of divine truth arises directly out of the doctrine of the incarnation, with its reminder that the Word became flesh in a specific cultural context (John 1:14). As the incarnate one, Jesus ministered to culturally embedded people in first-century Palestine in a culturally sensitive manner. The incarnation points to the contextualization of revelation and the missional purpose of God. As René Padilla observes, God does not shout the message of the gospel from the heavens but instead enters into the human situation as a human. "The climax of God's revelation is Emmanuel. And Emmanuel is Jesus, a first-century Jew! The incarnation unmistakably demonstrates God's intention to make himself known from within the human situation. Because of the very nature of the Gospel, we know this Gospel only as a message contextualized in culture."[21]

Following this pattern, Paul readily drew from the Greek cultural setting, including the works of pagan poets, in his conversation with the Athenian philosophers (Acts 17:28). John Goldingay remarks, "Paul is *the* great discursive theologian in scripture, but his systematic, analytic thinking characteristically takes the form of contextual theological reflection." He notes that this is especially apparent in Paul's first letter to the Corinthians, in which he addresses a series of issues in the life of the church. "What it does is declare the results of reflection on these in the light of a Christian understanding of creation, the story of Israel, the incarnation, the cross, the resurrection, and the future appearing of Jesus."[22] Newbigin pushes the point home, commenting that a missionary does not come "with the pure gospel and then adapt it to the culture where she serves: she comes with a gospel which is already embodied in the culture by which the missionary was formed." He goes on to say that this was the case from the very beginning. "The Bible is a book which is very obviously in a specific cultural setting. Its language is Hebrew and

---

20. Justo L. González, *Out of Every Tribe and Nation: Christian Theology at the Ethnic Roundtable* (Nashville: Abingdon, 1992), 30.

21. René Padilla, "The Contextualization of the Gospel," in *Readings in Dynamic Indigeneity*, ed. C. H. Kraft and T. N. Wisley (Pasadena: William Carey Library, 1979), 286.

22. John Goldingay, *Models for Scripture* (Grand Rapids: Eerdmans, 1994), 365.

Greek, not Chinese or Sanskrit. All the events it records, all the teachings
it embodies, are shaped by specific human cultures."[23]

To illustrate the interaction between theology and culture and the
situatedness of Christian thought, we will consider the life and work
of one of the most prominent early Christian writers, Origen of Alexandria, particularly as they relate to an interpretation of the Bible. Of
particular interest here is observation of the ways in which his social
and historical contexts and intellectual assumptions shaped his understanding of Scripture.

Theology and Culture: Origen and the Interpretation of the Bible

Few figures in the history of the church have stimulated the level of
debate and controversy that surrounds Origen of Alexandria. To some, he
was a brilliant intellectual as well as a passionately committed disciple
of Christ, the most influential and seminal thinker in the history of the
early church. Others regard him as a dangerous heretic whose interest in
spiritual and philosophical speculation unleashed a string of teachings
that stand in stark opposition to orthodox Christian faith. In light of this
spectrum of opinion, it is worth pointing out that Origen believed the
Bible was the Word of God, and as such it occupied a central place in
his life and thought, serving as the touchstone for all his beliefs. Indeed,
one of the major concerns of Origen's work was to assist Christians
facing the intellectual challenges of the third century by providing answers to the questions posed by Hellenistic philosophy and culture that
were in keeping with the teaching of Scripture. However, in spite of his
intentions and clear commitment to the principle of biblical authority,
many believe that Origen's *use* of Scripture significantly compromised
that authority and provided fertile conditions for the germination and
growth of heresy. To better understand the conflicted nature of Origen's
legacy and to observe the relationship between Christian thought and
culture, we will consider his approach to the interpretation of Scripture
in the context of his life and career.

Origen was born in either 185 or 186 in Alexandria and was raised
in a Christian home. His father was most likely a prosperous and influential man, who provided his son with an education that was both
Hellenistic and Christian, centered on the study of the classic literary
works of ancient Greece and the Bible. Hence, young Origen grew up
as both a learned Greek and a devoted Christian. This dual education

23. Newbigin, *Gospel in a Pluralist Society,* 144–45.

undoubtedly caused something of an internal tension in Origen as he sought to reconcile his commitment to Christian faith and the Bible with a Hellenistic outlook. From the perspective of Hellenism, Christianity was little more than another barbarous superstition, and the Bible constituted an inferior collection of texts that were not worth serious consideration from the standpoint of Greek aesthetic standards. Origen was not the first to grapple with this tension, and he was able to learn from previous Jewish and Christian engagements with Hellenism, particularly Platonic philosophy, in his own attempt to affirm the Bible and its teaching in the context of the Greek intellectual milieu. Indeed, as a student at the catechetical school in Alexandria, Origen likely had as a teacher Clement of Alexandria, who was well known for his attempts to relate Christian teaching to Greek philosophical thought.

When Origen was about seventeen, his father was arrested and imprisoned during an outbreak of persecution and was eventually executed for his profession of Christian faith. According to tradition, Origen intended to turn himself in to the authorities and to join his father in martyrdom but was prevented from doing so by his mother, who hid his clothes and thus prevented him from leaving the house. Later, he is said to have written to his father in prison, exhorting him not to turn from the martyr's calling for the sake of his family. Many Christians fled Alexandria to escape the fate of Origen's father, including Clement, who had been the head of the catechetical school. The combination of Origen's manifest Christian commitment in the face of persecution and his growing reputation as an outstanding student and thinker led Demetrius, the bishop of Alexandria, to entrust him with the leadership of the school at the age of eighteen.

During his tenure, the pursuit and execution of Christians in Alexandria continued, and Origen was under threat on numerous occasions, living the life of a wanted man and enduring the martyrdom of several of his students. In addition to the pressures brought about by persecution, Origen lived an austere life characterized by extreme self-discipline and ascetic practices. Of particular note, he apparently had himself castrated in accordance with a literal reading of Matthew 19:12 concerning those who had made themselves eunuchs for the sake of the kingdom of heaven. As one might imagine, this action was highly controversial even by the standards of the time and was later used against Origen as a reason to prohibit his ordination. In the midst of all this, Origen was immensely productive, teaching, preaching, traveling, and writing numerous scholarly and intellectual works concerning theology, philosophy, apologetics, and the Bible.

Among his many works, two are of particular importance in the history of the early church and Christian thought. *On First Principles* is an ordered and systematic account of Origen's theological and philosophical positions concerning God, creation, Jesus Christ, the Logos of God, and salvation. It is one of the great classics of Christian thought and constitutes both a philosophical discussion on the relation of God to the world and an attempt at developing a coherent set of theological teachings that may be derived from the logical elaboration of the basic doctrines of the Christian faith. As such, it may be construed as the first formal attempt at systematic theology in the history of the church. The second, *Against Celsus,* is a detailed apologetic defense of the Christian faith against the critique of the Roman philosopher Celsus. In it Origen attempts to demonstrate the superiority of the teaching and wisdom of the Bible over against that of Greek philosophy. This thorough point-by-point response to Celsus stands as an apologetic milestone in the history of the church and made an important contribution to the growing cogency and respectability of Christian faith in the ancient world. These works effectively refuted the contention that Christianity was simply another superstitious folk religion and helped to establish the intellectual credentials of the faith in relation to Greek philosophy and Hellenistic culture.

While Origen appreciated a great deal of Plato and the Greek philosophical tradition, he argued that at its best it merely anticipated the fullness of truth that was found in divine revelation. Further, he maintained that for all the benefits of philosophy, it could not finally lead to a true and proper knowledge of God because it was contaminated with too much false and erroneous teaching that could not be separated from the good. In spite of his reservations concerning philosophy, Origen believed that Christian faith itself was a kind of divine philosophy that, while surpassing and superseding all other philosophies, could make use of them by leading persons to a true knowledge of God and to salvation. Thus, Greek philosophy or other pagan learning could be studied and engaged with profit by Christians, who could "borrow" truth from these sources to explicate the meaning of the gospel and the Christian faith. Origen used an analogy from the Old Testament to make this point. In the same way that the Israelites took the property of the Egyptians with them in the exodus, so the people of God are permitted to make use of the truths of pagan culture and philosophy, the "spoils of the Egyptians," in the work of theology and biblical interpretation.

This willingness to make use of Greek thought is perhaps nowhere more evident than in Origen's spiritual or allegorical approach to the interpretation of Scripture. He maintained that the Bible contains three levels of meaning corresponding to the tripartite conception of a human being, consisting of body, soul, and spirit, derived from Platonic philosophy and the writings of Paul. The bodily level of Scripture is the bare letter of the text or its literal meaning, which is particularly useful in meeting the needs of the more simpleminded. The psychic level can be understood as the moral meaning of the text, providing guidance concerning right and proper conduct, although some ambiguity exists as to the exact ways in which Origen made use of this sense. In many cases, he simply maintained that biblical narratives contain ethical and moral principles that may be derived from or hidden beneath the surface of the literal and historical meaning of the text. The third and most important level of meaning is the spiritual or allegorical, which concerns the deeper meaning of the text and points to Christ and the relationship of the Christian with God. Origen believed that this spiritual/mystical meaning, while often hidden, is always present in the text. The task of the Christian interpreter is to attempt to uncover it. The allegorical method of interpretation sought to yield this hidden, symbolic meaning, and Origen became the leading figure in its establishment as the dominant method of biblical interpretation in the history of the church until the sixteenth century.

Examples of this approach abound in Origen's writings, particularly in his commentaries and homilies. For instance, in Origen's twenty-seventh homily on the book of Numbers, he provides a detailed exposition of growth in the spiritual life based on the forty-two stopping places of Israel in the wilderness mentioned in Numbers 33. Origen begins by asking why the Lord wanted Moses to write this passage down: "Was it so that this passage in Scripture about the stages the children of Israel made might benefit us in some way or that it should bring no benefit? Who would dare to say that what is written 'by the Word of God' is of no use and makes no contribution to salvation but is merely a narrative of what happened and was over and done a long time ago, but pertains in no way to us when it is told?"[24] For Origen, because the Bible is the inspired Word of God, it is never merely concerned with mundane matters of history and factual occurrences. Rather, it expounds the mysteries of God in Christ and gives direction to the spiritual life. Hence, the Christian interpreter must probe the text in various ways to uncover its true and deepest significance. According to Origen, the stopping places of the wandering Israelites were recorded in Numbers so that we can understand the long spiritual journey we face as Christians. In light of this knowledge, we must not "allow the time of our life to be ruined by sloth and neglect."[25] Further, each stopping place has particular spiritual significance until the sojourn ends on the banks of the Jordan, making

24. Origen, *Homilies on Numbers* 27.2, in *Origen: An Exhortation to Martyrdom, Prayer, and Selected Works*, ed. Rowan A. Greer (New York: Paulist, 1979), 248.
25. Ibid., 27.7, 254.

us aware that the entire journey takes place and "the whole course is run for the purpose of arriving at the river of God, so that we may make neighbors of the flowing Wisdom and may be watered by the waves of divine knowledge, and so that purified by them all we may be made worthy to enter the promised land."[26]

Another example is found in Origen's eleventh homily on Joshua with respect to his interpretation of the five kings who attack Gibeon in chapter 10 and end up hiding in the cave at Makkedah. "Now these five kings indicate the five corporeal senses: sight, hearing, taste, touch, and smell; for it must be through one of these that each person falls away into sin. These five senses are compared to those five kings who fight the Gibeonites, that is, carnal persons." As to their choice of refuge: "That they are said to have fled into caves can be indicated, perhaps, because a cave is a place buried in the depths of the earth. Therefore, those senses that we mentioned above are said to have fled into caves when, after being placed in the body, they immerse themselves in earthly impulses and do nothing for the work of God but all for the service of the body."[27]

This approach to interpretation often strikes contemporary readers as strange, unwarranted, and potentially dangerous. Why did Origen adopt such an approach? First, it must be pointed out that allegory is a legacy of Greek thought and would have been one of the staples of Origen's Hellenistic education. It was initially used to defend belief in the inspired character of the Homeric writings, the *Iliad* and the *Odyssey,* in the face of charges against such a claim because of the suspect morals they contained and the changing religious convictions of Greek culture. Homer's supporters maintained that the poems were symbolic and when read in their true, allegorical sense contained no moral or religious difficulties. Over time, allegorical interpretive methods became increasingly sophisticated with the development of the Platonist contention that myths and symbols were necessary components in the communication of truths that were otherwise inaccessible. This Platonist appreciation for the value of myths and symbols became an essential part of Origen's outlook, in which allegory served as a powerful and important means of conveying religious and philosophical truth.

On top of this general philosophical appreciation for allegorical interpretation, Origen was exposed to a lengthy tradition of spiritual exegesis of the Bible that began with the Jewish community in Alexandria, who used the method to demonstrate that their Scriptures were compatible

---

26. Ibid., 27.12, 268.

27. Origen, *Homilies on Joshua* 11.4, in *Origen: Homilies on Joshua*, ed. Cynthia White (Washington, DC: Catholic University Press of America, 2002), 118.

with Greek philosophy. The leading Jewish proponent of this movement was Philo, and although his work eventually fell out of favor with the Jews, it was accepted enthusiastically by Christians and certainly taught to Origen. Hence, he inherited a strong belief in the appropriateness and effectiveness of allegory as a tool to communicate the deepest and most profound philosophical and theological truths as well as the assumption that the Bible, the inspired Word of God, must be subject to such allegorical interpretation in order to yield its spiritual significance.

In addition to his indebtedness to Hellenistic philosophy and culture, Origen found ample evidence in Scripture itself for the practice of spiritual exegesis, beginning with the Christian conviction that the entire Old Testament is a prophecy concerning Christ, who is the interpretive key to understanding the Hebrew Bible. In 2 Corinthians 3, we read that the Jewish people who reject Christ have a veil before their faces and over their hearts that hides the true meaning of Scripture from their perception and limits them to the letter of the text that kills. Only through Christ can the veil be removed and the spiritual meaning of the text that gives life be revealed. Only when Jesus explains the Scriptures to his disciples on the road to Emmaus and shows that they speak of him can their true meaning be revealed. For Origen, allegorical exegesis clearly provided the true meaning of the Old Testament.

Among the most significant New Testament passages that Origen cited as justifying spiritual exegesis is 1 Corinthians 10, in which the crossing of the Red Sea, the manna, the water from the rock, and death in the wilderness represent baptism, the eucharist, and punishment for sin. Verse 11 sums up these events, explaining that each of these things happened to the Hebrews as a *typos*, a figure or example, that could be written down for those who live at the end of the age. For Origen, this implied that the Old Testament was written for Christians. They need to seek the spiritual interpretation that continues to apply because many of the ceremonies and legal precepts are no longer binding in the literal sense.

In Galatians 4, another important passage, Sarah and Hagar symbolize the two covenants in which the Christians are prefigured by Isaac, the son of Sarah the free wife, and the Jews by Ishmael, the son of Hagar the slave. The significance of this passage arises from its explicit use of allegory. Other examples mentioned by Origen include Matthew 12:39–40, in which the three days Jonah spent in the fish symbolize the three days Jesus spent in the heart of the earth; Matthew 26:61 and John 2:19–21, in which the temple symbolizes the body of Christ; Galatians 3, in which the posterity of Abraham is portrayed in Christ, who fulfilled the promises made to the patriarchs; and Hebrews 8, in which the ceremonies of the old covenant are but shadows of heavenly realities. For Origen, it was clear that the New Testament authorized and validated the spiritual interpretation of the Old Testament and, by extension, all of Scripture.

Together, the cultural assumptions of the Hellenistic world, the Christian belief in the inspired nature of the Bible, the centrality of Christ, and the teaching of the New Testament itself virtually demanded the practice of spiritual interpretation to Origen. In this context, three additional apologetic or pragmatic impulses sealed his commitment to allegory. First, in the context of Hellenistic Alexandria, the assertion that the Bible was divinely inspired required its allegorical interpretation. To assert that it could not or should not be interpreted in such a fashion would have been tantamount to denying its inspired character. Affirming the Bible as the Word of God entailed the assumption that its form and teaching were consistent with the highest cultural standards. Second, the Jewish critics of Christianity stressed Christ's failure to fulfill many of the prophecies concerning the Messiah. Origen believed that only a spiritual interpretation of the Old Testament prophecies that perceived their deeper sense and meaning could overcome these objections. Third, the Gnostic sects rejected the Old Testament on the grounds that it revealed a God different from the one revealed in Christ. They believed that in contrast to the New Testament God of love, the deity of the Old Testament was vengeful, jealous, capricious, and often directly responsible for sin and evil. Given his philosophical assumptions, Origen considered this conclusion unavoidable if the biblical texts were accepted as literal. Hence, he asserted that they must be understood allegorically. In fact, he argued that they were in many cases intentionally obscure and incoherent to coax and compel readers to seek their true, spiritual meaning. Finally, in response to those who argued that the multiplicity of meanings generated by this approach resulted in interpretive chaos, Origen insisted that the practice of Christian spiritual exegesis must always be conducted within the framework of the rule of faith, a brief summary of orthodox Christian teaching such as the Apostles' Creed, which was allegedly taught by the apostles themselves and subsequently preserved in the church.

Origen's significance as a biblical commentator, coupled with his intellectual acumen and ability as a teacher, should have ensured him an esteemed and permanent place in the history of the Christian church. Origen, however, was eventually condemned as a heretic and has been regularly regarded as heretical throughout much of the history of the church, particularly in the West. Recently, this negative judgment has been reconsidered and altered considerably in some quarters. In assessing his theological legacy, it is most important to remember that in Origen's context Christian theological beliefs were not well developed or respected. Origen's work was a decisive factor in changing this state of affairs, both in terms of establishing the intellectual credibility of the faith in the Hellenistic setting and of exploring the internal coherence of the Christian faith as well as its relationship to broader philosophical and cultural questions and aspirations. That he must sometimes be judged as mistaken in these explorations should hardly be surprising or a cause for great concern. Origen was one of the first Christian thinkers to give sustained attention to many of the issues he addressed. While he certainly taught some unorthodox positions by later standards, it is important to remember that he was a seminal thinker in the process of trial, error, revision, and refinement from which an orthodox consensus emerged. It is also worth remembering that Origen was always faithful to the standards of orthodoxy that pertained to his time. It would be less than charitable to hold him culpable for all the ways in which he failed to see the implications his views would have for future generations.

With respect to biblical interpretation, the point here is not to commend or to condemn Origen's approach to exegesis but rather to try to understand how an outlook that appears so foreign in the contemporary setting seemed appropriate in another context. Many histories of theology and biblical interpretation have pointed out the way in which Origen provided us with an object lesson in the pitfalls of accommodation, the practice of too closely associating the Bible and Christian faith with the values and presuppositions of a particular social, cultural, or philosophical outlook. Having said that, it is important to remember that all human forms of thought are situated and embedded in social contexts. In the last analysis, Origen is perhaps most guilty of the assumption that the Bible, as the Word of God, had to be interpreted in conformity with the highest standards and aspirations of his particular Hellenistic setting. Before we judge too quickly, though, we must ask a similar question of ourselves. Have we too readily conformed our conceptions of the Bible and its interpretation to the assumptions and aspirations of our culture? Further, given our participation in our culture, on what basis are we able to make such an assessment?

The history of theology provides numerous other examples of the interaction between theology and culture. It also serves to remind us that while an emphasis on the contextual nature of theology is a departure from standard approaches to theology in the last two centuries, it is also, in another sense, very traditional. As Stephen Bevans remarks, "While we can say that the doing of theology by taking culture and social change in culture into account is a departure from the traditional or classical way of doing theology, a study of the history of theology will reveal that every authentic theology has been very much rooted in a particular context in some implicit or real way."[28] In other words, according to Douglas John Hall, the process of contextualization "is the sine qua non of all genuine theological thought, and always has been."[29]

Theology and Culture: Models of Interaction

Observations such as these have led to a call for theology that is relevant to the specific circumstances from which it emerges. In seeking to address the relationship between theology and its particular circumstances, two approaches have gained widespread attention: correlation and translation. At the headwaters of the method of correlation is Paul Tillich, who proposed a model that "explains the contents of the Christian faith through existential questions and theological answers in mutual interdependence."[30] Because the questions are raised by philosophy through careful examination of human existence, a theologian must first function as a philosopher. In a second step, the theologian draws on the symbols of divine revelation to formulate answers to the questions implied in human existence, which philosophy can discover but not answer. The theologian's task is to interpret the answers of revelation so that they remain faithful to the original Christian message while being relevant to the questions asked by secular men and women. Recently, several theologians have offered variants on the general theme of correlation. One important example is Gordon Kaufman, who understands theology through its connection to the universal human question of meaning posed within the context of the mysteriousness of life. Theology provides the Christian response to the quest for a pattern of fundamental categories (a worldview) that can orient, guide, and order human life so as to promote "human flourishing and fulfillment," that is, "human wholeness, well-being, or salvation."[31] In a somewhat similar manner, David Tracy seeks to correlate the specific symbols and categories of Christianity with what he sees as universal human realities.[32]

---

28. Stephen B. Bevans, *Models of Contextual Theology*, rev. ed. (Maryknoll, NY: Orbis, 2002), 7.

29. Douglas John Hall, *Thinking the Faith: Christian Theology in a North American Context* (Minneapolis: Fortress, 1991), 21.

30. Paul Tillich, *Systematic Theology*, vol. 1 (Chicago: University of Chicago Press, 1951), 60.

31. Gordon Kaufman, *In Face of Mystery* (Cambridge: Harvard University Press, 1993), 41–42, 47.

32. David Tracy, *The Analogical Imagination: Christian Theology and the Culture of Pluralism* (New York: Crossroad, 1981), 405.

Tillich's method of correlation has received mixed reviews. While it certainly provides for a substantial engagement with issues pertaining to context, critics maintain that it gives autonomous philosophy too much independence from and authority over revelation. More specifically, they wonder how such an approach, disrupted by the tensions inherent in finite reason, can be trusted to formulate the right questions in a proper manner. They maintain that the substance and the form of the questions set forth by philosophy, if not revised in light of Christian thought, would have a distorting effect on the supposedly Christian constructions that emerge from the procedure.[33] In addition, the entire correlationist approach has come under recent criticism for its inability to take seriously the specificity and plurality of cultures, an emphasis of contemporary cultural anthropology. Rather than searching for the characteristics of a universal culture in general, anthropologists are interested in particular cultures. This development in anthropology would seem to disallow an attempt to engage in a method of correlation that formulates human universals as the context into which theological constructions are subsequently fitted. Instead, contemporary cultural anthropology encourages theologians to focus on the particular and to see theology as part of a concrete, specific, communally shaped way of life.[34]

One of the concerns with this approach is that it can easily lead to the acquiescence of Christian faith to dominant cultural values and assumptions. Appealing to the example of the prophets, Douglas John Hall calls for a theology that seeks engagement and dialogue with culture but remains "inherently suspicious of dominant values and trends" and is characterized by "neither a priori approval nor a priori disapproval of society."[35] This concern is also shared by David Kelsey, who warns, "In being conditioned by the limits culture sets on what is seriously imaginable, theological proposals may turn out to be merely restatements of what is already imagined in the culture apart from Christianity's central reality."[36] While acknowledging that culture must be engaged, Hall also warns that theology must not become narrowly focused on its own social setting. He notes that the Christian community in its intention to be relevant to its own time and place may come to find itself "the captive of currents and ever-changing trends within its host society. Because it seeks to respond concretely to these currents and trends, it may lose sight

---

33. George F. Thomas, "The Method and Structure of Tillich's Theology," in *The Theology of Paul Tillich*, ed. Charles W. Kegley (New York: Pilgrim Press, 1982), 137–38.

34. Kathryn Tanner, *Theories of Culture: A New Agenda for Theology* (Minneapolis: Augsburg Fortress, 1997), 66–67.

35. Hall, *Thinking the Faith*, 84.

36. David H. Kelsey, *The Uses of Scripture in Recent Theology* (Philadelphia: Fortress, 1975), 173.

of long-range questions to which its greater tradition tried to speak." In this context, a tendency to permit contemporary issues to determine its message and witness may emerge. When this happens, the theological community may fail to recognize the transience of the contemporary questions as well as the significance of other issues that were "hidden by the surface concerns with which it has busied itself. Perhaps it will even go so far as to let its context, rather glibly conceptualized, become the touchstone for any kind of theological 'relevance,' so that it retains out of the long tradition only what seems pertinent to the moment, and disposes of the rest as being *passé*."[37]

Another model for the engagement between theology and culture is the translation model. Stephen Bevans sees the translation model of contextual theology as the one "most commonly employed and usually the one most people think of when they think of doing theology in context."[38] One of the significant figures in articulating this approach is evangelical missiologist Charles Kraft. He begins with the anthropological principle that meanings can be conveyed to humans only through cultural forms or symbols. Humans, in turn, develop and perpetuate cultural forms within a cultural system because these forms serve as conveyers of meaning from and to those who use them. According to Kraft, the forms are essentially neutral, in contrast to the "non-neutral, subjective use that human beings make of their cultural patterns."[39] This distinction provides Kraft with the basis for contextualization in that it allows him to conclude that Christian meanings can be communicated through human cultural forms. Hence, he asserts that "relative cultural forms" are able to serve as the vehicles for expressing "absolute supracultural meanings," for the divine message, "while appropriately expressed in terms of those forms, transcends both the forms themselves and the meanings previously attached to those forms."[40]

Evangelicals and other conservatives have been especially interested in this approach, welcoming it as a way of overcoming the ahistorical nature of conservative theologies that, by focusing on the transcultural nature of doctrinal construction, fail to take seriously the social context of the theological task and the historicity of all theological reflection. Evangelical proponents of contextualization fault the approach of their conservative forebears for its tendency to promote a repetition of traditional formulations of biblical doctrine rather than to offer appropriate

37. Hall, *Thinking the Faith*, 111–12.
38. Bevans, *Models of Contextual Theology*, 37.
39. Charles H. Kraft, *Christianity in Culture: A Study in Dynamic Biblical Theologizing in Cross-Cultural Perspective* (Maryknoll, NY: Orbis, 1979), 391.
40. Ibid., 99.

recontextualizations of the doctrine in response to changing cultural and historical conditions. Commenting on this approach, Bevans observes that while in many ways every model of contextual theology is a model of translation, in that there is always a context to be adopted or accommodated, this model is particularly a translation model because of its "insistence on the message of the gospel as an unchanging message."[41] In the same way that our historical and social context plays a part in the construction of the reality in which we live, our context influences our understanding of God, our interpretation of the Bible, and the expression of our faith.

The chief difficulty with both of these methods is their indebtedness to foundationalism. Rather than acknowledging the particularity of every human culture, correlationists are prone to prioritize culture through the identification of a universal experience and to fit theology into a set of generalized assumptions. In contrast, translationist approaches often overlook the particularity of every understanding of the Christian message and too readily assume a Christian universal that then functions as the foundation for the construction of theology, even though it will need to be articulated in the language of a particular culture. This is especially evident in models of translation that are based on a distinction between the transcultural gospel and its expression through neutral cultural forms. Yet with few exceptions, most approaches to theology and context that move in the direction of the translation model presuppose a form of foundationalism that assumes the existence of a pure, transcendent gospel.

Despite the debilitating difficulties these approaches share as a result of their foundationalist assumptions, taken together they point the way forward. The two models suggest that an appropriately contextual theology must employ an interactive process that is both correlative and translational while resisting the tendencies of foundationalism. Neither gospel nor culture can function as the primary entity in the conversation between the two in light of their interpretive and constructed nature; we must recognize that theology emerges through an ongoing conversation involving both gospel and culture. While such an interactive model draws from both methods, it stands apart from both in one crucial way. Unlike correlation or translation, a dynamic and interactional model presupposes neither gospel nor culture as given, preexisting realities that subsequently enter into conversation. Rather, in the interactive process, both gospel and culture are viewed as particularized, dynamic realities that inform and are informed by the conversation itself. Under-

41. Bevans, *Models of Contextual Theology*, 37.

standing gospel and culture in this way allows us to realize that both our understanding of the gospel and the meaning structures through which people in society make sense of their lives are dynamic. In such a model, the conversation between gospel and culture should be one of mutual enrichment in which the exchange benefits the church in addressing its context as well as in the process of theological critique and construction.

The Second-Order Nature of Theology

The contextual nature of theology suggests the companion notion of theology as a second-order discipline and highlights its character as an interpretive enterprise. As such, the doctrinal, theological, and confessional formulations of theologians and particular communities are the products of human reflection on the primary stories, teachings, symbols, and practices of the Christian church. Therefore, these formulations must be distinguished from these "first-order" commitments of the Christian faith. For example, theological constructions and doctrines are always subservient to the content of Scripture and therefore must be held more lightly. In addition, the second-order nature of theology has entailed the development of conceptual vocabularies and sophisticated forms of argument that can appear to be far removed from idioms of Scripture. However, as John Webster notes, even though "technical sophistication is not without its attendant perils, it is only vicious when it is allowed to drift free from the proper end of theology, which is the saints' edification."[42] From this perspective, theology is a metadiscourse on the first-order language of the Christian story narrated and expounded in Scripture. The content of this theological metadiscourse should always be viewed as a second-order, interpretive venture subject to further clarification, insight, and correction.

This metadiscourse is linked to the meaning-making activity of the people who comprise the community of Christ. Hence, theology is related to the various Christian symbols and activities in their function as purveyors and conveyers of Christian cultural meaning and practice. Critical reflection on the beliefs and practices of the Christian community constitute what Hans Frei describes as "the Christian community's second-order appraisal of its own language and actions under a norm or norms internal to the community."[43] This reflection on the beliefs and

---

42. John Webster, *Holiness* (Grand Rapids: Eerdmans, 2003), 4.

43. Hans W. Frei, *Types of Modern Theology*, ed. George Hunsinger and William C. Placher (New Haven: Yale University Press, 1992), 2.

practices of the community includes the attempt to bring to light the meaning of the structures that inform them. It involves as well evaluating individual practices on the basis of the extent to which they reflect sound Christian teaching.[44] Of course, in this process, theologians are influenced by their own conclusions as to the meanings that ought to motivate and come to expression in Christian practices in general and the specific practice under scrutiny in particular.

Theologians not only reflect critically on the beliefs and practices of the community but also seek to express Christian communal beliefs and values as well as the meaning of Christian symbols in a more direct manner. That is, the theological enterprise entails not only a critical but also a constructive task. In its constructive dimension, theology is a cultural practice of the church. As Kathryn Tanner states, theology "is a material social practice that specializes in meaning production."[45] Connected as it is with the Christian community, such theological construction has as its goal the setting forth of a particular understanding of the framework of meaning and the mosaic of beliefs that are at the core of the Christian community. In this sense, theology can be understood as the "science of convictional communities."[46] In reflecting on the nature of theology as a second-order discipline, a potential distortion that must be avoided is the conclusion that theology is of little significance for the life and work of the church since it is "merely" a second-order, interpretive discipline subject to human frailty and fallibility.

To illustrate the second-order nature of theology and its function in the life of the church, let us consider the confessional tradition of the Christian faith. Christianity is a confessing religion that has produced a rich tradition of confessional and catechetical statements of belief. These statements arise out of the act of confession, one of the primary and defining activities of the church. In the act of confession, the church seeks, in dependence on the Spirit, to bind itself to the living God and the truth and hope of the gospel of reconciliation and redemption. This act of confession, which should be a regular and continual aspect of the life and activity of the church, produces confessions whose purpose is to bear witness to the gospel and to promote the ongoing confessional life and activity of the Christian community. In this way, confessional statements and formulas function as servants of the gospel in the life of the church in the form of second-order statements that reflect convic-

---

44. Ronald Thiemann, *Revelation and Theology: The Gospel as Narrated Promise* (Notre Dame: University of Notre Dame Press, 1985), 75.

45. Tanner, *Theories of Culture*, 72.

46. James William McClendon Jr. and James M. Smith, *Convictions: Defusing Religious Relativism*, rev. ed. (Valley Forge, PA: Trinity, 1994), 181–96.

tions concerning the meaning and implications of the primary stories, teachings, symbols, and practices of the Christian church. When the church attempts to engage in its appointed tasks apart from the act of confession, it runs the risk of losing sight of its relationship to the gospel.

This can occur in one of two ways. First, it can occur through the decision to marginalize the confessional tradition of the church and to function as though it did not exist by relegating it to the status of a museum piece. This marginalization, even elimination, of the confessional tradition has been pronounced in both liberal and conservative Protestantism since the nineteenth century. Suspicion toward tradition, an emphasis on objectivity, and the priority of the individual in the task of knowing form the basic characteristics of the liberal theological program spawned in the wake of the Enlightenment. Hence, one of the chief concerns of liberal theology is to render an account of Christian faith that is intelligible, credible, and convincing to an honest, objective inquirer.[47] In line with this concern, liberals came to view formulations of the past as a hindrance to the task of theology in that such formulations were based on conceptions of reality that had been superseded by those of the modern world. What is needed, according to the liberal perspective, is a reformulation or a revision of Christian doctrine consonant with modern sensibilities, not a retrieval of the particular doctrines of the ancient Christian past.[48]

In one sense, liberal theology is a logical trajectory of Protestantism. Luther, Zwingli, and especially Calvin critically appropriated and revised the traditions of the ancient church in their reformist theological programs. For Protestants, therefore, the call to scrutinize critically received traditions and confessions was not a new idea. Although liberalism can claim a certain degree of continuity with the aims and concerns of the Protestant Reformation, at least on the formal level, we dare not overlook the significant difference between the two. The Reformers were concerned that the Christian tradition had been deformed by the medieval church, and as the antidote, they appealed to one of the central premises of the tradition, the primacy of Scripture, as the corrective. They claimed that their reform program as developed on the basis of Scripture alone was rooted in a proper understanding of the tradition itself.

According to Brian Gerrish, the problem shifted in liberal theology "from the inside to the outside: it is not so much that the tradition itself

47. H. P. van Dusen, *The Vindication of Liberal Theology* (New York: Scribner's, 1963), 27.

48. Bernard M. Reardon, ed., *Liberal Protestantism* (Stanford: Stanford University Press, 1968), 73–78.

has been corrupted by the infidelity of the church as that the church's tradition in the modern world has become insecure."[49] The issue for liberalism, then, is not Scripture and tradition but the legitimacy of the classical Christian tradition itself, including its commitment to Scripture, as viewed from the perspective of modernity. The liberal stance almost inevitably leads to the denigration of the entire tradition prior to the Reformation, as well as that of the Reformation itself in terms of its material concerns, inasmuch as both are committed, in one way or another, to the centrality of Scripture. Gerrish asserts that liberal Protestantism is at once both "less and more radical than the classical, Reformation model: less radical because there is a stronger consciousness of continuing what is right in the tradition (rather than correcting what is wrong); more radical because the tradition is brought to the test of norms from outside the entire Christian heritage."[50] Although Gerrish is partially correct, liberalism can be thought less radical only in its stance toward the formal, revisionist character of the Reformation, which liberalism maintains, not in terms of the material commitments of the Reformation contained in its creeds and confessions, which liberals largely reject.

The standard liberal approach urges the cultivation of a skepticism and doubt with regard to the classical Christian tradition and for all intents and purposes mutes the voice of that tradition in theology. Where an appeal to tradition is made, liberalism tends to claim the heritage of the revisionist character of the Protestant Reformation. This liberal theological paradigm is characterized by a commitment to reason as an independent authority set over against the Christian tradition. The assumption that follows from this commitment is that the most responsible use of the Christian theological tradition is "initially to rebel against its authority, to test its worth, and only to afford it respect when one can establish the truth of its offerings on other independent grounds, and thereby commend its truth to those who do not belong to the tradition."[51]

In keeping with this paradigm, when liberal Protestants have discussed the Christian tradition, the focal point has not been the authority of that tradition but the question of the origins of the confessional tradition of orthodoxy. As Richard Lints notes, having cut themselves loose from the authority of the Bible and the church, "they sought to explain

49. B. A. Gerrish, *Tradition and the Modern World: Reformed Theology in the Nineteenth Century* (Chicago: University of Chicago Press, 1978), 7.

50. Ibid., 7.

51. Trevor Hart, *Faith Thinking: The Dynamics of Christian Theology* (Downers Grove, IL: InterVarsity, 1995), 168.

the development of doctrine in the history of the church in naturalistic terms, focusing on political, social and economic factors."[52] This interest in the historical development of doctrine, coupled with the concern of biblical scholarship to get behind the text in order to reconstruct the true history of the ancient faith communities, led to the conclusion that the church in its many expressions had corrupted the true meaning of the gospel. In the estimation of many liberals, the tradition of the church merely codifies and defines the prejudices of the past and the attempts of those in power to impose their will on the church. In this paradigm, the results of the struggle to define various doctrines are viewed as the products of an essentially political procedure.

Walter Bauer set forth this construal of orthodoxy and tradition, maintaining that doctrinal pluralism was the norm in the early church and was only later suppressed by the rise of orthodoxy. Bauer claimed, in keeping with nineteenth-century liberalism, not only that there were numerous and significant doctrinal differences between the pure teaching of Jesus and that of the early church but also that doctrinal diversity was at the center of the early tradition.[53] The widespread acceptance of Bauer's thesis among liberals effectively silenced the voice of the classical Christian tradition in contemporary liberal theology.[54] More recently, New Testament scholar Bart Ehrman has developed a similar approach to the tradition.[55] In their dismissal of the Christian tradition as a corruption of the true teachings of Jesus and genuine Christianity, liberal theologians seek to free themselves from the constraints of that tradition in order to open up the possibility of new formulations and interpretations of the faith that they believe to be more in keeping with contemporary cultural assumptions.

While the influence of the classical Christian tradition in contemporary theology has been largely negated in liberalism, the situation is somewhat different, although not altogether more positive, among evangelicals, who have often been characterized by a disdain for tradition despite their claims to hold to the faith of the ancient church. The biblical foundationalism of evangelical theology coupled with a reductionistic account

52. Lints, *Fabric of Theology*, 88.

53. Walter Bauer, *Orthodoxy and Heresy in Earliest Christianity*, ed. Robert A. Kraft and Gerhard Krodel (Philadelphia: Fortress, 1971).

54. On the continuing influence of Bauer's work, see Daniel J. Harrington, "The Reception of Walter Bauer's *Orthodoxy and Heresy in Earliest Christianity* during the Last Decade," *Harvard Theological Review* 77 (1980): 289–98.

55. Bart D. Ehrman, *Lost Christianities: The Battle for Scripture and the Faiths We Never Knew* (Oxford: Oxford University Press, 2003); and idem, *The Orthodox Corruption of Scripture: The Effect of Early Christological Controversies on the Text of the New Testament* (Oxford: Oxford University Press, 1993).

of the Reformation notion of *sola scriptura* has served to marginalize the influence of tradition in the evangelical church. In addition, evangelical theologian Richard Lints notes three fundamental characteristics of contemporary evangelicalism that work against the appreciation and the appropriation of tradition: (1) the emphasis on inductive methods of Bible study, (2) the pervasive parachurch or transdenominational orientation of the movement, and (3) its ahistorical devotional piety.

In many evangelical contexts, the emphasis on Bible study often focuses primarily on the meaning of the text for an individual reader. Although such an approach may well stimulate a greater interest in individual Bible study, it also encourages reading according to subjective interests. In such circumstances, the Bible can be enslaved by the whims of an individual reader whose only interest is in the "meaning" of the text for his or her particular situation. Lints points out that if this is the primary concern in the examination of the text, the church will have to contend with as many different interpretations of the biblical text as there are interpreters. He notes that in the elimination of all mediators between the Bible and believers, the evangelical community has allowed Scripture to be ensnared in a web of subjectivism. "Having rejected the aid of the community of interpreters throughout the history of Christendom, we have not succeeded in returning to the primitive gospel; we have simply managed to plunge ourselves back to the biases of our own individual situations."[56]

The parachurch orientation of evangelicalism causes the movement to have no cohesive tradition or ecclesiology of its own. The evangelical community is a patchwork of communities bound together in part by shared theological, social, and cultural concerns. The basis for the unity of the evangelical movement has typically been a narrow core of theological distinctives that represent a diversity of theological approaches and beliefs. This tendency has given evangelicalism its transdenominational character, with the result that "evangelical Presbyterians and Methodists typically locate their identity less in the Presbyterian or Methodist heritage than in the nebulous theological heritage of evangelicalism."[57] To a significant extent, this transdenominational orientation effectively severs evangelicalism from the richness of the many theological traditions that are part of the movement. The result is a truncated theology that emphasizes certain "essentials" while virtually ignoring other elements of traditional Christian faith. Above all, the neglect of ecclesiology characteristic of the movement effectively eliminates tradition from playing a major role in evangelical theology.

56. Lints, *Fabric of Theology*, 93.
57. Ibid., 94.

The final factor that Lints cites as inhibiting the reception of tradition in the evangelical movement is the ahistorical character of its devotional piety. He writes that the classics of evangelical devotional literature go back no farther than the 1950s and suggests that evangelicals have removed themselves from the works of Christian writers from the nearly two thousand years of prior Christian history. Evangelicals "have convinced themselves that every important thing has happened in the present century and every important book (excepting the Bible, of course) has been written in their own lifetime."[58] The history of the evangelical movement as a largely twentieth-century coalition works against the appropriation of the more distant past and leaves evangelicalism less able to critique the biases of its own perspective.

The second way in which the church can fail in the act of confession and so risk losing sight of its relationship to the gospel is through the claim that a particular confessional statement can be viewed as virtually, if not absolutely, infallible. Many conservative Protestants have continued to affirm their roots in the creeds of the magisterial Reformation, whether Lutheran, Reformed, or Anglican. Thus, while much of contemporary evangelicalism has evidenced little place for tradition, another segment of conservative evangelical Protestantism has continually maintained a strong confessional approach to tradition as a vital component of theology. It is this wing of the movement that explains why evangelicals are "so often accused by the larger theological community of having a Roman Catholic view of tradition" and why it is "a common perception of modern theologians that the evangelical movement relies on its confessions as infallible interpreters of the Scriptures."[59]

Finding their theological bearings in the authority of the confessions and catechisms of their various traditions, these groups have often been critical of the disregard for the traditions of confessional Protestantism they see in evangelicalism. Yet such groups often give evidence of a static rather than a living view of tradition. As a consequence, the theology that often emerges in such circles routinely is little more than a confessional variety of the foundationalism that typifies modern theology in general. This is particularly the case among churches and institutions that maintain theological and doctrinal standards that require a strict confessional subscriptionism.

Each of these approaches is problematic for the confessional nature of the church. In the first instance, the act of confession is severed from its connection to the past operation of the Spirit and so is easily held captive to the cultural, social, and intellectual norms of a particular age,

58. Ibid., 96.
59. Ibid., 91.

leading to the accommodation of the gospel. In the second, an awareness of the ongoing need for confession is blunted as a past confessional formulation, implicitly if not explicitly, is taken to be an adequate confession for all times and places. As John Webster comments, "The creed is a good servant but a bad master: it assists, but cannot replace, the act of confession." The church cannot bypass the act of confession and yet retain the creed, "for to do so is to convert the event of confession into an achieved formula, graspable without immediate reference to the coming of the Holy Spirit. Whatever else we may say by way of commending the place of the creed in the life of the church, we must not promote the notion that the creed's significance is merely statutory."[60]

The creeds and confessions of the Christian church are second-order interpretive reflections on the primary stories, teachings, symbols, and practices of the Christian faith that, under the guidance of the Spirit, provide a hermeneutical trajectory in which the discipline of theology is pursued in conversation with the normative witness of Scripture and the contemporary cultural situation. From this perspective, we can summarize the second-order nature of church confessions as subordinate and provisional, open-ended, and eschatologically directed.

First, the creeds and confessions of the church are subordinate. They are subordinate to God and Scripture. They are responses to the revelation of God in Scripture and as such are normed norms. However, this should not lead to the conclusion that confessions and creeds are merely poor, fallible human attempts to bear witness to the truth of the gospel. Webster reminds us that to say that confessions and creeds are conditional or provisional is "worlds apart from the idea that the creed is merely one not-very-good attempt at pinning down a God whom we cannot really know."[61] Speaking of the provisionality of confessions is not an expression of skepticism or an attempt to undermine genuine confession. It is simply a sober consequence of the fact that finite and sinful human beings cannot fully comprehend the revelation of God and an acknowledgment of the need for the ongoing reformation of the church's thought and speech. However, such a reforming theology is not a matter of promoting the instability "of having everything open to revision all the time; such an attitude risks denying the reality of the gift of the Spirit to the church. All we are saying is that the creed is not God's Word, but ours; it is made, not begotten."[62]

60. John Webster, "Confession and Confessions," in *Nicene Christianity: The Future for a New Ecumenism*, ed. Christopher R. Seitz (Grand Rapids: Brazos, 2001), 120.
61. Ibid., 129.
62. Ibid.

The provisional, subordinate nature of confessional statements stands as a challenge to those who ascribe binding authority to them. Such an approach runs the risk of transforming past creeds into de facto substitutes for Scripture. Furthermore, in the interest of securing an absolute and final authority in the church, this approach can actually hinder such a community from hearing the voice of the Spirit speaking in new ways through the biblical text. A helpful distinction may be drawn between open and closed confessional traditions. A closed confessional tradition holds a particular statement of beliefs to be adequate for all times and places. In contrast, an open confessional tradition, in the words of Jack Stotts, "anticipates that what has been confessed in a formally adopted confession takes its place in a confessional lineup, preceded by statements from the past and expectant of more to come as times and circumstances change."[63] Such an approach also understands the obligation to develop and adopt new confessions in accordance with shifting circumstances. Although such confessions are "extraordinarily important" for the integrity, identity, and faithfulness of the church, "they are also acknowledged to be relative to particular times and places."[64]

To understand the confessional heritage of the church as a second-order language that provides a hermeneutical trajectory in the task of interpreting Scripture and doing theology is to acknowledge the importance of confessions without elevating them to a position of final authority because of the ongoing life of the church as it moves toward its eschatological consummation. It is also to acknowledge the second-order nature of contemporary theological reflection, which takes its place in the ongoing theological conversation about the meaning and implications of the revelation of God in Jesus Christ. Throughout the course of the ebb and flow of the history of the church, the Spirit is at work completing the divine program and bringing the people of God as a community into a fuller comprehension of the implications of the gospel. This activity of the Spirit will reach consummation only in the eschatological future. Until then the church must grapple with the meaning and the implications of the biblical message for its context as it listens patiently and expectantly for the voice of the Spirit speaking afresh through Scripture and yet in continuity with the Spirit-guided trajectory of the tradition and confessional heritage of the church.

Gabriel Fackre describes the ongoing theological dynamic that characterizes the life of the church and contributes to the development of

63. Jack L. Stotts, "Introduction: Confessing after Barmen," in Jan Rohls, *Reformed Confessions: Theology from Zurich to Barmen*, trans. John Hoffmeyer (Louisville: Westminster John Knox, 1998), xi.
64. Ibid.

church tradition prior to the consummation: "The circle of tradition is not closed, for the Spirit's ecclesial Work is not done. Traditional doctrine develops as Christ and the gospel are viewed in ever fresh perspective. Old formulations are corrected, and what is passed on is enriched. The open-endedness, however, does not overthrow the ancient landmarks. As tradition is a gift of the Spirit, its trajectory moves in the right direction, although it has not arrived at its destination."[65] In short, at the heart of tradition, which is discussed more fully in the next chapter in connection with the task of theology, and the ongoing work of confession is the eschatological directedness of the Spirit's work. The Spirit is at work guiding the community of faith into the truth, purposes, and intentions of God for the church and the world. This divinely given *telos* is anticipated in the present through the life of the church but is ultimately realized only at the consummation. The contextual, interpretive, and eschatological dimensions of theology point to the ongoing nature of its character.

The Ongoing Nature of Theology

Because the situation into which the church proclaims the message of the gospel is constantly changing, the task of theology in assisting the church in the formulation and application of its faith commitments in the varied and shifting context of human life and thought is an ongoing enterprise. In the same way that our historical and cultural contexts shape our understanding and perceptions of reality, so they influence our understandings of God and the expression of our faith. As we saw with Origen, the dominant and pervasive assumptions of a particular time shape and influence the thoughts, hopes, beliefs, and expectations of the people who live within it. However, since these assumptions are always a part of our outlook, they shape our instincts and intuitions in ways that are often unnoticed and unexamined. Huston Smith suggests that this state of affairs can be metaphorically compared to "the pair of glasses which, because they are so often on the wearer's nose, simply stop being observed." The fact that the wearer ceases to be cognizant of their function, however, does not mean that they have no effect. "Ultimately, assumptions which underlie our outlooks on life refract the world in ways that condition our art and our institutions: the kinds of homes we live in, our sense of right and wrong, our criteria of success, what we conceive our duty to be, what we think it means to be a man

65. Gabriel Fackre, *The Christian Story: A Narrative Interpretation of Basic Christian Doctrine*, 3rd ed. (Grand Rapids: Eerdmans, 1996), 18–19.

or a woman, how we worship our God or whether, indeed, we have a God to worship."[66]

To understand the ways in which the dominant and pervasive assumptions of our context shape our outlooks on life and the world, and consequently our theology, we must understand something of the nature and function of culture. In recent years, the notion of culture as traditionally conceived has come under such strident and thoroughgoing criticism that some thinkers have come to believe that the term has been compromised and should be discarded. While a few favor this radical surgery, most anthropologists agree with James Clifford's grudging acknowledgment that culture "is a deeply compromised idea I cannot yet do without."[67] Thus, rather than causing the concept to be eliminated entirely, the criticisms of the term have led to a postmodern understanding of culture that takes the historical contingencies of human life and society more seriously.

Postmodern anthropologists have discarded the assumption that culture is a preexisting social-ordering force that is transmitted externally to members of a cultural group who in turn passively internalize it. They maintain that this view is mistaken in that it isolates culture from the ongoing social processes that produce and continually alter it.[68] Culture is not an entity standing above or beyond human products and learned mental structures. In short, culture is not a "thing."[69] This older understanding also focused on the idea of culture as that which integrates the various institutional expressions of social life and binds individuals to society. This focus on the integrative role of culture is now facing serious challenges. According to Anthony Cohen, it has become one of the casualties of the demise of "modernistic grand theories and the advent of 'the interpretive turn' in its various guises."[70] Rather than viewing cultures as monolithic entities, postmodern anthropologists view cultures as being internally fissured.[71] The elevation of difference that typifies postmodern thinking has triggered a heightened awareness of the role of persons in culture formation. Rather than exercising determinative power over people, culture is conceived as the outcome and product of

---

66. Huston Smith, *Beyond the Post-Modern Mind*, 2nd ed. (Wheaton: Theosophical Publishing House, 1989), 3–4.

67. James Clifford, *The Predicament of Culture: Twentieth-Century Ethnography, Literature, and Art* (Cambridge: Harvard University Press, 1988), 10.

68. Tanner, *Theories of Culture*, 50.

69. Roy G. D'Andrade, *The Development of Cognitive Anthropology* (Cambridge: Cambridge University Press, 1995), 250.

70. Anthony P. Cohen, *Self Consciousness: An Alternative Anthropology of Identity* (London: Routledge, 1994), 118.

71. Tanner, *Theories of Culture*, 56.

social interaction. Consequently, rather than being viewed as passive receivers, human beings are seen as the active creators of culture.[72]

Clifford Geertz provided the impetus for this direction through his description of cultures as comprising "webs of significance" that people spin and in which they are then suspended.[73] Geertz defines culture as "an historically transmitted pattern of meanings embodied in symbols, a system of inherited conceptions expressed in symbolic forms by means of which people communicate, perpetuate, and develop their knowledge about and attitudes toward life."[74] According to Cohen, Geertz was responsible for "shifting the anthropological view of culture from its supposedly objective manifestations in social structures, towards its subjective realisation by members who compose those structures."[75] Culture resides in a set of meaningful forms and symbols that, from the point of view of a particular individual, appear as largely given.[76] Yet these forms are only meaningful because human minds have the ability to interpret them.[77] This has led contemporary anthropologists to look at the interplay of cultural artifacts and human interpretation in the formation of meaning. They suggest that, contrary to the belief that meaning lies in signs or in the relations between them, meanings are bestowed by the users of signs.[78] However, this does not mean that individuals simply discover or make up cultural meanings on their own. Even the mental structures by which they interpret the world are developed through explicit teaching and implicit observation of others. Consequently, cultural meanings are both psychological states and social constructions.[79]

The thrust of contemporary cultural anthropology leads to the conclusion that its primary concern lies in understanding the creation of cultural meaning as connected to world construction and identity formation. This approach leads to an understanding of culture as socially constructed. The thesis of social constructionists such as Peter Berger is that, rather than inhabiting a prefabricated, given world, we live in a social-cultural world of our own creation.[80] At the heart of the pro-

72. Cohen, *Self Consciousness*, 118–19.

73. Clifford Geertz, *The Interpretation of Cultures* (New York: Basic Books, 1973), 5.

74. Ibid., 89.

75. Cohen, *Self Consciousness*, 135.

76. Geertz, *Interpretation of Cultures*, 45.

77. Ulf Hannerz, *Cultural Complexity: Studies in the Social Organization of Meaning* (New York: Columbia University Press, 1992), 3–4.

78. Claudia Strauss and Naomi Quinn, *A Cognitive Theory of Cultural Meaning* (Cambridge: Cambridge University Press, 1997), 253.

79. Ibid., 16.

80. Peter L. Berger, *The Sacred Canopy: Elements of a Sociological Theory of Religion* (Garden City, NY: Doubleday, 1969), 3–13.

cess whereby we construct our world is the imposition of a meaningful order on our variegated experiences. For the interpretive framework we employ in this task, we are dependent on the society in which we participate.[81] In this manner, society mediates to us the cultural tools necessary for constructing our world. Although this constructed world gives the semblance of being a given, universal, and objective reality, it is actually, in the words of David Morgan, "an unstable edifice that generations constantly labor to build, raze, rebuild, and redesign."[82] We inhabit socially constructed worlds to which our personal identities are intricately bound. The construction of these worlds, as well as the formation of personal identity, is an ongoing, dynamic, and fluid process in which the forming and reforming of shared cultural meanings play a crucial role. Culture includes the symbols that provide the shared meanings by which we understand ourselves, pinpoint our deepest aspirations and longings, and construct the worlds we inhabit. Through the symbols of our culture, we express and communicate these central aspects of life to one another while struggling together to determine the meaning of the very symbols we employ in this process.

To be human is to be embedded in culture and to participate in the process of interpretation and the creation of meaning as we reflect on and internalize the cultural symbols that we share with others in numerous conversations that shape our ever-shifting contexts. As we have seen, the question of the relationship between culture and theology has been implicit throughout the history of Christian theology. The constantly changing nature of culture and the world in which we live means that the challenge of relating the gospel to different and shifting circumstances is an ongoing process. "The time is past when we can speak of one, right, unchanging theology, a *theologia perennis*. We can only speak about a theology that makes sense at a certain place and in a certain time. We can certainly learn from others (synchronically from other cultures and diachronically from history), but the theology of others can never be our own."[83] Therefore, no matter how persuasive, beautiful, or successful past theologies or confessions of faith may have been, the church is always faced with the task of confessing the faith in the context of the particular circumstances and challenges in which it is situated. In this way, the nature of theology is ongoing, and theology will continue to wrestle with the challenges of culture and context until the eschaton.

81. Ibid., 20. See also Peter L. Berger and Thomas Luckmann, "Sociology of Religion and Sociology of Knowledge," *Sociology and Social Research* 47 (1963): 417–27.

82. David Morgan, *Visual Piety: A History and Theory of Popular Images* (Berkeley: University of California Press, 1998), 9.

83. Bevans, *Models of Contextual Theology*, 4–5.

As Garrett Green concludes, "Like all interpretive activity, theology will therefore be historically and culturally grounded, not speaking from some neutral vantage point but in and for its human context. One corollary is that the theological task will never be completed this side of the Eschaton, since human beings are by nature historical and changing."[84] This leads to the conclusion that in one sense all theology is local in that all attempts at doing theology are both influenced by the particular thought forms and practices that shape the social context from which it emerges and bear the distinctive marks of that setting.[85]

An awareness of the local character of theology and the nonfoundational relationship between gospel and culture raises a challenge for the practice of an appropriately catholic theology: the attempt to teach and bear witness to the one faith of the entire church. How do we do theology that is not simply accommodated to our own cultural assumptions and aspirations? Lesslie Newbigin has addressed this question by observing that while the ultimate commitment of a Christian theologian is to the biblical story, such a person is also a participant in a particular social setting whose way of thinking is shaped by the cultural model of that society in ways that are both conscious and unconscious. These cultural models cannot be absolutized without impairing the ability to properly discern the teachings and implications of the biblical narrative. Yet as participants in a particular culture, we are not able to see many of the ways in which we take for granted and absolutize our own socially constructed cultural model. Given this state of affairs, Newbigin maintains that the unending task of theology must be to be wholly open to the biblical narrative in such a way that the assumptions and aspirations of a culture are viewed in its light. This is done in order to find ways of expressing the biblical story in terms that make use of particular cultural models without being controlled by them. He concludes with the assertion that this can be done only if Christian theologians are "continuously open to the witness of Christians in other cultures who are seeking to practice the same kind of theology."[86] This means that while theology is genuinely local in the sense that it is shaped and marked by its particular context, it is also responsible in its local iterations to the entire church

84. Garrett Green, *Imagining God: Theology and the Religious Imagination* (San Francisco: Harper & Row, 1989), 186.

85. For an extended discussion on the character of local theology, see Robert J. Schreiter, *Constructing Local Theologies* (Maryknoll, NY: Orbis, 1985); and Clemens Sedmak, *Doing Local Theology: A Guide for Artisans of a New Humanity* (Maryknoll, NY: Orbis, 2002).

86. Lesslie Newbigin, "Theological Education in a World Perspective," *Churchman* 93 (1979): 114–15.

in its historical and global expressions. The local character of theology must not become the basis for sectarianism in the church.

As noted in the first chapter, the task of theology in its various historical, cultural, ecclesial, and confessional contexts and expressions is to offer its particular witness to the Christian faith as an ecumenical enterprise for the purpose of contributing to the common task of the church to clarify the teaching of the one faith. The next chapter considers the task of theology as critical and constructive reflection on the beliefs and practices of the Christian church. It suggests a model for theology that is inherently reforming in its openness to the Word of God and the multicultural Christian witness of the historical and global church and in keeping with the nature of theology as an ongoing, second-order, contextual discipline.

4

The Task of Theology

As concluded in the previous chapter, the unending task of theology is to find ways of expressing and communicating the biblical story in terms that make use of the intellectual and conceptual tools of a particular culture without being controlled by them. This suggests the need for both critical and constructive reflection on the beliefs and practices of the church in order to scrutinize continuously the life of the church by the standard of the biblical witness and to envision all of life in relationship to God and the mission of God in the world. This task of envisioning must also be done in continuity with the work of the Spirit throughout the history of the church and in the context of the global church, meaning that attention must be paid to past and present itera-tions of theology. Thus, while theology is in one sense local, and as such particularly concerned with addressing its own situation, it cannot be responsibly pursued in isolation from the church universal. To do so is to disregard the work of the Spirit in the life of the entire church and to fail to promote the unity of the church. This chapter maintains that the constructive task of theology involves the development and articulation of models of the Christian faith that are biblically normed, culturally relevant, and historically informed. This suggests three sources that must be taken into account in the formulation and construction of theology: canonical Scripture, the cultural contexts in which theology is developed, and the tradition of the church.

As observed in the previous chapter, the contextual nature of theology means we must be not only aware of our own circumstances but also alert to the importance of context with respect to the content of Scripture and the shape of the Christian tradition. Conclusions concerning the ongoing, second-order, and contextual nature of theology significantly alter the ways in which theology has traditionally been done in Western culture. In other words, to quote Stephen Bevans, "When we say that there are three sources for theology, we are not just adding context as a third element; *we are changing the whole equation.*"[1] An appropriate model for the task of theology must be open and flexible in accordance with the contextual nature of the discipline as understood in light of the knowledge of God and of ourselves. The principal concern in this chapter is to outline the shape of the theological task as it relates to the relationship among Scripture, culture, and tradition. However, first a few words are needed regarding the focal point of the critical and constructive reflection that constitutes the theological task: the church.

Theology's Focal Point: The Church

Chapter 2 maintained that the subject of Christian theology is the Triune God revealed in Jesus Christ. However, this should not lead to the conclusion that theology is an abstract undertaking simply concerned with ascertaining a series of right beliefs about God. The church is entrusted with the missional task of proclaiming and living out the gospel and its implications in the world. The nature of the church and its missional calling are tied up with the church's relationship with God and its role in the *missio Dei*. As suggested, God is social and missional in character, and these aspects of the divine nature have implications for the church and the task of theology. The nature of the church is connected with the understanding that humans are created in the image of God. Hence, Christian theologians have traditionally constructed theological anthropology around the concept of the *imago Dei*. Human identity is bound up with the idea that human beings are created in the image of God and therefore are bearers of the divine image.

In keeping with this conviction, theologians have offered various suggestions concerning the nature or content of the *imago Dei*. Perhaps the most long-standing interpretation of the image sees it as a structure of the human person. In this understanding, the divine image consists of the properties that constitute human beings as human with special

---

1. Stephen B. Bevans, *Models of Contextual Theology*, rev. ed. (Maryknoll, NY: Orbis, 2002), 5, emphasis in original.

emphasis placed on their capacity for rationality and their moral nature. This view is widespread in the history of Christian theology and continues to be influential, particularly in traditions influenced by Protestant scholasticism. In spite of its impressive and venerable pedigree, however, the substantialist view ultimately fails to do justice to the dynamic nature of the divine image. The concepts of relationality and destiny have shifted the conversation away from a substantialist understanding. The first finds its genesis in the Reformers, who placed primary focus on the special standing before God that characterizes human existence rather than on a formal structure supposedly found within the human person. The relational view suggested by the Reformers found increasing support in the twentieth century.

The Reformers also opened the door to the idea that the *imago Dei* is linked to human destiny. For example, Martin Luther maintained that although the image was distorted through sin, restoration is possible through the ministry of Word and Spirit. This restoration, which begins in the present and reaches completion only in the consummation, raises humans to a stature that is even higher than what was lost in the fall. This perfection of the divine image is the eternal life for which Adam was created.[2] In this sense, the *imago Dei* is ultimately God's intention and goal for humanity. The more formal development of the anthropological concept of destiny arose in the context of German romanticism and was worked out in the twentieth century by theologians such as Wolfhart Pannenberg, who suggests a link between the biblical concept of the image of God and the future human destiny.[3] This link introduces a dynamic dimension into the concept of the divine image. The image of God is a destiny toward which human beings are moving and entails what they are en route to becoming. It is what resurrected humans will bear in the new creation. Hence, it is a future reality that is present now only as a foretaste or only in the form of human potential. As Daniel Migliore states, "Being created in the image of God is not a state or condition but a movement with a goal: human beings are restless for a fulfillment of life not yet realized."[4]

The creation narratives of Genesis suggest that the destiny of human beings begins with a special standing before God. As created in the divine image, human beings are the recipients of God's commands and

2. Martin Luther, *Lectures on Genesis,* in *Luther's Works,* ed. Jaroslav Pelikan (St. Louis: Concordia, 1958), 1:64–65.

3. Wolfhart Pannenberg, *Systematic Theology,* vol. 2, trans. Geoffrey W. Bromiley (Grand Rapids: Eerdmans, 1991), 218–31.

4. Daniel L. Migliore, *Faith Seeking Understanding: An Introduction to Christian Theology* (Grand Rapids: Eerdmans, 1991), 128.

have a unique responsibility before God. The Old Testament links this responsibility with the notion of representation. Using the context of the setting in which the Old Testament was written, Gerhard von Rad draws a parallel between humanity as the image of God and the practices of kings in the ancient Near East. These kings often left images of themselves to represent their majesty and power in cities or territories where they could not be present in person. "Just as powerful earthly kings, to indicate their claim to dominion erect an image of themselves in the provinces of their empire where they do not personally appear, so man is placed upon earth in God's image as God's sovereign emblem. He is really only God's representative, summoned to maintain and enforce God's claim to dominion over the earth."[5] God has entrusted to humans a special task of serving as God's representatives and to reflect the character of God to creation.

While all persons are created in the image of God and share in the one human *telos,* the New Testament writers apply the concept of the divine image particularly to Jesus Christ (2 Cor. 4:4–6; Col. 1:15), who is the clear representation of the character and glory of God. By extension, those who are united to Christ share in his role as the *imago Dei.* All who are "in Christ" are being transformed into the image of Christ so that their lives may reflect his glory (2 Cor. 3:18). In fact, it is to conformity to Christ (as the likeness of God) that God has destined us (Rom. 8:29; 1 John 3:2). For this reason, Paul proclaims the hope that "just as we have borne the likeness of the earthly man, so shall we bear the likeness of the man from heaven" (1 Cor. 15:49), which will be accomplished through participation in Christ's resurrection (1 Cor. 15:50–53). This encapsulates the witness of the biblical narrative, which presents the mission and purpose of God as that of bringing into being a people who reflect the divine character as the *imago Dei.* At the eschaton, God will bring to completion the divine intention, and humanity will reflect fully the divine image as God's representatives after the pattern of the Triune God revealed in Christ.

This dynamic conception of the image of God may be combined with the social nature of the Triune God, biblical exegesis, and the postmodern turn to relationality to establish that the divine image is a shared, communal reality. It leads to the conclusion that the image of God is fully present only in community.[6] As seen in the discussion of the

5. Gerhard von Rad, *Genesis,* ed. G. Ernest Wright (Philadelphia: Westminster, 1972), 58.

6. For a detailed development of this thesis, see Stanley J. Grenz, *The Social God and the Relational Self: A Trinitarian Theology of the* Imago Dei (Louisville: Westminster John Knox, 2001).

Trinity, God is inherently relational in that throughout all eternity God is a triune community of love. In turn, God's goal for humanity is that we represent God by reflecting the divine nature, which is our destiny in Christ. In this context, the church is viewed as the foretaste of the new humanity. Hence, the divine design for Christ's community is that we be a people who, because we share in the Holy Spirit and thereby participate in the eternal love of God, represent God in the midst of a fallen world through lives that reflect God's own loving character. Only through relationships and in community can we truly show what God is like, for God is the community of love, the eternal relational dynamic enjoyed by the three persons of the Trinity.

Hence, the divine reign consists of God at work redeeming, reconciling, and transforming creation into God's intended ideal, thereby constituting the world as God's realm. This reign both transcends history and works within history as the power bringing about the new order. However, the new order God purposes for creation is communal in scope, meaning that when the reign of God is manifested and the will of God is done, we will see the emergence of community. In short, the emergence of community marks the presence of God's rule and the accomplishment of God's will. From creation to consummation, the biblical drama concerns the establishment of a community in the highest sense of the word, a reconciled and redeemed people living within a reconciled and redeemed creation in the presence of and in fellowship with the Triune God. The story of community is articulated at the opening of the biblical narrative with God's declaration, "It is not good for the man to be alone." God's activity from that point forward is directed toward bringing into being the community envisioned in the act of creation. As sociologist David Lyon observes, "It is clear from the creation account that sociality and interdependence are part of being human."[7] Further, at the heart of community, as depicted throughout the biblical narrative, is the idea of the presence of God among humans.

The covenant experience of the presence of God with Israel forms the context for the coming of Jesus as Immanuel, God with us (Matt. 1:22–23). In Jesus, the divine Word became flesh and "tabernacled" among us (John 1:14). Further, Jesus promised that he and his Father would take up their dwelling with the disciples (John 14:23) through the sending of another Comforter, who would be present among them (John 14:26). This promise provides the context for the work of the Spirit in fulfillment of the assurance of Jesus that he would be continually present with his followers. The Spirit comprises us individually and corporately

7. David Lyon, *Sociology and the Human Image* (Downers Grove, IL: InterVarsity, 1983), 128.

as the temple of God and the body of Christ. Because of the completed work of Christ and the continuing work of the Spirit, therefore, God is truly among us, even though our experience of that presence is partial. However, the biblical story does not end with a partial experience of God's presence. It reaches its climax only in the future, with the establishment of the new heaven and the new earth that will be characterized by community in the fullest sense. On that day, the peoples of the new earth will live together in peace, nature will again fulfill its purpose of providing nourishment for all the citizens of the earth (Rev. 22:1–3), and God will dwell with humans, thereby bringing to completion the divine design for creation.

In the present, the work of the Spirit is directed toward the establishment of a new people that transcends every human division, a people from every nation, every socioeconomic status, consisting of both male and female (Gal. 3:28). The completed work of Christ and the present work of the Spirit mean that the eschatological community that arrives in its fullness only at the consummation of human history is already present in a partial yet genuine manner. Although this present reality takes several forms, its focal point is the community of the followers of Christ. This observation brings us back to the concept of the divine reign in which the full manifestation of God's reign is in the community of Christ's disciples, in the fellowship of the people who by the Spirit have entered into covenant with the God of history and consequently live out their covenantal life through worship of the Triune God, mutual care, and mission in and for the world. As the church embodies the biblical vision of God's new community, its members reflect the character of God and are the *imago Dei*.

This vision and the New Testament characterization of the church as the body of Christ lead to the conclusion that the church is the focal point of the representation of the character of God in the world. In keeping with the discussion of the linguistically and socially constructed nature of reality, the church is the context in which the Spirit works to create a socially constructed "reality" that anticipates the ultimate reality of the consummated kingdom, a world centered on Jesus Christ. Christian theology is the explication of the interpretation of God and the world around which the Christian community finds its identity. Theology engages in this task for the purpose of facilitating Christ's disciples in fulfilling their calling to be the image of the social and missional God and thereby to be the community God desires and destines the church to become. A context in which the future world as God wills it to be is established in a proleptic fashion in the present as the church anticipates its participation in the trinitarian fellowship of love. The model of this love is that of Jesus Christ in his ministry of reconciliation characterized by obedience to God in the form of sacrificial love and service. The church is called to imitate this as the ongoing representative of Christ in the world, the metaphorical body of Christ (Phil. 2:5–11).

In addition to being called to imitate the love of Christ in anticipation of sharing in the trinitarian fellowship of love, the church is also called to share in the mission of Christ to the world. As shown in chapter 2, God has a mission to extend the fellowship of love to all creation. This mission reaches its revelatory climax in the life of Jesus Christ and continues through the sending of the Spirit as the one who empowers the church as the socially, historically, and culturally embodied witness to the gospel of Jesus Christ and the tangible expression of the mission of God. The call of the church to be imitators of Christ in his missional calling is expressed in the Gospel of John: "As the Father has sent me, I am sending you" (John 20:21). The church, the community of Christ's disciples, is sent into the world to be the representative of the mission of God after the pattern of the sending of the Son by the Father and the Spirit by the Father and the Son. Hence, the church is to represent the love and mission of God in the world through the proclamation of the gospel. In its beliefs and practices, it is called to be God's representative as the herald of reconciliation to a fallen and broken world. This calling makes the church the focal point for theological reflection. The task of theology is to serve the church by assisting in the process of coherently articulating the content and implications of the gospel and the Christian faith so that the church might faithfully reflect the image of God in the world and faithfully carry out the mission of God to the world through the guidance and power of the Spirit. This is done in anticipation of the eschatological consummation of God's creative purposes.

Theology's Task as Critical and Constructive

In keeping with its ongoing, second-order, and contextual nature, the task of theology involves reflection on the beliefs and practices of the church that is both critical and constructive. This section briefly comments on each of these in turn while bearing in mind that while they are distinguishable they are also interrelated and inseparable. Critical reflection involves the careful examination and scrutiny of the beliefs and practices of the church to ensure that they are coherent with the biblical narratives and the first-order commitments of the community and not enslaved to cultural practices and patterns of thinking that are not consistent with the gospel and the mission of the church. Critical reflection is necessary because of the nature of the church. As Karl Barth puts it, "The Christian Church does not exist in heaven, but on earth and in time." Hence, while the church is indeed a gift from God, it has been situated in the midst of human and earthly circumstances, and that reality shapes all that occurs in the church. In spite of the high calling entrusted to it by God, it often experiences temporal failure in its vocation as the representative of God. In possession and administration of this high calling, the church "passes on its way through history, in strength and in weakness, in faithfulness and in unfaithfulness, in obedience and in disobedience, in understanding and in misunderstanding of what is said to it."[8]

In short, critical theological reflection is necessary because the church, as a human institution, is prone to error and in danger of going astray. Hence, theology engages in an ongoing critical assessment of the beliefs and practices of the church guided by a norm or complex of norms internal to the life of the community. Of primary significance for the church is Scripture, which functions as theology's norming norm. While the next section examines the function of Scripture in the task of theology, here we simply note that the task of theology requires that the church, in the midst of its particular context, must take account of its beliefs and practices according to the standard of canonical Scripture and with guidance from its tradition and confessions. This critical reflection is not something done once for all. It is an aspect of theology that is returned to again and again in a ceaseless effort to ensure that the proclamation and the life of the church are in accordance with the gospel. This is another reminder that theology must not be viewed as "a matter of stating certain old or even new propositions that one can take home in black and white."[9] Instead, theology always begins again at the beginning in the interest of bearing faithful witness to its subject.

This critical reflection demands constant attention to the exegesis of Scripture and openness to what one finds in its pages. That said, one of the great challenges to the critical aspect of the theological task is the sheer familiarity, or presumed familiarity, of the biblical text. In addition, patterns of reading and deeply ingrained intuitions and assumptions can make the assertion that we always subject the beliefs and practices of the church to the teaching of Scripture little more than an abstract and empty formality. In this way, the gospel and the witness of Scripture can become domesticated by the standards of a particular culture or tradition. In seeking to address this challenge, we must keep in mind that theology must remain open to the witness of Christians in other cultures and contexts in the forms of biblical exegesis, theological reflection, and ecclesial practice. This openness can provide the context

8. Karl Barth, *Dogmatics in Outline* (New York: Harper & Row, 1959), 10–11.
9. Ibid., 12.

in which our own assumptions and presuppositions can be challenged and corrected where necessary for the sake of the proclamation of the gospel and the mission of the church. From this perspective, and in light of the opportunities and resources available in an increasingly global environment, engagement with the theological reflection and witness of the church in history and in other cultural settings can no longer be viewed simply as a luxury item or a specialist enterprise that most churches can safely disregard and ignore. Rather, it should be viewed as a crucial component of critical theological reflection that seeks to be attentive to the guidance of the Spirit in the church throughout its history and in its contemporary iterations.

The critical aspect of the theological task implies the constructive. The task of theological reflection is not simply to find inconsistencies or errors in the faith, life, and practices of the community. It is also to provide insight into appropriate ways of assisting the church to live out its calling in particular settings. Constructive reflection involves the development and the articulation of coherent models of Christian faith that are appropriate to the contemporary social-historical context. These models should be faithful to the biblical narratives and teachings, relevant to the contemporary setting, and informed by and in continuity with the historic position of the church. Hence, the sources for such a theology are the canonical Scriptures, the thought forms of the contemporary context, and the tradition of the church. The goal in this process is to envision all of life in relationship to the Triune God revealed in Jesus Christ through the articulation and practice of biblically normed, culturally relevant, and historically informed models of the Christian faith. Such models should express and communicate the biblical story in terms that make sense of it through the use of contemporary cultural tools and concepts without being controlled by them. The use of models in the constructive aspect of theology's task is particularly significant and deserves a brief explanation.

It has become commonplace to speak in terms of the construction of models in the theological task, and numerous works have appeared in recent years that employ this approach to theology.[10] Of particular importance is the work of Avery Dulles, *Models of the Church*, in which he demonstrates the effectiveness of employing models to address issues

---

10. For example, Avery Dulles, *Models of the Church* (Garden City, NY: Doubleday, 1974); idem, *Models of Revelation* (New York: Doubleday, 1983); John F. O'Grady, *Models of Jesus* (Garden City, NY: Doubleday, 1981); Raymond Collins, *Models of Theological Reflection* (Lanham, MD: University Press of America, 1984); Sallie McFague, *Models of God: Theology for an Ecological, Nuclear Age* (Philadelphia: Fortress, 1987); and Bevans, *Models of Contextual Theology*.

in theology. He suggests five models for construing the nature of the church and delineates the entailments of each with respect to a variety of theological questions. Dulles notes that through the use of models as heuristic devices complex theological issues and questions can be opened up for expression, reflection, and critical scrutiny. Dulles defines a model as "a relatively simple, artificially constructed case which is found to be useful and illuminating for dealing with realities that are more complex and differentiated."[11] While models are not able to capture fully all the complexities and nuances of the phenomenon under consideration, they are able to stimulate engagement and interaction with it. Hence, as Ian Barbour points out, models should be viewed "seriously but not literally."[12]

Models are constructions and not exact representations of particular phenomena. For example, the doctrine of the Trinity described in chapter 2 serves as a model of God and the relationship between Father, Son, and Holy Spirit. It does not provide a direct and literal picture of God, but it does, based on God's self-revelation, disclose actual features of God's character and the divine life. It is a second-order linguistic construction that, while not an exact replica of God, provides genuine comprehension concerning the nature and character of God. As Stephen Bevans puts it, models function like images and symbols and "provide ways through which one knows reality in all its richness and complexity. Models provide knowledge that is always partial and inadequate but never false or merely subjective."[13] The work of chemists in studying molecules provides a helpful analogy. Chemists study and learn about molecules and molecular structure through the construction of models, but we do not think that the pictures of these models found in science textbooks are simply large-scale replicas of molecules. They are analogue models with structural similarity to molecules that facilitate genuine engagement and understanding with the phenomena we refer to as molecules and molecular structure.

The results and the products of the constructive work of theology function in a similar fashion. As analogue or heuristic models of God and the relationship between God and the created order, they facilitate engagement and provide accurate insight and understanding without claiming that they provide an exact representation of God. God is transcendent and unique and categorically different from anything in creation. As the early church theologian Irenaeus once remarked, "God

---

11. Dulles, *Models of Revelation*, 30.
12. Ian G. Barbour, *Myths, Models, and Paradigms: A Comparative Study in Science and Religion* (New York: Harper & Row, 1974), 7.
13. Bevans, *Models of Contextual Theology*, 30.

is light and yet unlike any light that we know."[14] As George Hunsinger points out, "God's cognitive availability through divine revelation allows us, Irenaeus believed, to predicate descriptions of God that are as true as we can make them, while God's irreducible ineffability nonetheless renders even our best predications profoundly inadequate."[15] This points to the metaphorical nature of language, particularly with respect to the infinite and transcendent God of Christian faith.

Yet the revelation of God as social and missional calls us to speak of God as representatives of God and participants in the divine mission of reconciliation and the establishment of community. Thus, we construct models of God that are in keeping with God's self-revelation and that, as such, have analogical affinity with the nature and character of God and the relationship between God and the world.

In discussing the use of models in theology, it is also helpful to make a distinction between exclusive and inclusive models. Proponents of exclusive models may very well accept all that has been said thus far with respect to the use of models in theology and their analogical character. But they also maintain that the task of theology is to identify the single most appropriate model and to employ it to the exclusion of others. Proponents of inclusive models suggest the importance of multiple perspectives and angles of vision in the exploration and interpretation of theological truth. Bevans comments that due to "the complexity of the reality one is trying to express in terms of models, such a variety of models might even be imperative." He goes on to suggest that "an exclusive use of one model might distort the very reality one is trying to understand."[16] In light of the finite and fallen character of human knowledge and the divine subject matter of theology, a proper conception of God defies a unique description and requires a diversity of perspectives. From this perspective, all constructions are inadequate on their own and need to be supplemented by other models. This does not preclude the possibility of the adoption of one particular model as the most helpful from a particular vantage point, but as Avery Dulles comments, even this procedure does not require one to "deny the validity of what other theologians may affirm with the help of other models. A good theological system will generally recognize the limitations of its own root metaphors and will therefore be open to criticism from other points of view."[17]

14. Irenaeus, *Against Heresies* 11.13.4.
15. George Hunsinger, "Postliberal Theology," in *The Cambridge Companion to Postmodern Theology*, ed. Kevin J. Vanhoozer (Cambridge: Cambridge University Press, 2003), 47.
16. Bevans, *Models of Contextual Theology*, 30.
17. Dulles, *Models of Revelation*, 34–35.

In other words, no one model is able to account for all the diversity of the biblical witness, the diversity of perspectives on it, and the complexity in the interaction between gospel and culture that gives rise to theology. This observation brings us back to the critical aspect of the theological task and leads to the assertion that in the same way that the critical aspect of the theological task gives rise to the constructive, so the constructive gives rise to the critical. The task of theology must involve both critical and constructive reflection to bear faithful witness to its unique subject. Hence, the constructive aspect of the theological task involves the articulation of biblically normed, culturally relevant, and historically informed models of the Christian faith that are inherently self-critical and reforming in keeping with the character of human knowledge and the subject of theology. In addition, the task of theological construction may be characterized as an ongoing conversation participants in the faith community share regarding the meaning of the symbols through which they express their understanding of the world. This constructive theological conversation involves the interplay of three components: Scripture, the cultural context, and the tradition of the church. The following sections examine the interactions between these three, beginning with a consideration of Scripture as theology's norming norm and then an examination of the interrelationships between Scripture, culture, and tradition in the task of theology. Throughout, this discussion focuses on the work of the Spirit in seeking to develop a nonfoundationalist, contextual, and inherently reforming approach to theology by means of an inclusive and pneumatological model of the theological task.

Scripture: Theology's Norming Norm

The Christian tradition has been characterized by a commitment to the authority of the Bible. Christian communal identity is bound up with a set of literary texts that together form canonical Scripture. According to David Kelsey, acknowledging the Bible as Scripture lies at the heart of participating in the community of Christ. The decision to adopt the texts of Christian Scripture as "canon" is not "a separate decision over and above a decision to become a Christian."[18] To be a Christian is to participate in a community that acknowledges the authority of Scripture for life and thought. The question that arises is how this authority ought to be construed. This question leads us to consider how the Bible

18. David H. Kelsey, *Proving Doctrine: The Uses of Scripture in Modern Theology* (Harrisburg, PA: Trinity Press International, 1999), 165.

ought to function in theology by pursuing the traditional assertion that Scripture is theology's "norming norm." The point of departure for this affirmation of Scripture as the norming norm for theology lies in the Protestant principle of authority articulated in confessions such as the Westminster Confession of Faith, which states, "The Supreme Judge by which all controversies of religion are to be determined, and all decrees of counsels, opinions of ancient writers, doctrines of men, and private spirits, are to be examined, and in whose sentence we are to rest, can be no other than the Holy Spirit speaking in the Scripture."[19] This statement reflects the concern of the Protestant tradition to bind Word and Spirit together as a means of providing the conceptual framework for authority in the Christian faith. It also brings into focus the sense in which the Bible is conceived of as the norming norm for theology.

It is worth noting here that in the sixteenth century Protestant theologian John Calvin identified two tendencies with respect to the separation of Word and Spirit. Humanist scholarship was inclined toward the study of the Word apart from the Spirit, while the radical Reformers and the Roman Catholic Church were viewed as boasting of the Spirit apart from the Word. Calvin, of course, responded that Word and Spirit were inseparably linked.[20] Thus, drawing on Calvin, we can conclude that two errors must be avoided in the construal of theological authority with respect to Word and Spirit: "collapsing" the Spirit into the text and ignoring the text in the name of following the Spirit. In his "Reply to Sadolet," Calvin asserts that the church is to be governed by the Spirit. Yet he also maintains that the Spirit is bound to Scripture to ensure "that this government might not be vague and unstable."[21] It would seem more appropriate to say that Scripture is bound to the Spirit, who, in the divine economy, inspired it and continues to speak through it. Saying that the Spirit is bound to Scripture runs the risk of collapsing the Spirit into the text and allowing human beings to move from a position of epistemic dependency with respect to the knowledge of God to one of mastery. In this sense, the proposal to follow is in continuity with Calvin and the Protestant tradition in its insistence on binding Word and Spirit, but it also seeks to amend an aspect of the tradition by prioritizing the role of the Spirit in relation to Scripture.

The assertion that our final authority is the Spirit speaking in and through Scripture means that Christian belief and practice cannot be

19. The Westminster Confession of Faith, 1.10, in *The Creeds of the Churches*, 3rd ed., ed. John H. Leith (Atlanta: John Knox, 1982), 196.

20. John Calvin, "Reply to Sadolet," in *Calvin: Theological Treatises*, ed. J. K. S. Reid (Philadelphia: Westminster, 1954), 229–31.

21. Ibid., 229.

determined merely by appeal either to the exegesis of Scripture carried out apart from the life of the believer and the believing community or to any "word from the Spirit" that stands in contradiction to biblical exegesis. The reading and interpretation of the text is for the purpose of listening to the voice of the Spirit, who speaks in and through Scripture to the church in the present. This implies that the Bible is authoritative in that it is the vehicle through which the Spirit speaks. In other words, the authority of the Bible, as the instrument through which the Spirit speaks, is ultimately bound up with the authority of the Spirit. Christians acknowledge the Bible as Scripture because the Spirit has spoken, now speaks, and will continue to speak with authority through the canonical texts of Scripture. The Christian community confessed the authority of Scripture because it experienced the power and truth of the Spirit of God through writings that were, according to their testimony and confession, "animated with the Spirit of Christ."[22] Following the testimony of the church of all ages, we too look to the biblical texts to hear the Spirit's voice. Hence, as John Webster puts it, the work of biblical interpretation or exegesis "is of supremely critical importance, because the chief instrument through which Christ publishes the gospel is Holy Scripture. Exegesis is the attempt to hear what the Spirit says to the Churches; without it, theology cannot even begin to discharge its office."[23]

In declaring the biblical canon closed at the end of the fourth century, the church implicitly asserted that the work of the Spirit in inspiration had ceased. However, this did not mark the end of the Spirit's activity in connection with Scripture. On the contrary, the Spirit continues to speak to succeeding generations of Christians through the text in the ongoing work of illumination. On the basis of biblical texts that speak of the continuing guidance of the Spirit to the earliest believers, subsequent generations of Christians have anticipated that the Spirit would guide them as well. The Puritan pastor John Robinson proclaimed his famous and frequently quoted belief that God had yet more truth and light to break forth from his holy Word. This Puritan notion of additional light has been expressed in the language of literary theory by Northrop Frye, who notes that, to an extent unparalleled in any other literature, the biblical texts seem to invite readers to bring their own experiences into a conversation with them, resulting in an ongoing interpretation of each in light of the other.[24] For this reason, Frye suggests that readers

22. Thomas A. Hoffman, "Inspiration, Normativeness, Canonicity, and the Unique Sacred Character of the Bible," *Catholic Biblical Quarterly* 44 (1982): 457.

23. John Webster, *Holiness* (Grand Rapids: Eerdmans, 2003), 3.

24. Northrop Frye, *The Great Code: The Bible and Literature* (New York: Harcourt Brace Jovanovich, 1982), 225.

properly approach the text with an attitude of expectation, anticipating that there is always more to be received from the Bible.[25] Through Scripture, the Spirit continually instructs the church as the historically extended community of Christ's followers in the midst of the opportunities and challenges of life in the contemporary world.

The Bible is the instrumentality of the Spirit in that the Spirit appropriates the biblical text for the purpose of speaking to believers today. This act of appropriation does not come independently of what traditional interpretation has called "the original meaning of the text." Careful exegesis is required in an effort to understand the "original" intention of the authors. However, the speaking of the Spirit is not bound up solely with the supposed "original intention" of the authors. Contemporary proponents of "textual intentionality" such as Paul Ricoeur explain that although an author creates a literary text, once it has been written, it takes on a life of its own.[26] While the ways in which the text is structured shape the "meanings" readers discern in the text, the author's intentions come to be "distanced" from the "meanings" of the work. In this sense, a text can be viewed metaphorically as "having its own intention." This textual intention has its genesis in an author's intention but is not exhausted by it. Therefore, we must not conclude that exegesis alone can exhaust what the Spirit can say through the text. While the Spirit appropriates the text in its internal meaning, the goal of this appropriation is to guide the church in the variegated circumstances of particular contemporary settings. Hence, the Spirit's speaking does not come through the text in isolation but rather in the context of specific historical-cultural situations and as part of an extended interpretive tradition.

The assertion that the Spirit appropriates the text of Scripture and speaks in and through it to those in the contemporary world leads to the question of the goal or effect of the Spirit's speaking. What does the Spirit seek to accomplish in the act of speaking through the appropriated text of Scripture? A proper response to this inquiry suggests that through the process of addressing readers in various contemporary settings the Spirit creates the "world." Sociologists point out that religion plays a significant role in world construction through a set of beliefs and practices that provide a particular way of looking at reality. Wesley Kort suggests that certain specific types of beliefs, such as those about temporality, other people, borders, norms, and values, are essential for the development of an adequate and workable world. He maintains that

25. Ibid., 220.
26. For a discussion of the significance of Ricoeur's work for the task of theology, see Dan R. Stiver, *Theology after Ricoeur: New Directions in Hermeneutical Theology* (Louisville: Westminster John Knox, 2001).

these types of beliefs are closely connected to languages and texts and "can be textually identified because they and their relations to one another are borne by language." This observation leads to the importance of "scriptures" in that such texts function by articulating "the beliefs that go into the construction of a world."[27] For this reason, Ricoeur asserts that the meaning of a text always points beyond itself. The meaning is "not behind the text, but in front of it." Texts project a way of being in the world, a mode of existence, a pattern of life, and point toward "a possible world."[28]

In the Christian tradition, the Bible stands in a central position in the practice of the faith. The Christian community reads the biblical text as Scripture and looks to it as the focal point for shaping the narrative world it inhabits. As Walter Brueggemann maintains, the biblical text "has generative power to summon and evoke new life" and holds out an eschatological vision that "anticipates and summons realities that live beyond the conventions of our day-to-day, take-for-granted world."[29] This points to the capacity of the text to speak beyond the context in which it was originally composed. In short, as John Goldingay declares, the text "calls a new world into being."[30] The point that needs to be stressed here, however, is that this capacity for world construction, while bound closely to the text, does not lie in the text itself. Instead, this result is ultimately the work of the Spirit speaking through the text as the instrumentality of world creation. Further, the world the Spirit creates is not simply the world surrounding the ancient text or the contemporary world but rather the eschatological world God intends for creation as disclosed, displayed, and anticipated by the text. The claim that the Spirit speaks in and through the text, not in abstraction but in the context of particular cultural circumstances, leads to an inquiry about the relationship between Scripture and culture in the formulation of theology.

Before addressing this question, however, we must first consider the relationship between Scripture and the interpretive constructions of the biblical texts that make up the content of theology. The previous chapter discussed the nature of theology as a second-order discipline. Here theology's second-order nature comes into view in the context of understanding that theology functions as a part of the socially constructive world-forming action the Spirit accomplishes in speaking through

27. Wesley A. Kort, *Take, Read: Scripture, Textuality, and Cultural Practice* (University Park, PA: Pennsylvania State University Press, 1996), 10–14.
28. Paul Ricoeur, *Interpretation Theory: Discourse and the Surplus of Meaning* (Fort Worth: Texas Christian University Press, 1976), 87.
29. Walter Brueggemann, *Finally Comes the Poet* (Minneapolis: Fortress, 1989), 4–5.
30. John Goldingay, *Models for Scripture* (Grand Rapids: Eerdmans, 1994), 256.

the text of Scripture. This notion has significant implications for an understanding of the connection between the biblical text and various second-order theological constructions. Of particular significance is the implication that the purpose of the text is not to provide the raw materials for the construction of a theological system. Rather, theologians engage in the theological task as servants of the Spirit and ministers within the community of those who are intent on discerning the voice of the Spirit speaking through the text of Scripture. As Stanley Hauerwas points out, theological constructions and doctrines "are not the upshot of the stories; they are not the meaning or heart of the stories." Instead, they should be understood as tools whose purpose is to assist the community in hearing the Spirit's voice and "to help us tell the story better."[31] Put another way, the task of theology is not an attempt to identify and codify the true meaning of the text in a series of systematically arranged assertions that then function as the only proper interpretive grid through which to read the Bible. Such an approach is characteristic among those who hold confessional statements in an absolutist fashion and claim that such statements teach the "system" of doctrine contained in Scripture. The danger here is that such a procedure can hinder the ability to read the text and to listen to the Spirit in new ways. Theology should always lead us back to the Bible. Its goal is to place the Christian community in a position to be receptive to the voice of the Spirit speaking in and through the biblical text to refashion the world after the eschatological mission and purposes of God.

In light of this, the principle that the text of Scripture takes primacy over theological construction provides the basic parameter for understanding the interface between exegesis and theological reflection. If our working presupposition is not that the text exists primarily for the sake of theology but that theology serves the reading of the text, then we can no longer follow the commonly held view that the logical flow of Christian thought moves from biblical studies to a form of systematic theology. From this perspective, biblical scholars deliver to theologians the authentic biblical teachings in their unsystematic multiplicity, and theologians, in turn, bring these materials together into a systematic statement of what purports to be the doctrinal system taught in the Bible. Such an approach reminds us of the importance of solid biblical scholarship in the theological task. In fact, theological construction ought never proceed apart from a careful exegesis of the biblical texts. In this way, exegesis is an indispensable participant in the theological

31. Stanley Hauerwas, *The Peaceable Kingdom: A Primer in Christian Ethics* (Notre Dame: University of Notre Dame Press, 1983), 26.

task such that it is not an overstatement to assert that theology is dependent on exegesis.

However, the unidirectional pattern that moves from biblical studies to theology suffers from some serious deficiencies, such as a naïveté about the purported objectivity of exegesis that springs from modernist hermeneutical assumptions. As George Aichele asserts, "Biblical scholars have been slow to awaken from the dream in which positivist science occupies a space apart from interests and values, to awaken to the realization that our representations of and discourse about what the text meant and how it means are inseparable from what we *want* it to mean, from how we *will* it to mean."[32] While this realization may have dawned slowly, it is becoming much more common. Robert Fowler observes that the presupposition of exegetical objectivity has come under severe attack, and there is a growing recognition in recent biblical scholarship "that reading and interpretation is always interested, never disinterested; always significantly subjective, never completely objective; always committed and therefore always political, never uncommitted and apolitical; always historically bound, never ahistorical. The modernist dream of disinterested, objective, distant, abstract truth is fading rapidly."[33] Rather than a strict unidirectional model, a more helpful theological engagement involves a dialogue between the text and theological construction. Such a dialogical approach is necessitated by the situated and contextual nature of all biblical exegesis. We simply cannot bracket our commitments, values, and assumptions in an attempt to approach the text as uninvolved, neutral observers.

More significantly, this dialogical engagement arises out of the very purpose for engaging the Bible. We read knowing that the Spirit speaks through Scripture in order to create a communal world. While the world the Spirit fashions is specific to our situation and hence is not merely a transplanting of the world of the text into the present, the Spirit-constructed world we are to inhabit is nevertheless shaped by the world disclosed in the text. Our world is to be the contemporary embodiment of the paradigmatic narrative of Scripture constructed through the interpretive framework that emerges from the Bible as a whole. For this reason, the goal must always be to read Scripture theologically so that the world with which we are confronted through our reading is the future, eschatological world that arises from the vision of the whole of Scripture.

32. George Aichele et al., *The Postmodern Bible* (New Haven: Yale University Press, 1995), 14.
33. Robert M. Fowler, "Postmodern Biblical Criticism," *Forum* 5, no. 3 (September 1989): 22.

The philosophical basis for dialogical engagement was articulated in the nineteenth century by the German thinker Wilhelm Dilthey. Dilthey argued that the goal of the hermeneutical enterprise is to understand the social and cultural meaning systems that underlie past expressions of human experience that remain available for study in the present, especially as disclosed through writings.[34] Dilthey noted, however, that this task is complicated at its inception by what he called the "hermeneutical circle": We can comprehend a complex whole only by appeal to its parts, but the parts acquire their meaning only within the whole.[35] Dilthey admitted that the circle is theoretically unresolvable. Nevertheless, he believed that in practice we can untangle complex situations through an inductive, to-and-fro movement by means of which we make and then revise provisional conclusions. From the parts we obtain a preliminary idea of the sense of the whole. We then use this sense of the whole to determine more precisely the significance of the parts, which in turn serves to test and correct our idea of the whole.

Yet the construal of a Christian interpretive framework on the basis of exegesis of the biblical text does not bring the theological task to its culmination. Rather, the purpose of theological constructions is to bring us back to the text, acknowledging that the final authority in the church is not the theology based on the text but the Spirit speaking through it. Thus, we read the text aware that theological constructions are always partial, incomplete, and subject to revision. At the same time, we read with the conviction that the Spirit speaks through Scripture in such a way that the text bears witness to the eschatological world the Spirit displays and calls into being through the agency of Scripture.

Theology, therefore, participates in the process of discerning the Spirit's voice through Scripture by contributing to the hermeneutical process of reading Scripture. A central aspect of theology's role in this process is related to the exegesis of the text on the basis of theological themes that, according to Francis Watson, "guide and shape the form and content of exegesis." At the same time, they are "clarified and corrected by the progress of exegesis in accordance with the inescapable working of the hermeneutical circle."[36] However, if the goal of reading is to discern the work of the Spirit, then the hermeneutical center of Scripture is not found as much in theology per se as in the overarch-

34. Wilhelm Dilthey, "Construction of the Historical World," in *Dilthey: Selected Writings*, ed. H. P. Rickman (Cambridge: Cambridge University Press, 1976), 228.

35. Wilhelm Dilthey, "The Development of Hermeneutics," in *Dilthey*, 259. See also Robert C. Solomon, *Continental Philosophy since 1750: The Rise and Fall of the Self* (Oxford: Oxford University Press, 1988), 106–7.

36. Francis Watson, *Text, Church, and World: Biblical Interpretation in Theological Perspective* (Edinburgh: T & T Clark, 1994), 241.

ing mission and purposes of God to create in the present a world that anticipates the eschatological world of the consummated kingdom of God. Theology provides a provisional guide in the attempt to assist and participate in the work of the Spirit in bringing this world into being in the midst of the Christian community in its various social and cultural expressions. Based on this conception of Scripture as theology's norming norm and the discussion of culture and the contextual nature of theology in the previous chapter, we are now in a position to discuss the relationship among Scripture, culture, and theology.

Scripture, Culture, and Theology

Karl Barth reportedly suggested that good theology and effective preaching must be done with the Bible in one hand and today's newspaper in the other. This is consistent with his assertion, cited earlier, that theology is concerned to address what we must say in our time to our generation on the basis of the apostles and prophets. This raises the question of the relationship among Scripture, culture, and theology. As suggested, theology emerges through an ongoing conversation involving both gospel and culture in which neither enters into the conversation as given, preexisting realities but rather as particularized, dynamic realities that inform and are informed by the conversation itself. In this model, the conversation between gospel and culture is characterized by mutual enrichment in which the exchange is beneficial to the church in its ability to address its context as well as to the ongoing process of theological critique and construction.

One purpose of theological reflection is to facilitate the ability of the church to address the message of the gospel to the contemporary situation. If we inhabit a socially constructed reality, culture must become a crucial component of theological work. Discerning what constitutes the socially constructed worlds people inhabit places us in a better position to address the generation God calls us to serve. Doing so, however, necessitates that we understand and articulate the Christian faith in a manner that contemporary people can understand and that is in continuity with the faith of the church. That is, we must express the gospel through the language of the culture—the cognitive tools, concepts, images, symbols, and thought forms through which contemporary people discover meaning, construct the world they inhabit, and form personal identity. The missional calling of the people of God to proclaim and to live out the meaning and the implications of the gospel is also enhanced as we come to understand how the Christian faith addresses the problems, longings, and ethos of contemporary people, knowing that the social context in which we live raises issues that are theological in nature.

Viewed from this perspective, the task of theology includes an attempt to understand and interpret the times theologically in order to assist the church in living as the people of God in the wider contemporary social setting and in proclaiming the gospel message in that context. To this end, those who engage in the theological task draw from existing cultural artifacts and interpret them. The task of listening to the culture entails being observant of the various venues and events that provide a cultural voice, that give expression to the ethos of the day, and that embody the often unexpressed inner longings and structure of meaning indicative of people in society. Examples of these venues and events include literature, music, film, television programming, art, newspapers, and magazines as well as expressions of institutional life such as elections or the observance of holidays. In the process of this examination of culture, we must bear in mind that exegesis of cultural phenomena will not be objective. Rather than viewing culture as neutral observers, we will engage with our context as participants in the faith community. We will bring the categories of our own meaning structures and beliefs to the conversation we seek to have with culture. In short, just as there is no culture-free reading of the biblical text and no culture-free construction of Christian theology, so also there can be no interpretation of culture and cultural artifacts apart from the theological commitments we bring to the task.

This examination of culture also involves subjecting cultural phenomena to critical scrutiny, bringing to the surface the particular assumptions, beliefs, or meaning structures lying behind, motivating, or being expressed in cultural phenomena. The goal of this scrutiny is to gain a window into what people think, sense, and believe about themselves and the world they inhabit as well as to determine what cultural meanings are exercising a molding influence on people today. To this end, we engage cultural artifacts in conversation by asking the specific questions that a particular theological stance raises. Hence, we seek to understand the conceptions of God, ourselves, and the world that are bound up with the cultural items under scrutiny. We raise such questions as, How does this cultural item disclose what people today believe about themselves, the world, and transcendent meaning? In this process, we seek to determine why particular aspects of culture resonate among its participants within its meaning structures.

This critical engagement with culture also involves the task of formulating an appropriate response. This includes a theologically informed appraisal of the beliefs and meaning structures expressed in cultural phenomena. Hence, we seek to determine the extent to which the cultural meanings and underlying belief assumptions are related to the meanings and implications of the Christian faith. This response also involves ascertaining the extent to which the cultural artifacts under examination offer a bridge for connecting the Christian faith with those who find these cultural artifacts to be an expression of their own sensitivities. Of course, the task of listening and responding to culture is difficult and challenging and, like theology itself, ongoing and contextual. As Robert Schreiter points out, "In ideal circumstances the process of constructing local theologies begins with a study of the culture, rather than with possible translations of the larger church tradition into the local circumstance."[37] In this process, theology seeks not only to respond to the cultural situation but also to learn from it.

If we view interpretations of the gospel and culture as particular contextual constructions rather than as given, established realities, we are aware that both an understanding of the gospel and the meaning structures through which people in society make sense of their lives are dynamic and that the conversation between them can be one of mutual enrichment. The theological interplay between the gospel and culture not only optimizes our ability to address our context but also enhances our theological constructions. For this reason, we must consider the extent to which cultural context in general and a cultural expression in particular ought to lead us to reconsider our understanding of the Christian faith. Indeed, whether occurring directly or, more likely, in an indirect manner, culture can be a means through which we gain theological insight. In short, reading the culture can assist us in reading the biblical text so as to hear more clearly the voice of the Spirit in a particular circumstance.

As maintained earlier, Scripture functions as theology's norming norm because it is the instrument of the Spirit, who speaks in and through the text for the purpose of creating a world that is concretely and particularly centered on the present and future lordship of Jesus Christ. However, this speaking is always contextual in that it always comes to its hearers within a specific social and historical setting. The ongoing guidance of the Spirit always comes as a specific community of believers in a specific setting listens for and hears the voice of the Spirit speaking in and to the particularity of its social and historical context. This conception of the work of the Spirit was operative in the earliest church and in the establishment of the biblical canon, which is the product of the early Christian community hearing the Spirit speaking within its changing contexts, often through literary materials they had gathered

37. Robert J. Schreiter, *Constructing Local Theologies* (Maryknoll, NY: Orbis, 1985), 39.

and preserved. The specificity of the Spirit's speaking means that the conversation with culture and cultural context is crucial to the theological task. We seek to hear the voice of the Spirit through Scripture, which comes to us in the particularity of the social-historical context in which we live. Consequently, because theology must be in touch with life in the midst of present circumstances, the questions, concerns, and challenges it brings to Scripture are not necessarily identical with those of contemporary exegetes or even the ancient writers themselves. Douglas John Hall states that what theology seeks "from its ongoing discourse with the biblical text is determined in large measure by its worldly context" in order that it might address that setting from "the perspective of faith in the God of Abraham, Isaac, and Jacob."[38]

This hermeneutical process occurs in part as contemporary construals of knowledge and the discoveries and insights of the various disciplines of human learning inform theological construction. For example, theories about addictions and addictive behavior can provide insight into the biblical teaching about sin. Likewise, current discoveries about the process of human identity formation can assist us in becoming aware of the many dimensions entailed in the new identity the Spirit seeks to create in us through union with Christ. Hence, theological reflections and constructions are able to draw from the resources of other disciplines, even those that have generally been more "secular" in orientation and practice. This corresponds to Origen's principle of drawing on the "spoils of the Egyptians" in the work of theology and biblical interpretation. This perspective is theologically appropriate, as Wolfhart Pannenberg maintains, because God is the ground of all truth, and therefore all truth ultimately comes together in God. Theology, therefore, draws from all human knowledge, for in so doing it demonstrates the unity of truth in God.[39]

In light of this conclusion, we are able to say that in addition to listening for the voice of the Spirit speaking through Scripture, theology must also be attentive to the voice of the Spirit speaking through culture. While Western theology has tended to focus on the church as the sole repository of all truth and the only location in which the Spirit is operative, Scripture appears to suggest a much broader understanding of the Spirit's presence, a presence connected to the Spirit's role as the life giver. The biblical writers speak of the Spirit's role in creating and sustaining life as well as enabling it to flourish. Because Spirit-induced

38. Douglas John Hall, *Thinking the Faith: Christian Theology in a North American Context* (Minneapolis: Fortress, 1991), 263.

39. Wolfhart Pannenberg, *Systematic Theology*, vol. 1, trans. Geoffrey W. Bromiley (Grand Rapids: Eerdmans, 1990), 59–60.

human flourishing evokes cultural expression, we can anticipate in such expressions traces of the Spirit's creative and sustaining presence. Consequently, theology should be alert to the work of the Spirit manifest in the artifacts and symbols of human culture. However, it should be added that the speaking of the Spirit through the various media of culture never comes as a speaking against the text. Setting the Spirit's presence in culture against the text is to follow the foundationalist agenda and to elevate a dimension of contemporary experience or thought as a criterion for accepting or rejecting aspects of the biblical witness. Darrell Jodock notes this danger: "The problem here is not that one's world view or experience influences one's reading of the text, because that is inescapable. The problem is instead that the text is made to conform to the world view or codified experience and thereby loses its integrity and its ability to challenge and confront our present priorities, including even our most noble aspirations."[40]

Therefore, while acknowledging the Spirit's voice wherever it may be found, we must still uphold the primacy of the text as theology's norming norm. While we cannot hear the Spirit speaking through the text except by listening within a particular social-historical setting, the Spirit speaking through Scripture provides the normative context for hearing the Spirit in culture. Having said this, it must be affirmed that the speaking of the Spirit through Scripture and through culture do not constitute two communicative acts but rather one unified speaking. Consequently, theology must listen for the voice of the Spirit, who speaks normatively and universally through Scripture but also particularly and locally in the variegated circumstances of diverse human cultures. Hence, Scripture, which functions as theology's norming norm, is always in conversation with culture, which functions as theology's embedding context. In this way, the Spirit continually speaks to the believing community in its present situation through the witness of Scripture to the events of God's revelation in Jesus Christ as a means of providing ongoing guidance for the church as it grapples with constantly changing circumstances. From this perspective, the tradition of the church is viewed, in the words of Robert Schreiter, "as a series of local theologies, closely wedded to and responding to different cultural conditions."[41] This raises the question of the role of these local theologies that make up the Christian tradition, as the historical witnesses to the speaking of the Spirit, in the task of contemporary theological construction. It is to this aspect of

---

40. Darrell Jodock, "The Reciprocity between Scripture and Theology: The Role of Scripture in Contemporary Theological Reflection," *Interpretation* 44, no. 4 (October 1990): 377.

41. Schreiter, *Constructing Local Theologies*, 93.

the constructive task of theology that we now turn, beginning with the relationship between Scripture and tradition.

Scripture and Tradition: The Catholic-Protestant Divide

In attempting to address the question of the role of tradition in theology, we must acknowledge the historical background that has shaped the interpretation of this issue ever since the sixteenth-century Reformation and the debate between Roman Catholics and Protestants concerning the relationship between Scripture and tradition. The genesis of this debate, however, is rooted in historical developments that took place well before the sixteenth century. The discussion of this issue in the later medieval period focused particularly on the question of the authority of *extrascriptural* tradition. Prior to Basil in the East and Augustine in the West, the concept of an extrascriptural tradition functioning authoritatively in the life of the church would have been viewed as highly problematic. In the early church, Scripture and tradition were not seen as mutually exclusive but as coinherent.[42] Scripture and tradition completely coincided in the thinking of the early church. The church proclaims the gospel that is contained in written form in the canonical documents and is preserved and handed down in living form through the tradition of the church. The whole of the *kerygma* is found in both Scripture and tradition. From this perspective, tradition is viewed not as an addition to the message contained in Scripture but as the living, socially embodied expression of that message.

The conception of the coinherence of Scripture and tradition came as the result of the assumption that both issue from the common source of divine revelation. This understanding constitutes an explicit repudiation of an extrascriptural tradition on a par with Scripture as authoritative for the church. Writing in the latter half of the second century, Irenaeus set forth the most complete refutation of the appeal to traditions beyond Scripture in his work *Against Heresies*. He identified appeals to revelatory truth apart from Scripture as a form of heretical Gnostic practice and maintained that only the "tradition which is derived from the apostles" contained in Scripture and preserved in the church was to serve as authoritative for the faith and practice of the Christian community.[43] However, starting with Basil the Great, a transition occurred concerning

---

42. George H. Tavard, *Holy Writ or Holy Church: The Crisis of the Protestant Reformation* (New York: Harper & Brothers, 1959), 22.

43. Jaroslav Pelikan, *The Emergence of the Catholic Tradition (100–600)* (Chicago: University of Chicago Press, 1971), 115.

how the understanding of tradition is to be formulated. In his treatise *De Spiritu Sancto*, Basil stated that some aspects of Christian faith and practice are not found in Scripture but in the tradition of the church.[44] Historian Heiko Oberman pinpoints the significance of this work for the Catholic understanding of tradition: "We find here for the first time explicitly the idea that the Christian owes equal respect and obedience to written and unwritten ecclesiastical traditions, whether contained in canonical writings or in a secret oral tradition handed down by the Apostles through their successors."[45]

Oberman also highlights the importance of Augustine in the establishment of this new conception of tradition. On the one hand, Augustine reflects the coinherence of Scripture and tradition characteristic of the early church in that he repeatedly asserts the ultimate authority of Scripture yet not in such a way as to oppose the authority of the church. On the other hand, Augustine also reflects the view evidenced in Basil. In Oberman's words, "In contrast to Irenaeus' condemnation of extrascriptural tradition, in Augustine we find mention of an *authoritative* extrascriptural oral tradition." According to Augustine, the church "moves" the faithful to "discover the authority of Scripture," and Scripture in turn "refers the faithful back to the authority of the church with regard to a series of issues with which the Apostles did not deal in writing." Oberman notes that Augustine appeals to this extrascriptural principle in his discussion of the baptism of heretics and then indicates the role that this theological move would play in subsequent history: "Abelard in the same manner would later treat Mariology, Bonaventura the *filioque* clause, and Thomas the form of the sacrament of confirmation."[46]

In the fourteenth century, Basil's statement on the legitimacy of extrascriptural tradition and the two aspects of Augustine's thought gave rise to two competing conceptions regarding the authority of Scripture and tradition. Oberman labels these two understandings "Tradition I" and "Tradition II." Tradition I represents the single-source understanding in which the emphasis is on the sufficiency of Scripture as the exclusive and final authority in the church. Oberman explains, "The horizontal concept of Tradition is by no means denied here, but rather understood as the mode of reception of the *fides* or *veritas* contained in

44. St. Basil the Great, *De Spiritu Sancto* in *Patrologia Graeca*, ed. J. P. Migne (Paris: Migne, 1857–86), 32:188; and St. Basil the Great, *On the Holy Spirit* (Crestwood, NY: St. Vladimir's Seminary Press, 1980), 98–99.

45. Heiko Oberman, *The Harvest of Medieval Theology: Gabriel Biel and Late Medieval Nominalism*, rev. ed. (Grand Rapids: Eerdmans, 1967), 369.

46. Ibid., 370–71.

Scripture." Ecclesiastical tradition is not to be understood as "self-supporting"; rather, it "depends on its relation to the faith handed down by God in Holy Scripture." Tradition II maintains a two-source conception of authority in which both the written *and* the unwritten oral components of the apostolic message, as approved by the church, are deemed equally authoritative. Here the emphasis shifts from the interpreters, or doctors, of Scripture toward the bishops who determine the content of the authentic tradition. The church hierarchy is viewed as having its "own" oral tradition, which is, to cite Oberman's characterization, "to a certain undefined extent independent, not of the Apostles, but of what is recorded in the canonical books. Ecclesiastical traditions, including canon law, are invested with the same degree of authority as that of Holy Scripture."[47]

Prior to the fourteenth century, these two conceptions were held together without a conscious effort to distinguish between them or to integrate them. Nevertheless, a significant difference already existed between the theologians and the canon lawyers, a difference that was finally brought into relief during the fourteenth century. Throughout the early Middle Ages, canonists regularly referred to Basil's statement. In fact, the leading canon lawyer of the day, Ivo of Chartres, cited it in arguing for an equal standing for Scripture and extrascriptural oral tradition.[48] This argument, along with the Basilean passage from which it was derived, was included by Gratian of Bologna in his *Decretum*. From this highly influential source, the passage and its interpretation were widely disseminated into the standard textbooks of theologians as well as canon lawyers.[49] From the perspective of the canon lawyers, these developments were sufficient to establish the two-source theory with respect to canon law. Therefore, throughout the medieval period, canon law stood on the foundations of Scripture and tradition, the latter of which was understood as approved extrascriptural oral tradition handed down from the apostles and preserved in the church.

The medieval theologians, in contrast, did not adhere to this understanding. Because they conceived of theology as the science of Scripture, they elevated Scripture as the final authority for matters of faith, as indicated in the use of the term *sacra pagina* to denote theology. This was the case despite the increasing tendency of medieval theologians to comment on previous interpretations as though they had authority. Although their works reflect acceptance of a close connection between

---

47. Ibid., 371–73.
48. Ivo of Chartres, *Patrologia Latina*, ed. J. P. Migne (Paris: Migne, 1844–64), 161:283.
49. Oberman, *Harvest of Medieval Theology*, 369.

Scripture and its interpretation, the scholastic thinkers respected the distinction between text and gloss. They viewed the prior interpretive tradition as a vital and important component of theology without losing sight of the primacy of Scripture. These thinkers were convinced that final authority regarding questions of interpretation resided in the text of canonical Scripture.

In the fourteenth century, the prominence of canon lawyers resulted in a growing acceptance of the Basilean two-source theory in the church. Oberman points out that in the context of historical circumstances, namely, the Great Schism and the final phase of the struggle between pope and emperor, canon lawyers were in high demand and perhaps even surpassed theologians in status at the papal *curia* and the royal courts. In his estimation, it is not surprising "that the canon-law tradition started to feed into the major theological stream in such a way that the Basilean passage became a genuinely theological argument, and the foundation of the position which we have called Tradition II."[50] The development and hardening in the later medieval period of the position described by Tradition II can be seen as a response to the increasing acceptance of the two-source theory, which had its roots in Basil. In the struggle between the curialists and the conciliarists to reform the church in the aftermath of the Western schism, members of both groups supported the legitimacy of authoritative extrascriptural tradition. The two differed merely over the location of highest authority, pope or council, in determining and defining the extrascriptural tradition. With this development in the later Middle Ages, Tradition II was increasingly seen by the church as the more acceptable position. Those reformers who supported Tradition I, such as Bradwardine, Wycliffe, and Hus, were viewed as dangerous radicals by the church hierarchy because they challenged the authority of the pope and the received church tradition.

By the sixteenth century, the debate in the church regarding Scripture and tradition had undergone further development. Three main schools of thought can be identified. The first, corresponding to Tradition I, maintained that all truth necessary for salvation could be found either explicitly or implicitly in Scripture. Tradition was required for the task of correctly interpreting Scripture, particularly those elements regarding salvation that were deemed merely implicit in the text. This is often referred to as the classical view. The second position, which corresponds to Tradition II, asserted that Christian revelation is only partly contained in the canonical text, with another part lodged in the oral traditions of the apostles passed down through their disciples. A

---

50. Ibid., 372.

third outlook, which came to prominence among curial canonists and theologians in the late Middle Ages, taught that the Holy Spirit abides constantly with the church and gives new inspiration or illumination to the church. In this view, the teaching of popes and councils is binding on the faithful, even where such teaching is unsupported by Scripture or the oral traditions of the apostles.[51]

In response to the increasing emphasis on extrascriptural tradition and papal authority, the northern European humanists of the fifteenth and sixteenth centuries advocated a reformist agenda characterized by the slogan *ad fontes*, "back to the sources." This program gave clear priority to the teaching of Scripture as the source for Christian faith and was highly critical of the elevation of tradition in the practices of the medieval church.[52] The emphasis of the humanists on the sufficiency of Scripture and the related rejection of the distorting influence of the medieval tradition were adopted by early Reformers such as Luther and Zwingli and provided the basis for their appeal to the principle *sola scriptura*, that Scripture alone was normative for the faith and life of the church.[53] The elevation of *sola scriptura* effectively set the agenda for what became Protestant antitraditionalism, at least as it characterized the Protestant attitude toward the theological developments of the first fifteen hundred years of church history.[54]

Predictably, the Reformers often applied the implications of *sola scriptura* to one another when they believed that one doctrine or another had been too greatly affected by tradition. Thus, Luther was critiqued by Zwingli on the sacraments, Zwingli by the Zurich Anabaptists on the question of infant baptism, and Calvin by Servetus on the doctrine of the Trinity. The Reformers did not intend to sever themselves entirely from the Christian past. Calvin's writings in particular contain numerous references to the church fathers, and he clearly attempted to align the program of the Reformation with Augustine.[55] The significance of Calvin in this regard is noted by Jaroslav Pelikan, who states that the Geneva Reformer became the one figure who "more than any other, enabled the leaders of the Reformation to claim that they were not throwing over

51. These three positions and their proponents are described in greater detail in Tavard, *Holy Writ or Holy Church*, 47–66.

52. Ibid., 67–79.

53. For an account of the influence of humanism on the Reformation, see Alister McGrath, *The Intellectual Origins of the European Reformation* (Oxford: Basil Blackwell, 1987), 32–68.

54. Jaroslav Pelikan, *The Vindication of Tradition* (New Haven: Yale University Press, 1984), 11.

55. On Calvin's use of the early church and medieval traditions, see A. N. S. Lane, "Calvin's Use of the Fathers and Medievals," *Calvin Theological Journal* 16 (1981): 149–205.

the Christian past after all."[56] Yet in spite of attempts by some of the
Reformers to maintain a place, albeit a limited one, for the tradition
of the church, the *trajectory* of Protestantism coupled with its ongoing
polemic against the Catholic Church inevitably served to diminish, if
not eclipse, the significance of tradition for Protestant theology.

The separation of Scripture and tradition occasioned by the Protestant
insistence on Scripture as the *sole* source for theology was intensified by
the developments at the Council of Trent.[57] In addition to formulating
and clarifying official Catholic doctrine, the council was also clearly
concerned with the refutation of Protestantism. Thus, while the council engaged in lengthy deliberations about the precise nature of the
relationship between Scripture and tradition, the participants were in
fundamental agreement that the Protestant position was inadequate.[58]
The Catholic theologians at Trent almost unanimously agreed that the
canonical Scriptures were not in themselves sufficient as a source of
doctrine. The Tridentine formulation asserted that the Catholic Church
"accepts and venerates" apostolic tradition with the same sense of "loyalty
and reverence" with which it "accepts and venerates" all the writings of
Scripture.[59] In short, although Trent did not formally speak of Scripture
and tradition as two sources of revelation, it at least seemed to suggest
such a construction. It certainly held that the authority of tradition was
not in any way less than that of Scripture, insofar as both came from
God and therefore both carried divine authority.[60]

According to George Tavard, Catholic opposition to *sola scriptura*
became so strong in the wake of Trent that despite the council's careful attempt to set forth a doctrine of Scripture and tradition that did
suggest two separate sources of revelation, the classical or traditional
conception nearly vanished from the highly polemical theology of the
Counter-Reformation. Tavard goes so far as to suggest that a careful study
"would show that the main post-Tridentine theologians misinterpreted
the formula of the Council."[61] He maintains that for the most part later
Catholic theology followed these mistaken formulations and asserted

56. Pelikan, *Vindication of Tradition*, 19.

57. For a brief commentary on the doctrinal position of Trent on tradition, see Joseph
Ratzinger, "On the Interpretation of the Tridentine Decree on Tradition," in Karl Rahner and
Joseph Ratzinger, *Revelation and Tradition* (New York: Herder & Herder, 1966), 50–78.

58. For a discussion of the council's deliberations on Scripture and tradition, see
Tavard, *Holy Writ or Holy Church*, 195–209.

59. H. Denzinger and A. Schonmetzer, eds., *Enchiridion Symbolorum*, 33rd ed. (Frie-
burg: Herder, 1965), 1501.

60. Avery Dulles, *The Craft of Theology: From Symbol to System* (New York: Crossroad,
1992), 89.

61. Tavard, *Holy Writ or Holy Church*, 244.

that Scripture and tradition constitute two sources of revelation.[62] In addition, in response to the Protestant denial of the authority and infallibility of the Catholic hierarchy, Catholic polemical theologians placed great emphasis on this doctrine as an extension of the ongoing authority of the church's tradition.[63]

The post-Tridentine Catholic position on tradition that arose as a response to *sola scriptura* occasioned, in turn, the hardening of the Protestant attitude toward tradition. The Reformers asserted that theology must be subject only to the direct authority of God, who has spoken through the Bible, not to any merely human authority, such as the creeds and traditions of the church. They maintained that their teachings were based solely on Scripture apart from any other source.[64] Moreover, they developed hermeneutical principles, such as the perspicuity of Scripture and the idea that Scripture interprets Scripture, aimed at minimizing the need for human interpretation. In accordance with these principles, Protestant thinkers rejected the Catholic claim of an infallible ecclesiastical magisterium, arguing instead that the only infallible interpretive authority for Scripture is Scripture itself. In this way, Protestant theologians believed they had secured the sole authority of God in the church and could access divine commands and instructions in a relatively unmediated fashion through the Bible, without recourse to human traditions, which are subject to error.

On the basis of loyalty to Scripture, the Reformation mounted a serious theological challenge to tradition. Since the sixteenth century, Protestants have generally looked on tradition with considerable suspicion. The constant polemic against the Catholic position became, and continues to be in some contexts, a staple of Protestant theological exposition. In many respects, the denial of tradition as an authoritative source for theological construction has even constituted the Protestant raison d'être. This negative attitude toward tradition born in the Reformation came to maturation in three contexts: the elimination of tradition in Anabaptist theology, the devaluation of tradition in Protestant orthodoxy, and the undercutting of tradition in the Enlightenment. The emphasis on *sola scriptura* and the influences of these three contexts on the formation of North American Protestantism led to the virtual elimination of tradition in much of traditional Protestant theology.

However, in spite of the various attempts to minimize the human element in the reception of the Bible and the work of theology, the

---

62. Ibid., 245.

63. James P. Mackey, *Tradition and Change in the Church* (Dayton, OH: Pflaum Press, 1968), 138–39.

64. Pelikan, *Vindication of Tradition*, 11–12.

simple fact remains that Scripture must be interpreted, and this activity is always shaped by the theological and cultural context within which interpreters participate. It is simply not possible to step back from the influences of tradition and context in the act of interpretation or in the ascription of meaning. Interpretive communities that deny the reality of this situation and seek an interpretation unencumbered by the distorting influence of fallible human traditions are in fact enslaved by interpretive patterns that are allowed to function uncritically, precisely because they are unacknowledged. Such a mind-set has been labeled by Richard Lints as "antitraditional traditionalism," in which the disdain for tradition becomes an ironic form of tradition.[65] Trevor Hart comments that the notion of a "pure" reading of the text "must be shown up for the self-deception that it is."[66]

While recent conversations between Catholics and Protestants about the relationship between Scripture and tradition have started to close the breach of the sixteenth century, significant differences still remain, such as whether Scripture or the church has priority. This fundamental difference still animates contemporary dialogues between Catholics and Protestants. However, posing the difference in this manner is ultimately unhelpful in that it rests on foundationalist understandings of the derivation of knowledge. Shifting to a nonfoundationalist conception can assist in moving the discussion beyond this impasse. The Protestant principle of authority is bound up in the link between Word and Spirit, meaning that the authority of Scripture is finally the authority of the Spirit, who speaks in and through the text. Scripture is authoritative because it is the vehicle through which the Spirit speaks. That is to say, the authority of the Bible is ultimately the authority of the Spirit. This understanding of the relationship between Word and Spirit suggests the possibility of a parallel connection between the Spirit and tradition. The pathway to such an understanding, however, proceeds indirectly through ecclesiology. The same Spirit whose work accounts for the formation of the Christian community also guides that community in the production and authorization of the biblical texts. This characterization of the role of the Spirit points toward an appropriate pneumatological-ecclesiological understanding of tradition.

Crucial in the development of such an understanding is the observation of Catholic theologian Avery Dulles, who speaks about the process of "traditioning," which began before the composition of the inspired books

---

65. Richard Lints, *The Fabric of Theology: A Prolegomenon to Evangelical Theology* (Grand Rapids: Eerdmans, 1993), 91.

66. Trevor Hart, *Faith Thinking: The Dynamics of Christian Theology* (Downers Grove, IL: InterVarsity, 1995), 167.

and continues without interruption through the ages.[67] This stands as a reminder that the community precedes the production of the scriptural texts. In a certain sense, the faith community was responsible for both the content of the biblical books and the identification of particular texts for inclusion in an authoritative canon, to which the community has chosen to make itself accountable. Apart from the Christian community, the texts would not have taken their particular and distinctive shape. Apart from the authority of the Christian community, there would be no canon of authorized texts. In short, apart from the Christian community, the Christian Bible would not exist.

Viewed from the historical perspective, the Bible is the product of the community of faith that produced it. The compilation of Scripture occurred within the context of the faith community, and the biblical documents represent the self-understanding of the community in which they were developed. As Paul Achtemeier notes, the "major significance of the Bible is not that it is a book, but rather that it reflects the life of the community of Israel and the primitive church, as those communities sought to come to terms with the central reality that God was present with them in ways that regularly outran their ability to understand or cope."[68] Scripture witnesses to the claim that it is the final written deposit of a trajectory or a traditioning that incorporates a number of varied elements in its composition, including oral tradition and other source documents. The community of faith recognized these writings as authoritative materials, and these materials in turn were interpreted and reapplied to the various contemporary situations. Under the guidance of the Holy Spirit, the community engaged in the task of preserving the canonical documents for the sake of the community's continuity. These writings contain the literary witness to the events that gave shape to the community, the prophetic interpretation of those events, and the various context-sensitive instructions regarding the implications of those events for the community's ongoing life.

That same faith community has corporately confessed the Spirit-inspired character of the canonical texts as a distinctive collection of documents to which it makes itself accountable.[69] Awareness of the role of the community in the production of the writings of Scripture, that is, to the process of traditioning present already within the biblical era, leads to a broader concept of inspiration. While inspiration includes

67. Dulles, *Craft of Theology*, 96.
68. Paul J. Achtemeier, *The Inspiration of Scripture* (Philadelphia: Westminster, 1980), 92.
69. Gabriel Fackre, *The Christian Story: A Narrative Interpretation of Basic Christian Doctrine*, 3rd ed. (Grand Rapids: Eerdmans, 1996), 19.

the composition of particular writings produced by individuals, it also incorporates the work of the Triune God in the midst of the Hebrew and early Christian communities, leading these people to participate in the process of bringing Scripture into being. By extension, the direction of the Spirit permeated the entire process that climaxed in the coming together of the canon as the book of the Christian community. Thus, although the church precedes Scripture chronologically and is responsible for its formation, it has nevertheless, by its own corporate affirmation in the establishment of the canon, made itself accountable to Scripture as the norming norm for its life, faith, and practice. In this sense, the text shapes the community.

What unifies this relationship between Scripture and the communal tradition of the church is the work of the Spirit. It is the Spirit who stands behind both the development and the formation of the community as well as the production of the biblical documents and their coming together into a single canon as that community's authoritative text. The community found these documents to be the vehicle through which they were addressed by the Spirit of God. The illuminating work of the Spirit brought forth these writings from the context of the community in accordance with the witness of that community. This work of illumination did not cease with the closing of the canon. Rather, it continues as the Spirit attunes the contemporary community of faith to understand Scripture and to apply it afresh to its own context in accordance with the intentions of the Spirit.

The contemporary process of illumination parallels that experienced by the ancient faith community insofar as the Bible contains materials that represent the community's appropriation of the writings and oral traditions of its tradition. Some of these materials were rejected with respect to their inclusion in the canon insofar as they were deemed to be contrary to the established trajectory of the community. Hence, Scripture contains sharp critique and condemnation of some of the attitudes and actions of the ancient faith community. At the same time, however, there is also a significant difference between the experience of the ancient faith community and our relationship to Scripture. The people of Israel and the early Christian community engaged in the interpretive task *within* the process of the formation of the canon. Since the closure of the canon, the Christian community receives the illumination of the Spirit speaking through canonical Scripture. Thus, in terms of the relationship between Scripture and the tradition of the church, canonical Scripture is on the one hand constitutive of the church, providing the primary narratives around which the life and faith of the Christian community are shaped and formed. On the other hand, it is itself derived from that community and its authority. In the divine economy,

Scripture and tradition are in this manner inseparably bound together through the work of the Spirit.

For this reason, to suggest that the Protestant slogan *sola scriptura* implies an authority apart from the tradition of the church, its creeds, teachings, and liturgy is to transform the formula into an oxymoron.[70] Separating Scripture and the church in such a manner was certainly not the intention of the Reformers. Indeed, historian Heiko Oberman contends that the issue of the Reformation was not Scripture *or* tradition but rather the struggle between two differing concepts of tradition.[71] Commenting on the role of the community in the process that led to the production and identification of Scripture, Achtemeier notes, "If it is true, therefore, that the church, by its production of Scripture, created materials which stood over it in judgment and admonition, it is also true that Scripture would not have existed save for the community and its faith out of which Scripture grew. That means that church and Scripture are joint effects of the working out of the event of Christ."[72] This "working out" is carried on under the guidance and illumination of the Spirit.

In this conception, the authority of both Scripture and tradition is ultimately an authority derived from the work of the Spirit. Each is part of an organic unity so that even though Scripture and tradition are distinguishable, they are fundamentally inseparable. In other words, neither Scripture nor tradition is inherently authoritative in the foundationalist sense of providing self-evident, noninferential, and incorrigible grounds for constructing theological assertions. The authority of each, tradition as well as Scripture, is contingent on the work of the Spirit, and both Scripture and tradition are central components within an interrelated web of beliefs that constitutes the Christian faith. To misconstrue the shape of this relationship by setting Scripture over against tradition or by elevating tradition above Scripture is to fail to comprehend properly the work of the Spirit. Moreover, to do so is, in the final analysis, a distortion of the authority of the Triune God in the church.

The same illuminating work of the Spirit that served to guide the community in the process of the composition, compilation, and canonization of Scripture continues to lead and direct that community by speaking through the texts of Scripture. In this way, the action of the Spirit enables the Christian community to fulfill its task of living

70. Robert Jenson, *Systematic Theology*, vol. 1, *The Triune God* (New York: Oxford University Press, 1997), 28.

71. Heiko A. Oberman, "Quo Vadis? Tradition from Irenaeus to Humani Generis," *Scottish Journal of Theology* 16 (1963): 225–55.

72. Achtemeier, *Inspiration of Scripture*, 116.

as the people of God in the various historical and cultural locations in which it is situated. This broader conception of the Spirit's guidance and illumination in the production of Scripture and the ongoing life of the community leads not only to a more adequate understanding of the process by which Scripture came into being but also to a greater appreciation for the theological significance of the tradition of the Christian community.

The Christian tradition provides an important reference point and numerous resources for the contemporary community in its struggle to understand the meaning of Scripture and to engage in the task of theology in the context of the complex issues that characterize the present age. This raises the question, How does the Christian tradition provide these resources? Or put another way, How does the Christian tradition function in the task of theology?

Tradition: Theology's Hermeneutical Trajectory

In responding to this question, we must begin with the nature of tradition itself. According to Alasdair MacIntyre, a tradition begins with a contingent historical starting point, most often a text or a set of related texts, and develops as a historically extended, socially embodied argument as to how best to interpret and apply the formative text(s).[73] Based on this conception of tradition in general, we can conceive of the Christian tradition as the history of the interpretation and application of canonical Scripture by the Christian community, the church, as it listens to the voice of the Spirit speaking through the text. The Christian tradition is comprised of the historical attempts by the Christian community to explicate and translate faithfully the first-order language, symbols, and practices of the Christian faith, arising from the interaction among community, text, and culture, for the various social and cultural contexts in which that community has been situated. In this understanding, tradition is viewed not as a static but as a living, dynamic concept in which development and growth occur. A tradition grows as it confronts new challenges and as it faces new situations and difficulties over the course of time and in various contexts. The Christian tradition is thus characterized by both continuity and change as the faith community, under the guidance of the Spirit, grapples with the interaction

---

73. Alasdair MacIntyre, *Whose Justice? Which Rationality?* (Notre Dame: University of Notre Dame Press, 1988); and idem, *Three Rival Versions of Moral Enquiry: Encyclopaedia, Genealogy, and Tradition* (Notre Dame: University of Notre Dame Press, 1990).

between Scripture and the particular challenges of changing contexts and situations.

As we examine this past today, we gain wisdom and insight from the results of the Spirit-guided reflection of the community on Scripture. Gabriel Fackre rightly notes that the gift of the Christian community "comes to us in creed and council, catechism and confession, dialogue and proclamation. It meets us in the ancient lore of the Church and the present learnings of the Christian community. This common life and its wisdom, brought to us by the constant activity of the Holy Spirit, is a fundamental resource in our engagement with the biblical source."[74] Insofar as the tradition of the Christian church is the product of the ongoing reflection of the Christian community on the biblical message, it is in many respects an extension of the authority of Scripture. Thus, theologian Thomas Oden suggests that the history of theology may be viewed in large measure as the history of biblical exegesis.[75] In addition to mediating the *kerygma*, the narrative of God's redemptive action toward human beings, Scripture also provides a record of some of the basic Christian teachings and practices that developed in the earliest church. The canonical documents witness to these teachings and the concern of the early church that these basic teachings be communicated from one generation of Christian believers to the next. The narratives of God's redemptive activity and these basic teachings and practices of the early Christian community constitute what Scripture calls "the faith which was once for all delivered to the saints" (Jude 3). This sense of passing on the teachings of the community from generation to generation is the most basic expression of the operation of tradition. Speaking of this body of early Christian beliefs, Robert Webber notes that its content "is basic to and even prior to theological formulation."[76] The contemporary believing community stands in the tradition of the ancient community, who maintained and passed on the basic body of beliefs on which the church reflects theologically.

Although this commitment to pass on "the faith once delivered to the saints" is an important component of the Christian tradition, it can also be misconstrued and as a consequence used as the basis for oversimplifying a complex phenomenon. The assumption that tradition comprises an unchanged body of Christian doctrines articulated by the ancient church for all time fails to comprehend properly the dynamic

74. Fackre, *Christian Story*, 18.
75. Thomas C. Oden, *Systematic Theology: The Living God* (San Francisco: Harper & Row, 1987), xiii.
76. Robert Webber, *Common Roots: A Call to Evangelical Maturity* (Grand Rapids: Zondervan, 1979), 139.

character of tradition, viewing it instead in static terms. The dynamism of tradition, however, emerges out of its very nature within the life of the faith community. From its inception, the Christian community has been concerned with the task of proclaiming the message of the gospel to the world so that all people might know and experience the love of God. In keeping with this concern, the church has undertaken the mission of establishing communities of believers throughout the world. As a consequence, the Christian church has been located in a variety of social, historical, and cultural contexts, and it has faced the numerous challenges presented by these various situations. These challenges have called on the church to exercise wisdom and creative judgment in addressing questions in a manner that best promotes its mission to proclaim the gospel and to establish communities of Christ's disciples. A canonical example of this activity is the story of the Jerusalem Council (Acts 15), in which the church had to address the cultural issues raised by the conversion of Gentiles and their coexistence in the community of the new covenant with ethnic Jews who were concerned to preserve their social distinctiveness. Viewed from this perspective, tradition is comprised of the ongoing deposit of wisdom emerging from the dynamic movement of the community under the Spirit's guidance.

The multicultural character of the Christian community alerts us to an additional insight about tradition. As observed, all expressions of the faith are contextualized. This includes not only the confessions, creeds, and theological constructions of the church but also the content of the biblical documents themselves. All texts of the Christian faith were formulated within the social, cultural, linguistic, and philosophical frameworks of the times in which they were produced. This observation alerts us to the incarnational character of the Bible and the challenges of contextualizing its message in new, varied, and changing settings. It calls for a multifaceted understanding of the tradition of the church as a source for theology. The Christian tradition, viewed as a series of local theologies, serves as a resource for theology, not as a final arbiter of theological issues or concerns but by providing a hermeneutical context or trajectory for the theological task. These resources are available in the history of Christian theology, past theological formulations, the history of Christian worship, and the practices of the Christian community. They serve to assist the church in the task of proclaiming the faith in the contemporary setting.

An aspect of the tradition of the Christian church that is particularly beneficial to the task of theology is the complex and multifaceted story of theological history that describes the responses of the Christian community to past challenges. Throughout its history, the church has continually sought to proclaim and affirm the gospel in the context of specific cultural situations. The story of theological history is the narrative of the attempts by the Christian community to explicate the gospel message within these shifting historical circumstances. This theological history is important for contemporary theology for a number of reasons. Previous theological models and constructions are helpful for theology because they provide the present community with a record of the failures of past efforts. Ideas have consequences, but the long-term consequences of ideas are seldom fully discernible. The history of theology provides the opportunity to observe the long-term consequences of various theological formulations and approaches to theology in a number of contexts. Some of these formulations and approaches have clearly failed to sustain the community throughout its history. For example, overly accommodationist approaches to the relationship between theology and culture have had devastating consequences for the church. Perhaps the most telling example of such accommodation has been the close linking of Christian faith with the goals and aspirations of particular nationalities or political ideologies at the cost of faithfulness to the gospel and the integrity of the community.

The history of theology also brings us into contact with another type of failure, namely, what has traditionally been labeled heresy. Awareness of those thinkers whose ideas about theology and the Christian faith have been rejected by the Christian community remains instructive for contemporary theology. As Roger Olson points out, it is "almost impossible to appreciate the meaning of orthodoxy without understanding the heresies that forced its development."[77] The Christian community did not simply receive orthodox belief and pass it on in a static fashion. Rather, the community struggled to determine the content and the application of orthodoxy in ways that were faithful to the canonical narratives. This process grew through the challenges presented by those whose teachings were eventually deemed heretical. Paraphrasing Luther, God sometimes strikes significant blows with a crooked stick. In other words, those who have held views declared heretical by the church have often been of great importance in the development of theology. We saw a striking example of this in the work of Origen. While many of his ideas were eventually declared unorthodox, his contribution to the development of early Christian thought and his intellectual achievement place him among the most significant theologians in the history of the church. His speculative theology provided the impetus for much of the theological reflection of the early Christian community, and his essential vision

---

77. Roger Olson, *The Story of Christian Theology: Twenty Centuries of Tradition and Reform* (Downers Grove, IL: InterVarsity, 1999), 21.

of the Christian faith has remained highly influential throughout the history of the church.

More importantly, however, the history of theology suggests directions that may hold promise for contemporary attempts of the community to fulfill its calling. Especially important in this respect are those formulations, symbols, and practices that have emerged from the history of worship and theology and have come to be regarded as classic in the collective memory of the Christian church. Such theological formulations, symbols, and communal practices have survived the test of time and have remained an integral part of the life of the Christian community in its various cultural locations. For example, the near universal acceptance by the worldwide Christian community of ecumenical statements such as the Apostles' Creed and the Nicene Creed makes these symbols of the faith a vital resource for theology. Fackre highlights this aspect of the tradition viewed as an ecumenical consensus inherited from the past: "Found in both official documents and formal statements of the undivided Church, such as the Apostles' and Nicene Creeds, the doctrines of the Person of Christ and the trinity, the patterns of affirmation implicit in the worship and working of faith of the church universal, tradition is a weighty resource in Christian theology."[78] These statements and symbols of the historical community stand as milestones in the thought and life of the church universal and therefore have a special, ongoing significance for the work of theology.

The role of classic theological formulations is made clearer when we recall the broader historical implications of Christian confessions of faith for our own confession and our own theological statements. Throughout the history of the church, Christian believers from successive generations and various locations have confessed and witnessed to faith in the God revealed in Christ. In this act, they have participated in the faith of the one church and have been co-confessors with all who have acknowledged the one faith throughout the ages. In confessing the one faith of the church in the present, we become the contemporary embodiment of the legacy of faith that spans the ages and encompasses all the host of faithful believers. Rather than standing alone in this act, we confess our faith in solidarity with the entire company of the church universal. Hence, although our expression of faith is contemporary, in keeping with the task of proclaiming the gospel to the age in which we live, it also places us in continuity with the faith of the one people of God, including both our forebears, who made this confession in ages past, and our successors, who will do so in the future.

78. Fackre, *Christian Story*, 18.

When we engage in the second-order task of theology, therefore, we do so conscious that we stand in the context of a community of faith that extends through the centuries and that has engaged in this task before us. Because we are members of this continuous historical community, the theological tradition of the church must be a crucial component in the construction of contemporary theological statements. In this way, we maintain our theological or confessional unity with the one church of Jesus Christ. Formulations and symbols that have stood the test of time and have received broad affirmation among Christians of many generations and in many contexts comprise a type of "ecumenical theology." This ecumenical theology has come to expression as well in the great corpus of theological literature written over the centuries. The library of theological literature can be read with great benefit in the contemporary context, providing a considerable resource for the task of theology.

Having asserted the essential significance of these past symbols of the faith, we must now voice an important reminder in keeping with the second-order nature of theology discussed in the previous chapter. These past creeds, confessions, and theological formulations are not binding in and of themselves. They are helpful in providing insight into the faith of the church in the past and in making us aware of the presuppositions of our own context. In addition, they stand as monuments to the community's reception and proclamation of the voice of the Spirit. Despite their great stature, such resources do not take the place of canonical Scripture as the community's constitutive authority. Moreover, they must always be tested by the norm of canonical Scripture. In addition, in reading the great theological literature, we must keep in mind the culturally situated nature of all such statements and that therefore they must be understood within their particular historical and cultural contexts. For this reason, it is the *intent* of the creeds, confessions, and formulations and not the specific construction and order of their wording that is significant for contemporary theology.

In these ways, the ongoing tradition of the Christian community provides the context in which to hear the Spirit's voice speaking through the canonical texts of Scripture in continuity with the church universal. This context establishes and provides a Spirit-directed hermeneutical trajectory for theological reflection. This hermeneutical trajectory is not institutionalized, as Roman Catholic theologians have argued, but must be discerned through participation in the fellowship of the Christian community and its practices of worship, prayer, Bible reading, and service, as well as through study of and reflection on the symbols and literature of the tradition. That is to say, the task of Christian theology begins with a commitment to and participation in the tradition of the church. To participate in the fellowship of the Christian community is to participate in this hermeneutical trajectory and to embrace the joint responsibilities of maintaining continuity with the community of the past and addressing the context in which the community is situated. Many thinkers are now aware that they can read and interpret Scripture properly only in light of hermeneutical history and the way in which the church uses the Bible. Clark Pinnock points out that in this way tradition becomes "a defense in the church against individualism in interpretation."[79] Concerning the function of *sola scriptura* in Protestantism, D. H. Williams warns that it "cannot be rightly and responsibly handled without reference to the historic Tradition of the church, and when it is, any heretical notion can arise taking sanction under a 'back to the Bible' platform."[80] Scripture and tradition must function together as coinherent aspects of the ongoing ministry of the Spirit.

These aspects of tradition are focused primarily on the beliefs of the church expressed in the history of theology and in classic formulations of Christian faith. Of course, these expressions of belief occupy a central place in the ongoing life of the Christian community. However, it is also important to remember that the beliefs are closely related to practices. While the two are distinguishable, they are not easily separated. Practices not only reflect formal beliefs but also shape them, such that it is not a simple matter to determine whether practices flow from beliefs or beliefs from practices. What need to be maintained are the ways in which beliefs and practices are inextricably bound together and are mutually reflective of each other. A focus on the practices of the church leads to two additional aspects concerning the resources of tradition in the task of theology: the history of Christian worship and the ongoing performance of the Christian church through the ages.

One of the most significant though often overlooked aspects of the Christian tradition is the history of worship and liturgy. The content and form of Christian worship throughout the history of the church provides an understanding of the context in which theologians have worked and insight into the primary commitments of the church. Recently, a renewed emphasis on the role of faith for theology has reminded us that theologians have not worked in isolation from the church, producing systems of theology untouched by the concerns of the community. Theologians are part of the community that prays and worships, and this context informs the nature and the shape of their theological reflection. The

79. Clark H. Pinnock, *The Scripture Principle* (San Francisco: Harper & Row, 1984), 217.

80. D. H. Williams, *Retrieving the Tradition and Renewing Evangelicalism: A Primer for Suspicious Protestants* (Grand Rapids: Eerdmans, 2001), 234.

phrase *lex orandi, lex credendi,* the way you pray determines what you believe, addresses the intimate connection between the life of prayer and the content of faith, pointing to the interaction between theology and worship. What Christians believe shapes the content and the approach of their worship, and their worship reflects what they believe. This points to the importance of liturgical history as providing insight into the first-order commitments of the Christian community that have shaped its theological reflection.

Contemporary theologians have recently developed a renewed interest in the relationship between worship and theology. Of particular significance is the work of Geoffrey Wainwright, whose systematic theology is written from the perspective of the liturgical forms of the church.[81] He examines the connection between liturgy and theology and draws attention to the ways in which the earliest Christian communities incorporated theological motifs into worship. He points out that the liturgy of the church is not simply or purely emotive in character; it includes intellectual elements as well, and the connection between the two is entirely natural. Thus, Wainwright suggests that doing theology from a liturgical perspective grounds theology in the life and faith of the historical and ecumenical Christian community by pointing to the beliefs and the concerns that have been expressed and emphasized in the forms and practices of Christian worship.

One final aspect of the function of the hermeneutical trajectory in the task of theology remains to be noted. This dimension emerges through the metaphor of performance. Tradition provides an interpretive context for the task of living out or "performing" the deepest intentions of an established, historical community. The ultimate purpose of theology is not simply to establish "right belief" but to assist the Christian community in its vocation to *live* as the people of God in the particular social-historical context in which it is situated. The goal of theology is to facilitate and enable authentic "performance" of the Christian faith by the community in its various cultural locations. Tradition provides an essential component in this process.

Like a Mozart symphony that has only one score but many possible interpretations, the text of Scripture has been subject to numerous interpretations over the centuries. While the score of a symphony is authoritative, it demands performance so that the intention for which it was produced can be realized. Performance requires interpretation. However, not all interpretations of Mozart have equal integrity in the history of the performance of his works; some are too radical or idio-

---

81. Geoffrey Wainwright, *Doxology: The Praise of God in Worship, Doctrine, and Life* (New York: Oxford University Press, 1980).

syncratic. Determinations as to the legitimacy or the illegitimacy of particular interpretations and performances emerge in the context of tradition. Frances Young offers a helpful perspective on the performative metaphor: "For classic performance, tradition is indispensable. A creative artist will certainly bring something inspired to the job, but an entirely novel performance would not be a rendering of the classic work. Traditions about appropriate speed and dynamics are passed from master (or mistress) to pupil, from one generation to another, and a radical performance will be deliberate reaction against those traditions if it violates them."[82] The tradition of the Christian community functions in much the same manner. It establishes a context for authentic interpretation and performance of the biblical message and its implications, which allows for creativity in addressing new situations while providing a basis for identifying an interpretation that is not consonant with the historic position of the community.

N. T. Wright suggests a model of biblical authority that moves along similar lines.[83] He uses the analogy of a five act Shakespeare play in which the first four acts are extant but the fifth has been lost. In this model, the performance of the fifth act is facilitated not by the writing of a script that "would freeze the play into one form" but by the recruitment of "highly trained, sensitive, and experienced Shakespearean actors" who immerse themselves in the first four acts and then are told "to work out a fifth act for themselves."[84] The first four acts serve as the "authority" for the play, but not in the sense of demanding that the actors "repeat the earlier parts of the play over and over again." Instead, the authority of the extant acts functions in the context of an ongoing and unfinished drama that "contained its own impetus, its own forward movement, which demanded to be concluded in the proper manner but which required of the actors a responsible entering in to the story as it stood, in order to first understand how the threads could appropriately be drawn together, and then to put that understanding into effect by speaking and acting with both *innovation* and *consistency*."[85] Wright then suggests that this model closely corresponds to the pattern of the biblical narratives.

Such a model brings the role of Christian tradition in the task of theology into sharp relief. A key component of Wright's model, although

82. Frances Young, *The Art of Performance: Toward a Theology of Holy Scripture* (London: Darton, Longman, & Todd, 1990), 45.

83. N. T. Wright, "How Can the Bible Be Authoritative?" *Vox Evangelica* 21 (1991): 7–32.

84. Ibid., 18.

85. Ibid., 19.

not one he emphasizes, is the role of tradition. His actors are immersed not only in the first acts of the play, the textual authority, but also in the Shakespearean interpretive *tradition*, which also functions in an authoritative fashion, albeit a secondary one, in the performance of the final act. The Christian tradition provides a historically extended, socially embodied context in which to interpret, apply, and live out the communally formative narratives contained in the canonical texts. In this manner, the biblical narratives function as the norming norm for Christian faith and life. Nevertheless, the tradition of the community, with respect to both its beliefs and its practices, provides a crucial and indispensable hermeneutical context and trajectory for the task of constructing Christian theology that addresses contemporary settings and concerns while remaining in continuity with the ministry and the witness of the church in its historical and global iterations.

In conclusion, this construal of the task of theology is intended to provide the context for the development of an open and flexible theology that is normed by the witness of canonical Scripture, sensitive and alert to the challenges and opportunities of various cultural contexts, and in continuity with the tradition of the church. Such an approach will result in the production of multiple models of local theological reflection that share in the commitment to follow the guidance of the Spirit and to bear faithful witness to the one faith. Insofar as they share this commitment, these models of Christian faith will find a broad coherence and a family resemblance in their various local and contextual interpretations of a trinitarian theology centered on Jesus Christ.

The construction of such models does not, however, constitute the end of the theological enterprise. Rather, the purpose of theology is to serve the believing community by assisting it in its missional vocation to live as the people of God in a particular setting. Theology does not simply serve itself; it should make a difference in the life and witness of the church. Christian theology ought to help clarify the ways in which Christian faith should be lived and provide motivation and encouragement for Christians, individually and corporately, to live in accordance with their commitments. Good theology must be related to life and ethics and should promote the love of God and nourish godly practice and living in the context of the Christian community as well as in society at large. It is to this purpose of theology that we now turn our attention.

The Purpose of Theology

In addressing the purpose of theology, we are asking the why question. Why do we engage in the task of theology? What is the point and intention of doing theology in the first place? Is it to acquire a proper set of beliefs concerning God? Is it to correct false teaching? Of course, these matters are important, and Scripture identifies each of them as an aspect of the Christian life and the work of the church that requires attention. But they do not provide an ultimate answer to the question of why we do theology. Why do we need a proper set of beliefs about God, and why is it important to seek to correct inappropriate teaching?

Scripture provides a number of other assertions that may be connected to the purpose of theology. We are called to love God with the entirety of our being, including through the use of our minds (Matt. 22:37); to resist conformity to the patterns of the world and to be transformed through the renewing of our minds in accordance with the will of God (Rom. 12:2); to bring every thought into obedience to Christ (2 Cor. 10:5); and always to be prepared to give an answer to anyone who inquires as to the reason for the hope we have in Christ (1 Pet. 3:15). While these responsibilities reveal important perspectives concerning the character of theology, they still do not provide an answer concerning theology's overarching purpose. Why love God, seek transformation, discipline our thoughts, and be ready to give a reason for our hope?

The assertion in this chapter is that the purpose of theology is mission. Theology that is faithful to its subject engages in the life and the work of the church by articulating, assisting, promoting, and participating in the missional vocation of the church. Hence, theology that is properly attuned to its subject (God) and its focal point (the church) will be missional theology. The critical and constructive task of theology is pursued not simply to secure right belief or to correct false teaching but to assist in the promotion and the accomplishment of the mission of God. The commands to love God, be transformed, discipline our thoughts, and be ready to account for our hope are all connected to the calling and the participation of the church in the mission of God. This missional vocation should shape and orient all the beliefs and practices of the Christian community. This chapter explores the purpose of theology as that of assisting Christ's followers in their missional vocation to live as the people of God in the particular social-historical context in which they are situated. It begins with a discussion of the purpose of theology with respect to the formation and the establishment of community.

The last chapter maintained that the focal point of the critical and constructive task of theology is the church. Here the focus is on the purpose of theology in assisting and promoting the establishment of community in keeping with the social character of God and the divine mission. In other words, the work of establishing and being a community that reflects and represents the image of God is part of the mission of the church, which is sent by God into the world under the guidance and empowerment of the Spirit. Theology participates in this mission by assisting the work of the Spirit in the formation and the development of Christian community. To facilitate the exploration of this aspect of theology's purpose, we must first examine the concept of community.

The Concept of Community

To appreciate the concept of community, we must understand something of the ongoing conversation between contemporary individualists and communitarians. It has become commonplace to speak of contemporary Western society as the heir of two traditions that bear a distinct set of values. In particular, the American mind has been deeply stamped by both the individualist impulse and a strong sense of the importance of communal relationships. The presence of these two traditions is reflected in Robert Nisbet's appraisal of the American experience in the middle of the last century. On the one hand, Americans valued "equalitarian democracy, moral neutrality, intellectual liberation, secular progress, rationalism, and all the liberating impersonalities of modern industrial and political society." On the other hand, they continued "to venerate tradition, secure social status, the corporate hierarchies of kinship, religion, and community, and close involvement in clear moral contexts."[1]

The individualist tradition asserts the primacy of the individual person in all forms of social life and views contracts between individuals as the basis of all social interaction. This tradition promotes such values as personal freedom, self-improvement, privacy, achievement, independence, detachment, and self-interest. Although the exercise of these values may bring a person into contact with others, the essential meaning of such values is not connected to interaction among persons but to the rights and needs of individuals separate from their relationships with others.[2] Thus, lying at the heart of this tradition is what Robert Bellah calls "ontological individualism," that is, "the belief that the truth of our condition is not in our society or in our relation to others, but in our isolated and inviolable selves."[3] The individualist tradition is closely connected to liberal political theory. The modern conception of the political order is based on social atomism and the idea of the social contract. According to this theory, autonomous selves come together to form a state, contracting with one another to give up certain individual prerogatives to the whole for the sake of personal advantage.

The individualist tradition finds its roots in seventeenth- and eighteenth-century thinkers who sought to cope with the demise of the rigid status systems endemic to feudal society and the rise of the modern world characterized by a market economy, industrialization, specialization, and urbanization.[4] In response to the changing situation, philosophers such as Thomas Hobbes, David Hume, and Jeremy Bentham sought to provide an understanding of human nature that could justify the loss of the older communal social relationships. The emerging understanding looked to the contract between free persons rather than to custom or tradition as the basis for all human interactions. These thinkers maintained that social rules, economic structures, and even the forming of families were artificial arrangements of convenience derived from contracts between individuals who were able to attain personal identity and self-consciousness without them. On this basis, Hobbes

---

1. Robert A. Nisbet, *The Quest for Community: A Study in the Ethics of Order and Freedom* (New York: Oxford University Press, 1953), 212–13.

2. Gerry C. Heard, *Basic Values and Ethical Decisions: An Examination of Individualism and Community in American Society* (Malabar, FL: Robert E. Krieger, 1990), 3.

3. Robert N. Bellah, "Community Properly Understood: A Defense of 'Democratic Communitarianism,'" in *The Essential Communitarian Reader,* ed. Amitai Etzioni (Lanham, MD: Rowman & Littlefield, 1998), 17.

4. Robert A. Nisbet, *The Sociological Tradition* (New York: Basic Books, 1966), 48–51.

broke with the past by elevating rights rather than responsibilities as
the foundational moral concept.[5]

In the American context, individualism took two forms. The first to
emerge was "utilitarian" individualism with its belief that in a society
that encouraged each person to vigorously pursue his or her own interests, "the social good would automatically emerge."[6] This attitude
was especially prevalent in the economic realm, where it fostered an
approach to capitalism that encouraged individuals to pursue their own
material interests. This utilitarian individualism spawned a reaction
among nineteenth-century thinkers such as Ralph Waldo Emerson and
Walt Whitman. They advocated a distinct form of individualism that
Donald Gelpi labels "expressive" individualism. "At the heart of each
person lies a unique core of intuition and feeling that demands creative expression and needs protection against the encroachments both
of other individuals and of social institutions."[7]

Individualism continues to be a powerful influence in contemporary
American society with its assumption that the autonomous self exists
independently of any tradition or community. For example, it continues
to be evident in the tendency of persons to define themselves primarily
through reference to the particular choices they make. According to
Robert Bellah and the other authors of the seminal study *Habits of the
Heart*, for most Americans, the meaning of life is "to become one's own
person, almost to give birth to oneself."[8] In keeping with this ideal,
American society encourages us "to cut free from the past, to define
our own selves, to choose the groups with which we wish to identify"
in order to participate in "the upward mobility of the middle-class individual who must leave home and church in order to succeed in an
impersonal world of rationality and competition."[9] The autonomous self
is understood by many contemporary observers as the primary context
in which the social and political structures of American culture have
taken shape.

Contrary to the views of individualism, the communal tradition emphasizes the social nature of human existence. It maintains that an
understanding of the self is formed by connections with other people,

---

5. Arthur J. Dyke, *Rethinking Rights and Responsibilities: The Moral Bonds of Community* (Cleveland: Pilgrim, 1992), 12.

6. Robert N. Bellah et al., *Habits of the Heart: Individualism and Commitment in
American Life* (New York: Harper & Row, 1986), 33.

7. Donald L. Gelpi, "Conversion: Beyond the Impasses of Individualism," in *Beyond
Individualism: Toward a Retrieval of Moral Disclosure in America*, ed. Donald L. Gelpi
(Notre Dame: University of Notre Dame Press, 1989), 2.

8. Bellah, *Habits of the Heart*, 82.

9. Ibid., 152–54.

institutions, and traditions. Thus, the communal tradition holds to the primacy of the group, elevates the importance of relationships for personal existence, and suggests that interaction among people takes on meaning only within the social context in which it occurs. It values relational qualities such as fellowship, belonging, dependence, social involvement, and the public good. Further, its advocates maintain that conceptions of what is right and proposals concerning the organization of society always presuppose a vision of the common good. Therefore, a society should promote civic ties and foster those institutions that form its citizens in accordance with the common good.[10] Until the Enlightenment, the communal tradition was deeply embedded in the fabric of society. Indeed, the notion that humans are social creatures was generally assumed from the time of Socrates until the seventeenth century.[11] After a period of decline coinciding with the rise of individualism, the communal tradition is undergoing a renaissance that can be traced to the work of thinkers such as Alasdair MacIntyre, Michael Sandel, and Charles Taylor, who are often referred to as "the new communitarians."[12] These thinkers have launched a sustained critique of liberal political theory and its orientation toward the language of rights.

From the communitarian perspective, the fundamental shortcoming of radical individualism is its disregard for the social dimension of life and its importance in the shaping of the self. Focused on the autonomous self, we have come to believe that we discover who we are and our deepest beliefs through intense self-examination and apart from the traditions and communities in which we participate. The language of radical individualism serves to blind us to the truth that we find ourselves "not independently of other people and institutions but through them. We never get to the bottom of our selves on our own." We come to know ourselves through our interaction with others and the activity that goes on "in relationships, groups, associations, and communities ordered by institutional structures and interpreted by cultural patterns of meaning." In short, "we are not simply ends in ourselves, either as individuals or as a society. We are parts of a larger whole that we can neither forget nor imagine in our own image without paying a high price."[13] In contrast to radical individualism, communitarians emphasize the notion of the social self and the importance of the social unit for certain crucial

10. David Fergusson, *Community, Liberalism, and Christian Ethics* (Cambridge: Cambridge University Press, 1998), 139.

11. Dyke, *Rethinking Rights and Responsibilities*, 12.

12. Amitai Etzioni, "Introduction: A Matter of Balance, Rights, and Responsibilities," in *Essential Communitarian Reader*, ix.

13. Bellah, *Habits of the Heart*, 84.

aspects of human existence. For instance, as mentioned earlier, community is integral to epistemology. Communitarians argue that we can no longer hold to the modern epistemological paradigm that focuses on the self-reflective, autonomous subject, since the knowing process is dependent on a cognitive framework mediated to the individual by the community. This critique forms the basis for the replacement of the individualistic, foundationalist rationalism of modernism with an understanding of knowledge and belief that views them as socially and linguistically constituted.

In the midst of this debate, some thinkers, such as Charles Taylor, have questioned the usefulness of the opposing labels, suggesting that the terms are too ill defined to be of genuine assistance.[14] Others are wary of the possible misunderstandings that the label communitarian may imply.[15] This is particularly a concern insofar as it is connected with either "majoritarianism," the view that "the values of the community or the will of the majority should always prevail," or "the idea that rights should rest on the values that predominate in any given community at any given time."[16] Hence, the concern to retain some of the significant gains of political and social liberalism and to avoid the pitfalls of majoritarianism is common even among those who embrace the communitarian tradition. Reflecting on the movement, Amitai Etzioni observes that the "new communitarians made the question of balance between individual rights and social responsibilities, between autonomy and the common good, a major concern." He also notes that they assumed that a notion of a good society needs "to deal simultaneously with both dangers: with a society whose communal foundations are crumbling and with one in which they have risen to the point that they block out individual freedoms."[17] Hence, most contemporary communitarians acknowledge that genuine community emerges only through the promotion of independent judgment and honest self-expression as well as by refusing to minimize or ignore differences among individuals.

In light of this, recent years have seen a degree of convergence in the liberal-communitarian debate,[18] leading many social theorists to conclude that "the concepts of individualism and community are inter-

14. Charles Taylor, "Cross-Purposes: The Liberal-Communitarian Debate," in *Liberalism and the Moral Life*, ed. Nancy L. Rosenblum, 159–82 (Cambridge: Harvard University Press, 1989).

15. Daniel Bell, *Communitarianism and Its Critics* (Oxford: Clarendon Press, 1993), 4.

16. Michael J. Sandel, *Liberalism and the Limits of Justice*, 2nd ed. (Cambridge: Cambridge University Press, 1998), ix–x.

17. Etzioni, "Introduction," xi.

18. Fergusson, *Community, Liberalism, and Christian Ethics*, 149–55.

dependent. Each needs the presence of the other to be able to reach its highest level."[19] In other words, the phenomenon of human experience is always, simultaneously and inextricably, both social and individual. "There is no human being apart from the social group in which he or she participates, and there is no group apart from the individual members who constitute that group."[20] Seyla Benhabib typifies thinkers who see value in both positions. She borrows the communitarian thesis that traditions, communities, and practices shape our identities. At the same time, she advances the liberal concern for maintaining reflective distance, on the basis that it facilitates the ability to criticize, challenge, and question the content of these identities and the practices they prescribe.[21]

However, in spite of the movement toward convergence, it is important to note that differences between the two traditions remain. Michael Sandel offers a succinct characterization that both sets forth the key issue dividing the two positions and indicates the contribution of the communitarian proposal to social thought. He notes that what is at stake in the debate is not simply whether rights are important but more pointedly whether rights can be identified and justified in ways that do not presuppose a particular notion of the good life. "At issue is not whether individual or communal claims should carry greater weight but whether the principles of justice that govern the basic structure of society can be neutral with respect to the competing moral and religious convictions its citizens espouse. The fundamental question, in other words, is whether the right is prior to the good."[22]

This ongoing conversation about community and its relationship to individualism leads to a discussion concerning an appropriate definition of community. Like many such terms, it does not readily lend itself to a single agreed-upon definition. Even contemporary communitarians are not agreed as to what they mean by the term. In a critical assessment of the movement in which he closely examined the writings of leading communitarian theorists, Derek Phillips concludes that a normative understanding of community in communitarian thought includes four central characteristics. "A community is a group of people who live in a common territory, have a common history and shared values, participate together in various activities, and have a high degree of solidarity."[23] Yet

19. Heard, *Basic Values and Ethical Decisions*, 103.

20. Daniel A. Helminiak, "Human Solidarity and Collective Union in Christ," *Anglican Theological Review* 70, no. 1 (January 1988): 37.

21. Seyla Benhabib, *Situating the Self: Gender, Community, and Postmodernism in Contemporary Ethics* (New York: Routledge, 1992), 74.

22. Sandel, *Liberalism and the Limits of Justice*, x.

23. Derek L. Phillips, *Looking Backward: A Critical Appraisal of Communitarian Thought* (Princeton: Princeton University Press, 1993), 14.

such a definition does not pass muster among many communitarians. The first characteristic is viewed as being particularly problematic in that communities do not necessarily need to be geographically concentrated.[24] Perhaps the most obvious example of this phenomenon is a religious community whose members are widely dispersed but maintain an acute sense of constituting a single whole. Some thinkers suggest that scientists are another counterexample in that they form a particular, worldwide community. For instance, Arthur Dyke maintains that the description of science offered by Michael Polanyi provides a living example of a particular group, represented throughout the world, that pursues truth and can do so only as a community. "Scientists constitute a community characterized by (1) a common tradition; (2) a common purpose; (3) an apprentice system of education; and (4) a network of publications, appointments, and research, all subject to peer review and well-represented in societally supported educational and research institutions."[25] The difficulty of getting a handle on the idea is further complicated by the realization that people are members of several communities simultaneously and that community boundaries are fluid, overlapping, and even intertwined.[26]

The challenges of defining community and the lack of uniformity concerning the use of a particular definition may lead to the conclusion that the concept of community is too compromised to be of value. However, the widespread use of the term and the place it has gained in contemporary thought suggest that the notion of community remains fruitful, particularly from a Christian perspective in light of the social character of God and the significance of the theme in the biblical narrative. Hence, three central characteristics should shape our understanding of the notion of community.

First, a community consists of a group of people who are conscious that they share a similar frame of reference. This perspective is evident in Amitai Etzioni's assertion that "communities are webs of social relations that encompass shared meanings and above all shared values."[27] Participants in a particular community tend to have a similar outlook toward life. They are inclined to view the world in a similar manner, to examine and construe the world in a common fashion. As Peter Berger observes, every worldview is a conspiracy in which the conspirators construct "a social situation in which the particular world view is taken for granted. The individual who finds himself in this situation becomes

24. Etzioni, "Introduction," xiv.
25. Dyke, *Rethinking Rights and Responsibilities*, 219.
26. Etzioni, "Introduction," xv.
27. Ibid.

more prone every day to share its basic assumptions. That is, we change our world views (and thus our interpretations and reinterpretations of our biography) as we move from one social world to another."[28] In addition, participants of a particular community construct the symbolic world they inhabit using similar linguistic and symbolic tools and concepts, even if they are not all agreed concerning the meaning of their world-constructing symbols.

Second, a sense of group focus is functional in all communities. This aspect is perhaps the most common in the various definitions of community. For instance, Bellah and company explain that a community is "a group of people who are socially interdependent, who participate together in discussion and decision making," and who together share certain common practices "that both define the community and are nurtured by it."[29] The group-centered focus is also present in the conception of Arthur Dyke, who notes that a community "is an affiliated and mutually beneficial network of interdependent human beings who, as human beings, share what is requisite for forming and sustaining such a network."[30] This focus on the group produces a shared sense of identity among the members, whose attention is directed toward the group and its significance in their lives. One important aspect of this group identity is the belief that as participants in the community they engage in a common task. This sense of group identity facilitates a type of solidarity among the members. Being a member of a community entails "interdependencies that impose nonvoluntary moral obligations and create relationships of reciprocity." Members of the community share "a general and diffuse sense of solidarity with everyone else in the community: from those with whom they are most intimate to those in circles most removed from them personally. As members of the community, their responsibilities should run both to all other individual members and to the community as a whole."[31]

However, the group focus does not demand unanimity and uniformity of opinion among all group members. Rather, what is indicative of a community is a shared interest in participating in an ongoing discussion as to what constitutes the identity of the group. Bellah highlights what might be called the ongoing argumentative character of community life, noting that a good community is one in which there is argument and even conflict about the meaning and the implications of the

28. Peter L. Berger, *Invitation to Sociology: A Humanistic Perspective* (Garden City, NY: Doubleday, 1963), 63–64.
29. Bellah, *Habits of the Heart*, 333.
30. Dyke, *Rethinking Rights and Responsibilities*, 126.
31. Phillips, *Looking Backward*, 17.

shared values and goals and the means by which they are made real in everyday life. "Community is not about silent consensus; it is a form of intelligent, reflective life, in which there is indeed consensus, but where the consensus can be challenged and changed—often gradually, sometimes radically—over time." He concludes that what makes a group a community and not just a contractual association is the shared concern among its members with making the group a *good* group. In this way, participants in a particular community share the intention of determining and attempting to bring into being a vision of what they imagine to be a good community that reflects particular goals and values.[32]

Finally, the group orientation of a community leads members to draw a sense of personal identity from the community. This aspect of a community is addressed by Michael Sandel's "constitutive" conception of community. He maintains that to say the members of a society are bound by a sense of community is not merely to imply that they profess and pursue communitarian sentiments and aims. Rather, they understand their identity as being defined to some extent by the community of which they are a part. "For them, community describes not just what they *have* as fellow citizens but also what they *are*, not a relationship they choose (as in a voluntary association) but an attachment they discover, not merely an attribute but a constituent of their identity."[33] With this conception of community in mind, we now turn our attention to the calling of the church to live as the people, or the community, of God and the role of theology in assisting the church in its vocation to be a missional community.

The Church, Missional Community, and Theology

Simply stated, the mission of the church is to be the image of God and to carry on the mission of God in the world. Thus, the missional vocation of the church is to be the community of God, the representative of God in the world. As such, this community is a particular kind of community, namely, a missional community in keeping with the missional character of God. That this calling is carried out around the world in numerous and divergent social, historical, and cultural settings means that the precise contours and iterations of this missional vocation are reflected in a variety of ways that share a family resemblance. This section reflects broadly on the nature of this missional vocation and comments on the role of theology as a missional activity of the

32. Bellah, "Community Properly Understood," 16.
33. Sandel, *Liberalism and the Limits of Justice*, 150.

church. It begins with a discussion of the calling of the church to be a true community.

It should be obvious from the discussion of the concept of community that a group is not a community simply because it contains a plurality of persons. This is certainly true of the church as well. Simply because a person attends a church on a Sunday morning does not mean that he or she is a part of a true community. Even formal membership is no guarantee of being part of a community in the sense described above. People attend church for a variety of reasons: as a social activity, out of a sense of duty, because they are struggling with difficult circumstances, or simply because they always have. However, many of these persons do not experience community in the sense of identity formation.

Communitarian accounts of personal identity formation generally begin with a reminder of the self's dependency on a group. George Herbert Mead asserted that meaning is not an individual matter but rather is interpersonal or relational. The mind is not only individual but also a social phenomenon. Hence, one's personal identity is socially produced.[34] According to Mead, human development is a product of the process of social interaction in that the mind, critical thinking, and a sense of self are facilitated by participation in the social group.

Another voice in articulating the role of community in identity formation was that of the early twentieth-century philosopher Josiah Royce, who noted that people come to self-consciousness under the persistent influence of others.[35] On this basis, he concluded, "My life means nothing, either theoretically or practically, unless I am a member of a community."[36] More recently, thinkers such as Alasdair MacIntyre have linked communitarian understandings of the self, such as those maintained by Mead and Royce, with narrative theory. Like contemporary narrative thinkers, MacIntyre argues that humans are storytellers and that identity develops through the telling of a personal narrative in accordance with which our lives make sense.[37] On this basis, MacIntyre concludes that "what I am . . . is in key part what I inherit, a specific past that is present to some degree in my present. I find myself part of a history and that is generally to say, whether I like it or not, whether I recognize it or not, one of the bearers of a tradition."[38]

---

34. George Herbert Mead, *Mind, Self, and Society*, ed. Charles W. Morris (1934; reprint, Chicago: University of Chicago Press, 1962), 118–34.

35. Josiah Royce, *The World and the Individual* (New York: Macmillan, 1901), 261.

36. Josiah Royce, *The Problem of Christianity*, vol. 2 (New York: Macmillan, 1913), 313.

37. Alasdair MacIntyre, *After Virtue: A Study in Moral Theory*, 2nd ed. (Notre Dame: University of Notre Dame Press, 1984), 216.

38. Ibid., 221.

George Stroup provides a more detailed treatment of the narrative theory of personal identity and its relationship to community. Stroup maintains that identity is the pattern that memory retrieves from one's personal history and projects into the future. Identity emerges as a person, through the exercise of memory, selects certain events from his or her past and uses them as a basis for interpreting the significance of the whole of his or her life. This identity is not created merely from the "factual data" or the "chronicle" of the events of one's life but requires an "interpretive scheme" that provides the "plot" through which the chronicle makes sense. The interpretive framework, likewise, cannot be derived from the data of one's own life. Instead, it arises from one's social context or "tradition." For this reason, according to Stroup, personal identity is never a private reality. It has a communal element; it is shaped by the community in which the person is a participant. Such a community contributes to the formation of the self by mediating the communal narrative necessary for personal identity formation.[39]

The identity-conferring aspect of community leads to what sociologists call a "reference group."[40] According to Robert Nisbet and Robert Perrin, a person's reference group is the social group to which an individual "refers," either consciously or unconsciously, in the shaping of his or her attitudes, beliefs, and values or in the formation of conduct. "It is the social entity toward which he orients his aspirations, judgments, tastes, and even at times his profoundest moral or social values."[41] In this manner, "the reference group serves as both a standard for *comparison* of one's self with a set of norms, that is, for self-appraisal, and also as the *source* of the varied norms and values that operate in a given individual's life." More important than geographic proximity, a community's role as a person's reference group is a function of "the degree of *symbolic* interaction that is involved."[42] This suggests that whereas people are members of a variety of communities at any given time as well as throughout their lives, only a select few function as a reference group in the full sense of the term. Consequently, the community that functions as the ultimate reference group is the particular community from which people draw their basic sense of identity. This community functions as the primary reference group. It is the "community of reference."

39. George W. Stroup, *The Promise of Narrative Theology* (Atlanta: John Knox, 1981), 101–98.

40. Berger, *Invitation to Sociology,* 118.

41. Robert Nisbet and Robert G. Perrin, *The Social Bond,* 2nd ed. (New York: Knopf, 1977), 100.

42. Ibid., 103.

Communitarians point out that the role of a group as a community of reference is connected with its ability to forge a link to both the past and the future. A community has a history and is, in an important sense, constituted by that history, which begins in the past and extends into the future. This "constitutive narrative" does not view time merely as a continuous flow of generally meaningless events and occurrences but rather as a story in which the community interprets the present with a sense of transcendent purpose and thereby presents time as a meaningful whole.[43] This constitutive narrative begins with the paradigmatic event(s) that called the community into being. A community does not forget its past. It retells the story of its beginnings and the crucial milestones that mark its subsequent trajectory. This narrative also calls to mind persons who have embodied or exemplified the meaning of the community and who thereby serve as models for life in the present. More important than merely articulating past events, recalling the narrative retrieves the constitutive past for the sake of personal and communal life in the present. Put another way, reciting the constitutive narrative of the past places the contemporary community within the narrative that constituted its forebears as this particular community. This act retrieves the past, bringing it into the present, and thereby makes the community in the present the contemporary embodiment of a communal tradition that spans the years. By articulating the narrative in this identity-forming manner, a community functions as a community of memory.

However, the communal history does not end in the past or even in the present. Rather, it extends into the future and anticipates the further development of the community. A community senses that it is moving forward toward an ideal that it has not yet realized. Hence, it expectantly looks forward to the time when the purpose and goals of the community will be fully actualized. This future expectation serves as an ongoing admonition to its members to embody the communal vision in the present. In keeping this vision before its members, a community acts as a community of hope. In this way, the constitutive narrative of the community stretches from the ancient past to the future and provides a vantage point for life in the present. The narrative offers a plausible explanation of present existence, for it provides the overarching theme through which members of the community can view their lives and the present moment in history as a part of a story that transcends the present. In this manner, as the community retells its constitutive narrative, it functions as an interpretive community.

The telling of the constitutive narrative is accentuated through sacred practices that anthropologists call "rites of intensification," rituals that

---

43. Bellah, *Habits of the Heart*, 282.

"bring the community together, increase group solidarity, and reinforce commitment to the beliefs of the group."[44] Perhaps a more descriptive designation is "practices of commitment," acts that define the community way of life as well as the patterns of loyalty and obligation that keep the community alive.[45] Through participation in these acts, a sense of community emerges among the members through "a fusion of feeling and thought, of tradition and commitment, of membership and volition."[46]

This discussion of the way in which a community provides personal identity formation through constitutive narratives leads to an inquiry about the nature of the church as it is understood in the contemporary setting. As noted above, individualism and social atomism gave birth to the modern conception of the social and political order. This conception views the state as the product of autonomous selves voluntarily entering into a social contract so as to gain certain personal advantages. Voluntarist contractualism in political theory finds its ecclesiological counterpart in the view that the church is a voluntary association of individual believers whose identity precedes their presence in the congregation; their identity is constituted prior to their joining together to form the church. According to this model, the church is constituted by its members rather than constituting them. The members of the church are deemed to be complete "Christian selves" prior to and apart from their membership in the church. The church, in turn, is an aggregate of the individual Christians who "contract" with one another to form a Christian society. This contractual view of ecclesiology continues to typify much contemporary church life and is borne out by the sociological study of Bellah and his associates, who conclude that most Americans "see religion as something individual, prior to any organizational involvement."[47] Such individualism not only reduces the local congregation to a voluntary society but also demotes participation in the visible community from an essential to an optional dimension of Christian discipleship.

Contractual political theory has played an undeniably beneficial role in the development of Western democracy. Despite the important gains it has engendered, its link to modern individualism has had devastating effects, as the new communitarians point out. In a similar manner, contractual ecclesiology followed the development of Western democracy. Under the impulse of individualism, the contractual view easily devalues

44. Stephen A. Grunlan and Marvin K. Mayers, *Cultural Anthropology: A Christian Perspective*, 2nd ed. (Grand Rapids: Zondervan, 1988), 222.

45. Bellah, *Habits of the Heart*, 152–54.

46. Nisbet, *Sociological Tradition*, 48.

47. Bellah, *Habits of the Heart*, 226.

the church, reducing the community of Christ's disciples to little more than a lifestyle enclave, a society formed by persons united by their shared interest in certain religious practices or who believe that membership in a Christian group will contribute to their individual good. For this reason, the establishment of community in the church has become a pressing challenge and a concern in contemporary ecclesiology.

While in one sense the contemporary Western church has struggled to manifest true community, in another sense the church is a community through the work of the Spirit. The sociological perspective sketched out above provides a helpful vantage point from which to understand the church as a community. The church is the fellowship of those persons who gather around the narrative of God at work in the world according to the witness of the Bible. What is important to remember is that the God of this narrative is the one who constitutes the church. More specifically, the church is formed by the work of the Spirit speaking through Scripture for the purpose of "world" creation. This world is a social-communal world in accordance with the nature of God as social. By speaking through Scripture, centered as it is on the narrative of God, who acts on our behalf to fashion a new creation, the Spirit brings into being a new community, a fellowship of persons who gather around the name of Jesus Christ. Hence, the church is more than the aggregate of its members. It is a particular people shaped by a particular constitutive narrative, namely, the Spirit-appropriated, community-fashioning narrative of Scripture, which spans the ages stretching from creation to consummation. As the church retells this constitutive narrative, it functions as a community of memory and hope and provides an interpretive framework through which its members find meaning in their personal and communal stories.

Through the Spirit, participation in the life of the church links the present with the full scope of God's action in history, which spans the ages from the beginning (Gen. 1:1) to the end, with the consummation of the ages and the establishment of "a new heaven and a new earth" (Rev. 21:1). As a consequence of this shared narrative, Christians are in solidarity with one another around the globe and throughout history. In the local church, this solidarity works its way out in the practical dimensions of fellowship, support, and nurture that its members discover through their relationships with one another as a communal people. In this process, the church becomes what Daniel Migliore calls an "alternative community" that "gives the world reason to hope."[48] In short, as James McClendon succinctly states, the church is a community "under-

---

48. Daniel Migliore, *Faith Seeking Understanding* (Grand Rapids: Eerdmans, 1991), 192.

stood not as privileged access to God or to sacred status, but as sharing together in a storied life of obedient service to and with Christ."[49]

Viewing the world through the interpretive framework of the constituting narratives of the Christian faith enables us to see that the various social groups in which people participate all fall short of the community God is fashioning. In comparison to the divine community, all human relationships and societies are merely, in the words of Stanley Hauerwas, "splintered and tribal existence."[50] However, the failure of community in the present leads to two realizations. First, the work of the Spirit in establishing a community in keeping with the divine intention is an ongoing process. Hence, while the Spirit constitutes the disciples of Christ as a community, the Spirit also continues to speak through Scripture in the ongoing task of world formation and the further realization of the true community that God intends. Second, the Spirit's work of establishing true community is eschatological in character and will be completed only at the consummation of the age and the corresponding fulfillment of God's creative intentions. This awareness tempers our expectations concerning the depth of community we will be able to experience in the present, and it ought to dissuade us from talking too glibly about our ability to construct true community in the present. As Nicholas Lash helpfully reminds us, "Christians continue, for the most part, to talk rather too easily about the fact or possibility of 'true community,' as if a situation in which the reality and appearance of social relationships wholly corresponded could be realized at almost any point in space and time, given a modicum of selflessness and goodwill."[51] Hence, while we seek to engage in the task of constructing community under the guidance of the Spirit, we nevertheless wait expectantly for God to complete the divine work of bringing creation as a whole and the people of God in particular into the enjoyment of the fullness of community.

In regard to the role of theology in assisting the church in the establishment of community, while categories from the discipline of sociology can inform an understanding of community, they are not the primary categories. It is important to remember not to let these insights function as a generic reality called "community" that can supposedly be discovered through objective observation of the world and then fit into the life of the church. Such a procedure would suggest that the com-

49. James William McClendon Jr., *Ethics: Systematic Theology*, vol. 1 (Nashville: Abingdon, 1986), 28.

50. Stanley Hauerwas, *A Community of Character: Toward a Constructive Christian Ethic* (Notre Dame: University of Notre Dame Press, 1981), 92.

51. Nicholas Lash, *A Matter of Hope: A Theologian's Reflections on the Thought of Karl Marx* (London: Darton, Longman, & Todd, 1981), 75.

munity of Christ is simply a particular example of a more general reality. This foundationalist approach to community assumes the priority of sociology, viewed as an objective science that sets both the agenda and the methodological direction for theological reflection and construction. As John Milbank states, no such objective account, in the sense of something neutral, rational, and universal, is available. Hence, he asserts that it is "theology itself that will have to provide its own account of the final causes at work in human history, on the basis of its own particular, and historically specific faith." He concludes that social theory that is properly Christian is "first and foremost an *ecclesiology*, and only an account of other human societies to the extent that the Church defines itself, in its practice, as in continuity and discontinuity with these societies. As the Church is *already*, necessarily, by virtue of its institution, a 'reading' of other human societies, it becomes possible to consider ecclesiology as also a 'sociology.'"[52] Theology, then, and not sociology, must be the ultimate basis for speaking of the church as a community. While ad hoc and descriptive use may be made of secular disciplines such as sociology, the character of Christian theology must remain distinctively Christian. Hence, talk about the Christian church as a community takes its cue from the particularly Christian conception of God that informs a particularly Christian ecclesiology. As maintained in the last chapter, the Christian understanding of community is connected to the character of the Triune God revealed in Jesus Christ.

Consequently, at the heart of understanding the missional vocation of the church is the realization that our calling is to reflect the character of the social God of love. Since God is none other than the divine trinitarian persons in relationship, a relationship characterized by a mutuality that can only be described as love, the *imago Dei* is ultimately human persons in loving relationship as well. Only in relationship, as persons in community, are we able to reflect the fullness of the divine character.[53] Because the followers of Jesus are called to be the divine image, the church is essentially a community characterized by love after the pattern of the Creator.[54] Hence, the Christian conception of God provides the perspective from which to speak about the church as community. In light of this, an understanding of community will always be particular,

52. John Milbank, *Theology and Social Theory: Beyond Secular Reason* (Oxford: Basil Blackwell, 1990), 380.

53. On the implications of the social Trinity for the image of God, see Cornelius Plantinga Jr., "Images of God," in *Christian Faith and Practice in the Modern World*, ed. Mark A. Noll and David F. Wells, 59–67 (Grand Rapids: Eerdmans, 1988).

54. On this theme, see Miroslav Volf, *After Our Likeness: The Church as the Image of the Trinity* (Grand Rapids: Eerdmans, 1998).

never generic. Christian theology is concerned with the formation of particularly Christian conceptions of community. From the perspective of Christian faith, all human relationships should be measured from the perspective of the quest for true community, the establishment of which indicates the presence of the reign of God. This means that we should evaluate every social group on the basis of its potential for being a contribution to or an anticipation of participation in the divine life that God destines for us. In so doing, we engage in the task of taking every thought captive in obedience to Christ.

Thus, the purpose of theology is to assist in the promotion of a community that is particularly Christian and to promote and support the work of the Spirit in creating and establishing a community in keeping with the divine intention. As observed in the last chapter, the focal point of this task is the church and its calling to be the people of God. This means that Christian theology arises from the Christian community in order to serve that community in its missional vocation to live as the people of God. Theology, therefore, is thoroughly enmeshed in the life of the Christian community and is shaped by it. Those who are concerned that this commitment amounts to a compromise of free intellectual inquiry should remember that there is no universal or neutral human reason and that reason, as Nicholas Wolterstorff maintains, is "person specific" and "situation specific."[55] To be human is to be situated in the context of particular cultures and communities such that our respective communities and traditions, be they religious or secular, play an indispensable role in shaping our conceptions of rationality as well as the beliefs we deem most basic and central to them. These communally derived conceptions of rationality and basic beliefs become those things to which we appeal in the assessment of new ideas.

Hence, Christian theology is communitarian in that it is linked to the life of a particular community, namely, the community of the disciples of Jesus Christ. Classically, theology has been understood as faith seeking understanding. While faith involves a personal response to the gospel, this does not mean that theology is solely the faith of an individual believer seeking understanding. Our particular beliefs, and hence the content of our faith, are dependent on the community in which we are situated. Being a Christian entails participation in the fellowship of those who have come to know the Triune God through Jesus Christ by the Spirit. Theology is the work of the community seeking to understand the faith its members share. Thus, James McClendon declares, "Theology is al-

---

55. Nicholas Wolterstorff, "Can Belief in God Be Rational If It Has No Foundations?" in *Faith and Rationality: Faith and Belief in God,* ed. Alvin Plantinga and Nicholas Wolterstorff (Notre Dame: University of Notre Dame Press, 1983), 155.

ways theology of the community, not just of the individual Christian."[56] As the shared faith of the community seeking understanding, Christian theology is communitarian in both its derivation and its intention.

As noted in the previous chapter, a central task of theology is to express communal beliefs and values as well as the meaning of the symbols of the faith community. Theological construction involves the articulation of the particular convictions that are at the heart of a particular community and their implications for the life of the community. The purpose of this articulation is to provide a specifically Christian way of viewing the world and living in it. From this perspective, Christian theology is by its very nature church dogmatics, the articulation and the proclamation of the convictions of the community as it continues to seek understanding from the perspective of its faith.

The communitarian derivation and purpose of theology come into concrete focus in an understanding of God. In addition to being faith seeking understanding, theology is also the study of God. As shown in chapter 2, however, this study is never simply generic. Instead, it is shaped by the assumptions of a linguistic and social context and is always the explication of the understanding set forth from a particular standpoint within a particular community. Hence, theology that is Christian speaks about the God known in the Christian community. Christian theology is the explication of the God witnessed to by the community, which has come to know God through Christ by the Spirit. Christians maintain that the only true God is the Triune God revealed in Jesus Christ and that Father, Son, and Holy Spirit participate in an eternal trinitarian fellowship of love. Hence, God is social, and the social character of God shapes the mission of the community of God to bear the divine image.

The concern for particularly Christian conceptions of community leads to an inquiry regarding the nature of community from a Christian perspective. As the metaphorical body of Christ, the Christian community is decisively shaped by the witness of Jesus in his life of intimate dependence on the Father and his ministry of self-sacrificial love. As such, the life of Jesus is the paradigmatic example of the life that Christians are called to lead and the witness they are to bear in the world for the sake of the gospel (Phil. 2:5–11). In this way, the Christian community is Christ-centered in its imitation of the life of Jesus. In its vocation to imitate Christ in the world by the power and guidance of the Holy Spirit, the church is also called to participate in the mission of God. As already discussed, God is not only social but also missional. The *missio Dei* was initially expressed in the act of creation, whereby the Triune God sought to extend the fellowship and the community of

56. McClendon, *Ethics*, 36.

love shared by Father, Son, and Holy Spirit. Thus, communities that are properly Christian are missional communities in keeping with the missional character of God.

In the same way that the church is called to be a community in response to the social character of God, the church is called to be a particular kind of commmunity in response to the missional character of God. Hence, all the beliefs and practices of the church are viewed in light of its missional calling. As we saw with respect to community, in one sense the church *is* a community by virtue of its constitution by God and the work of the Spirit. At the same time, the church can fail in its temporal situation to be what it is by divine constitution through the adoption of assumptions and practices that subtly (or not so subtly) undermine its central calling and convictions. The purpose of theology is to participate in the work of the Spirit and to assist the church in properly manifesting its calling as a contemporary community that anticipates the fullness of community that will be revealed at the consummation. In the same way, the church *is* a missional community as constituted by God and through the work of the Spirit, yet it can fail in its temporal situation to be what it is by divine constitution due to faulty beliefs and practices. Once again the purpose of theology is to participate in the work of the Spirit and to assist the community in realizing and working out its calling to be a missional community. As shown in chapter 2, the missional nature of the Christian community means that the church is missional in its very character, not simply that it engages in activities that are connected with a sense of mission. "A proper, biblical ecclesiology looks at everything the church is and does in relation to the mission of God in the world. The church does not exist for itself, but for participation in God's mission of reconciliation." From this perspective, mission is not simply "an activity carried out by special people in faraway places. Mission is the character of the church in whatever context it exists."[57]

In its critical and constructive reflection on the beliefs and practices of the church, the discipline of theology seeks to foster the missional character of the Christian community so that it can be faithful in its vocation before God. Put another way, theology that bears faithful witness to its subject views its purpose as serving the focal point of its reflective activity, the church, with the intention of helping and enabling the church to be faithful in its calling. Hence, theology participates in the work of the Spirit through the articulation and the promotion of communal beliefs and practices that fund a missional community. A

---

57. Lois Y. Barrett, ed., *Treasure in Clay Jars: Patterns in Missional Faithfulness* (Grand Rapids: Eerdmans, 2004), ix–x.

contemporary example of this understanding of the task and purpose of theology is found in the work of the Gospel and Our Culture Network, which seeks to call the church back to its missional vocation through theological reflection on the convictions that are internal to the life and tradition of the church. Chapter 2 referred to the work of this group, particularly the conclusions of *Missional Church*, authored collectively by members of the network. Here we note two features of a more recent work, *Treasure in Clay Jars*, which are particularly germane to this discussion.

First, in an effort to make theological reflection concrete in the life of the church and to promote the establishment of missional beliefs and practices, the authors provide twelve indicators of a missional church with a brief sketch of what these look like in the life of particular communities. These indicators include the following: the church proclaims the gospel; the church is a community in which all members are involved in learning to become disciples of Jesus; the Bible is normative; the church understands itself as different from the world because of its participation in the life, death, and resurrection of the Lord; the church seeks to discern God's specific missional vocation for the entire community and for all its members; a missional community is indicated by how Christians behave toward one another; the church practices reconciliation; people within the church hold themselves accountable to one another in love; the church practices hospitality; worship is the central act by which the church celebrates with joy and thanksgiving both God's presence and God's promised future; the church has a vital public witness; and there is a recognition that the church itself is an incomplete expression of the reign of God.[58]

In a list such as this, we see concrete ways of expressing the shape of a missional community. Of course, these activities must always be subject to ongoing critical and constructive scrutiny to ensure that they retain their missional focus because specific practices can be pursued in ways that fail to reflect the missional character of the church. Take for instance the indicator that the Bible is normative in a missional church. We would expect this conviction to be manifested in the concrete practice of Bible study, which is the natural outgrowth of belief in the formative and constitutive nature of Scripture in the life of the church. However, as Darrell Guder points out, while virtually every Christian tradition affirms the centrality of Scripture for the church, it is possible "to be biblically centered, to expect and to experience biblical preaching, and not to be a church that acknowledges, much less practices, its missional calling." He goes on to

---

58. Walter C. Hobbs, "Method," in *Treasure in Clay Jars*, 160–61.

add that this is precisely the dilemma faced in the Western church. It has appropriated Scripture in such a way that the central emphasis on formation for mission has been missed. In this context, it is possible to see the gospel as being primarily about what God's grace does for individuals. "It is possible to take the Bible seriously, persuaded that it is primarily about one's personal salvation. It is possible to preach the Bible in such a way that the needs of persons are met but the formation of the whole community for its witness in the world is not emphasized. It is, in short, possible to be Bible-centered and not wholeheartedly missional."[59]

In this way, the practice of Bible study, as well as other practices of the church, can fail to promote the missional character of the church. "In such congregations, mission tends to be one of the many programs done by the community, rather than to define the very purpose and character of the community."[60] A missional community is a community that is shaped and formed by participating in the mission of God, which is a mission of reconciliation and redemption that seeks to set things right in a broken and corrupt world. "A missional congregation lets God's mission permeate everything that the congregation does—from worship to witness to training members for discipleship. It bridges the gap between outreach and congregational life, since, in its life together, the church is to embody God's mission."[61] Thus, missional churches see themselves not so much as sending as being sent, after the pattern of Christ, whose life and work shape their sense of calling and mission. In this way, in their character, convictions, and practices, missional communities are Christocentric in focus.

A second important feature of *Treasure in Clay Jars* is the conviction that the calling to be a missional community is a contextual one. While a missional church exhibits certain common practices, patterns, and indicators, there is no one proper way to manifest the missional calling of the Christian community. Part of the missional calling involves the constant engagement of particular and changing social and historical circumstances so the church can be an effective witness to the gospel. The nature of this engagement, if it is to be effective, must be dynamic and ongoing rather than static and formulaic.

As shown in chapter 4, part of the task of theology is to construct models that help facilitate this conversational engagement for the sake of the mission of the church. These models should be understood as inclusive or complementary rather than exclusive. For example, in his

---

59. Darrell L. Guder, "Biblical Formation and Discipleship," in *Treasure in Clay Jars,* 60.

60. Ibid., 61.

61. Barrett, *Treasure in Clay Jars,* x.

classic work *Christ and Culture*, H. Richard Niebuhr proposes five models concerning the appropriate relationship between Christ and culture: Christ against culture; Christ of culture; Christ above culture; Christ and culture in paradox; and Christ the transformer of culture.[62] Each of these five models is developed in relationship to the witness of Scripture and its influence in the history and tradition of the church. But instead of being portrayed as inclusive models, they are presented as exclusive models in which the task is to settle on which of the models is the correct position for the church. The case can be made, however, that each of these models can be supported by Scripture and tradition and that any of the five, or a combination of several, can be construed in missional terms and may be appropriate in various settings, depending on the particular circumstances in which the church finds itself.

The point here is that the specific nature of a missional community varies from place to place in accordance with particular social contexts and traditions of theological reflection. The purpose of theology, then, is not simply to determine the one correct model for missional engagement but to assist the church in its vocation to be a missional community through ongoing critical and constructive reflection on its beliefs and practices. One of the implications of this is that judgments about the quality of theology, the question of whether it is "good" theology, can be finally made only in the context of its social embodiment in the life of a particular community. How is theology lived out in the church? Does it promote the concerns of community and mission? Does it assist and serve the church in the formation of an authentically missional community? Such questions can be answered only through the corporate life and witness of the church.

This suggests two final points. First, the entire community has a stake in the work of theology and is invited to participate in its work. Theology is not simply abstract reflection on the literary texts of the Christian tradition by highly trained academic specialists in search of answers to the mysteries of God and human life. This does not mean that there is no place for professional theologians in the life of the church, only that they should not be viewed as being solely responsible for the contextualization of the gospel and the work of theology in the community. As Krikor Haleblian asserts, "The believing community in each culture must take responsibility for contextualizing the gospel, but there is a place and a need for professionals who can act as 'brokers' in this difficult and ongoing task."[63]

62. H. Richard Niebuhr, *Christ and Culture* (New York: Harper & Row, 1951).

63. Krikor Haleblian, "The Problem of Contextualization," *Missiology: An International Review* 11, no. 1 (January 1983): 99.

Second, in keeping with its contextual nature and missional purpose, theology is not simply an academic discipline. It should not take only discursive forms such as textbooks, lectures, and scholarly articles, with which it has generally been associated in the Western church since the rise of universities in the Middle Ages. In keeping with its purpose, theology may take many other forms, and it is important to realize that "theology is a wider activity than just scholarship and that various cultures have other preferred ways of articulating their faith. Works of art, hymns, stories, dramas, comic books, cinema—all these media can become valid forms for theology in particular cultures."[64]

To sum up: The purpose of theology is to participate in the work of the Spirit by assisting the community of Christ's followers in its missional vocation to live as the people of God, namely, as a Christ-centered missional community, in the particular social-historical context in which it is situated. Theology provides this assistance and service through ongoing critical and constructive reflection on the beliefs and practices of the church and the articulation of biblically normed, culturally relevant, and historically informed models of missional Christian faith centered on Jesus Christ in order to promote the establishment of missional Christian communities. This entails two additional aspects of theology's purpose that are related to the work of the Spirit and the missional vocation of the church: the promotion of the unity of the church and truth.

The Unity of the Church and Truth

In its participation in the work of the Spirit and service to the church, theology must seek to promote both the unity of the church and truth. This assertion arises from an examination of the biblical witness concerning the work of the Spirit and its implications for the communal and missional character of the church. Sadly, it has often seemed difficult for many in the church to relate the twin concerns of unity and truth as they are expressed in the New Testament: The church is called to manifest visible unity and to proclaim the truth of the gospel in word and deed. Both of these concerns are addressed in the New Testament as being under the guidance of the Spirit. The task of theology is to provide models and formulations of the Christian faith that support the work of the Spirit in establishing the unity of the church and truth. Concerning the unity of the church, Jesus prays for his disciples and

---

64. Stephen Bevans, *Models of Contextual Theology*, rev. ed. (Maryknoll, NY: Orbis, 2002), 17.

the church and asks that they may be one as he and the Father are one so that the world may believe he was sent by the Father:

> My prayer is not for them alone. I pray also for those who will believe in me through their message, that all of them may be one, Father, just as you are in me and I am in you. May they also be in us so that the world may believe that you have sent me. I have given them the glory that you gave me, that they may be one as we are one: I in them and you in me. May they be brought to complete unity to let the world know that you have sent me and have loved them even as you have loved me.
>
> John 17:20–23

The unity for which Jesus prays is a visible one that will bear witness to the world that Jesus was sent into the world by the Father. This indicates that the unity of the church is vitally connected with its life and witness and as such is a central aspect of its missional vocation.

The New Testament also bears witness to the work of the Spirit in promoting the unity for which Jesus prayed. The Spirit is at work forming one body out of many parts in which a diversity of gifts is given for the edification of the entire body (1 Cor. 12). This should be understood with respect to both the local church and the church universal. In the same way that various members of the local church contribute to the edification of the particular community of which they are a part, so churches and traditions should see themselves as a part of the larger body of Christ, in which each has particular gifts to bear but none is able to fulfill the missional calling on its own. As the metaphor of the body suggests, each of the members is dependent on the others for its overall health. The gifts provided by the Spirit to one segment of the body of Christ are intended for the benefit and the edification of the entire church. Likewise, if one part of the body suffers, all parts suffer.

The letter to the Ephesians urges the church to adopt practices that will promote peace in the church and to maintain the unity of the Spirit. "Be completely humble and gentle; be patient, bearing with one another in love. Make every effort to keep the unity of the Spirit through the bond of peace. There is one body and one Spirit—just as you were called to one hope when you were called—one Lord, one faith, one baptism; one God and Father of all, who is over all and through all and in all" (Eph. 4:2–6). The letter to Titus warns of the dangers of foolish controversies and arguments about the law because they are unprofitable and can lead to division in the church. Hence, divisive persons are not to be tolerated in the church after a second warning because by their promotion of discord and dissension they show themselves to be warped and sinful. Clearly, according to the witness of Scripture, the unity of the church is a matter of utmost importance that the Spirit is jealous to protect and that the members of the community are called on to preserve and promote.

These texts point to the importance of the visible unity of the church as a testimony to the world of the truth of the gospel. As a result, the church is called to make every effort to preserve the unity of the Spirit and to be vigilant in opposition to those who promote division in the church. In this way, promotion and preservation of the unity of the church are parts of its missional vocation. The mission of the church is vitally connected with an appropriate and visible manifestation of its unity. Failure to maintain this unity significantly compromises its mission and witness to the world. Part of the challenge is connected to the pervasive individualism in society, which leads to not only personal individualism and the notion of the autonomous self but also a sectarian individualism with respect to the church. This occurs when people think that their particular church or tradition is the sole bearer of truth and the only proper way to bear witness to the gospel. Such notions are the products of individualistic ecclesiologies that fail to comprehend the interconnectedness of the entire church as the one body of Christ in the world, though with diversity in its expression.

Good theology, that is, theology that serves the church in ways that are consonant with its missional vocation, must seek to promote and preserve the unity of the church in accordance with the work of the Spirit and the witness of Scripture. Theology seeks to develop constructions and formulations of Christian faith that promote and maintain the unity of the church and the interconnectedness and solidarity that are called forth by the metaphor of the church as the body of Christ. It is not divided but one. The interconnectedness and solidarity among churches points to the dual responsibilities involved in the missional calling of the church. It must bear witness to the gospel in the context of particular social, cultural, and historical circumstances while remaining faithful to the entire church in its historical and global expressions. The decisions made by any one church, denomination, or tradition will have implications for the entire church and its witness to the gospel. While the one faith takes on multiple expressions, not all expressions of the one faith are appropriate.

The problematic nature of some expressions of the faith points to the critical and constructive work of theology in the ongoing process of assessing tradition and reform in the life of the church. This also means that the unity of the church is not to be sought merely as an end in itself but rather as a unity centered on the truth of the gospel. The same Spirit who is portrayed in the New Testament as the Spirit of unity is also the Spirit of truth. In John 14, Jesus speaks to his disciples of the Counselor, the Holy Spirit, whom the Father will send in the name of Jesus and who will teach the disciples "all things" and will remind them of everything that Jesus had taught them (v. 26). In John 15, Jesus again makes reference to the Spirit as the Counselor, "the Spirit of truth who goes out from the Father" (v. 26). In John 16, Jesus speaks of the promised Spirit as the "Spirit of truth" who will guide the disciples into "all truth" (v. 13). Finally, 1 John 2 contains the admonition to trust the work of the Spirit, who guides the church into all truth (v. 27). In the witness of the New Testament, the Holy Spirit is pictured as the Spirit of truth as well as the Spirit of unity. The Spirit is concerned with the promotion and the establishment of both unity and truth in the church. While it is certainly true that the full manifestations of these aspects of the Spirit's work will be realized only at the eschaton, it is also true that the church is called to pursue these concerns as part of its missional calling so that what is promised, the fullness of unity and truth, may be anticipated in the present life of the church. The purpose of theology is to assist in the calling and the task of this realization.

This raises the question of accounting for both the diversity of the church (in light of the work of the Spirit in promoting unity in the church) and the sovereignty of God as Lord of the church. In other words, how might we account for the diversity of the church theologically? The work of the Spirit and the sovereignty of God imply that the diversity in the Christian tradition is by divine design and that in some sense it must be a good thing. Diversity in the church is not a problem to be overcome but rather a gift of the Holy Spirit. Of course, not all developments in the history of the church and theology have been helpful. Yet the diversity of orthodox biblical, theological, and confessional perspectives in the Christian tradition is a necessary and appropriate manifestation of the church, the body of Christ in the world, since no single linguistic context or interpretive community is able to bear fully adequate witness to the truth of the living God. The traditions of the Christian tradition, bound together by their commitment to common ecumenical concerns, all bear their distinctive gifts and treasures for the instruction and edification of the church in the shared task of teaching and bearing witness to the one faith.

We have already suggested that the models that theology constructs should be inclusive rather than exclusive in keeping with the nature and character of the infinite God, who defies the possibility of adequate description in any particular linguistic context or by a single exclusive model. From this standpoint, a diversity of models and perspectives is necessary both to bear appropriate witness to God in various local contexts and to avoid the distortion of the divine reality that would result from reliance on one exclusive model. In this way, the diversity of the church can be construed as the only missionally appropriate way to bear witness to the numerous social and cultural contexts that comprise the human experience and the only theologically adequate way to bear faithful witness to the living and infinite God, who both calls forth the mission and witness of the church and yet also transcends all human attempts to bear such witness.

The transcendence of God should not lead to the conclusion that all witness is therefore invalid and not trustworthy but rather that faithful witness demands multiple perspectives in order to do justice to the nature and character of God. The unity of the church is important in this process so that the models produced through the constructive task of theology will be naturally viewed as inclusive and complementary rather than exclusive and subject to the ongoing scrutiny of the entire church. This leads to the conclusion that the diverse witness of the unified church is the most beneficial context for bearing faithful witness to the subject of theology. In the context of a fragmented and divided church, theological models are too often construed as exclusive models, and they become the basis for turning the diversity of the church into the rationale for a sectarian approach to Christian faith and witness.

The unity of the church is not to be found in full agreement concerning all the teachings and practices of the church but rather in the living presence of Christ in the church. What marks a particular community as a Christian community is its Christ-centered focus, which shapes the missional character of its life together. By the gift of the Spirit, Christ not only serves as the example of Christian life and witness but is also a living presence in the midst of the church. As Thomas Oden observes, "The circle of the Christian tradition has an unusually wide circumference without ceasing to have a single, unifying center. It is Christ's living presence that unites a diverse tradition, yet that single center is experienced in richly different ways." He goes on to identify the ways in which this presence has been experienced in the different traditions of the church: sacramentally in liturgical traditions, spiritually in charismatic traditions, morally inspiring in liberal traditions, as the ground of social experiment in pietistic traditions, as the doctrinal teacher in scholastic traditions, as the word of Scripture in evangelical traditions, as the sanctifying power of persons and society in the Greek Orthodox tradition, and as grace perfecting nature in the Roman Catholic tradition. He concludes that these diverse traditions of the church "have experienced the living and risen Christ in spectacularly varied ways. But nothing else than the living Christ forms the center of this wide circumference."[65]

---

65. Thomas C. Oden, *After Modernity . . . What? Agenda for Theology* (Grand Rapids: Zondervan, 1990), 176–77.

C. S. Lewis has provided a helpful way of thinking about the church along these lines in the opening pages of his classic work *Mere Christianity*. He describes the church using the metaphor of a house containing "a hall out of which doors open into several rooms." The hall represents "mere" Christianity, or, expressed in another way, the orthodox consensus of the ecumenical church, while the rooms represent the existing communions and traditions in the church. Lewis states that the goal of the book is to help readers find their way into the hall, but he also makes it clear that readers should not suppose that the content of mere Christianity or ecumenical orthodoxy is an alternative to the creeds and confessions of existing communions, as if one could simply choose it in preference to a particular tradition. As he puts it, "It is in the rooms, not in the hall, that there are fires and chairs and meals. The hall is a place to wait in, a place to try various doors, not a place to live in. For that purpose the worst of the rooms (whichever that may be) is, I think, preferable." In other words, while the hall serves the important function of providing the structures for Christian unity, the rooms are the places where the "whole counsel of God" is worked out in the life and fabric of particular communities. Hence, the hall is not a place to live but rather a place to wait on the Lord for guidance in the process of finding a room and to begin to obey the rules common to the entire house. These rules require that "you must be asking which door is the true one; not which pleases you best by its paint and paneling. In plain language, the question should never be: 'Do I like that kind of service?' but 'Are these doctrines true: Is holiness here?'" He concludes by saying that once one has reached a room, it is important to be kind to those who have chosen other doors. "If they are wrong they need your prayers all the more; and if they are your enemies, then you are under orders to pray for them. That is one of the rules common to the whole house."[66]

This metaphor provides a helpful way of viewing the diversity and the unity of the church that maintains the importance of truth. The church is pictured as bearing a diverse and contextual witness to the gospel, reflecting the variety of perspectives contained in the biblical narratives and the variety of social and historical contexts in which the message of Scripture is received. Yet it is unified around the presence of Christ, a shared ecumenical orthodoxy, and an ongoing commitment to truth. This commitment to truth means that part of the missional vocation of the church is the ongoing pursuit of truth in the midst of its particular circumstances. Theology shares this commitment and serves the Christian community through the unwavering promotion of truth in the church and the world.

66. C. S. Lewis, *Mere Christianity* (New York: Macmillan, 1952), 11–12.

Some Christian thinkers have raised questions concerning assertions of the situated and contextual nature of all knowledge and the nonfoundational approach to theology articulated in chapters 1 and 2. They are concerned that the adoption of such conclusions amounts to the capitulation of theology and Christian faith to postmodern thought and the corresponding abandonment of robust truth claims. However, affirmation of the situated character of knowledge and the corresponding critique of foundationalism are not a matter of capitulating to postmodern thought but rather an attempt to think theologically about epistemology. As with all theological matters, a properly theological epistemology must be appropriate to the subject of theology. As noted in the first two chapters, this entails affirmation of the primacy of God and the dependency of human beings in all epistemic relations concerning the knowledge of God.

The emphasis on the primacy of the Christian community for epistemology and an understanding of the nature, task, and purpose of theology, coupled with the commitment of theology to truth, raises the question of justification, particularly in the midst of the plurality of convictional communities. How are we able to justify our convictions about truth in the face of competing claims from other communities of discourse? As James McClendon and James Smith point out, "We can neither ignore communities other than our own, nor, given the embedding of personal convictions in communities that generate the meaning and determine the conditions of the possible justification of a set, can we easily justify our convictions in universally satisfactory ways if the challenge to our convictions comes from a rival community."[67] In other words, how are we able to adjudicate convictions and beliefs that are deeply intertwined with our lives and the lives of the communities in which we participate and derive our identity?

If, as argued earlier, epistemology must be theological, so must the conception of justification. We cannot follow the track of philosophers who seem to assume that they, in the words of McClendon and Smith, "have attained a grand cosmic neutrality, far above the strife of systems. With their clean, convictionless slates they would set out on the quest, inviting the open-minded to come along and promising at the end of the road there would be inscribed on their tablets nothing but the truth impartially discerned."[68] Instead, we must engage the task of justification in the context of Christian convictions concerning the knowledge of God and of ourselves. What might a theological and nonfoundational

---

67. James William McClendon Jr. and James M. Smith, *Convictions: Defusing Religious Relativism*, rev. ed. (Valley Forge, PA: Trinity, 1994), 101.

68. Ibid., 101–2.

construal of justification look like that takes seriously the situated nature of human knowledge, the socially constructed nature of reality, the limitations of language, the epistemic primacy of God, and Christian convictions concerning revelation? While space does not permit a full-scale discussion, what follows briefly sketches its main features.

A nonfoundational and contextual account of justification views its task as an ongoing participatory process involving convictional communities rather than something to be accomplished objectively in a once-and-for-all fashion. McClendon and Smith identify three components that make up an important part of such a process: the language of the process, the loci of the process, and the social matrix of the process.[69]

In their conception of the linguistic dimension of justification, McClendon and Smith move away from a referential theory of language and set forth a position that, drawing on speech-act theory, affirms the situated and contextual character of language and its role in shaping the narrative worlds of those who participate in particular linguistic communities. The loci of the process involve what are usually called "ultimate criteria" in justification, concepts such as truth, justice, and peace. As with language, the particular criteria and their content are contextual and are communally specific, meaning that no single list or exposition will satisfy all communities of inquiry. For this reason, they prefer to think of these concepts not as criteria but as "possible loci of justification" and note that in spite of their contextual nature, these and other central notions "will appear as main intersections, junction points of reflection, criticism, debate, and correction" to all those who seek to justify their convictions.[70] Hence, these possible loci of justification provide places of interaction in a pluralist world between competing convictional communities in the process of justification. Finally, McClendon and Smith note that the social matrix of the process means that the language of a particular community is "never a hermetically sealed system, that it is never even static, but is in a constant process of adjustment to external as well as internal pressure."[71] This allows for the possibility of reform within communities and for conversation with other convictional communities as well as with the broader social contexts in which they are situated.

Through these three components, McClendon and Smith provide a general procedure for the process of justification that is nonfoundational and contextual without retreating from a robust commitment to truth. A specifically Christian account of truth and justification requires

69. Ibid., 149–79.
70. Ibid., 155.
71. Ibid., 108.

that these concerns be situated in the context of particularly Christian convictions. For instance, Karl Barth works out an account of the Word of God and the knowledge of God that grows out of the doctrine of the Trinity. More recently, Bruce Marshall has set forth a proposal that takes the epistemic primacy of the communal Christian belief in the Trinity as the starting point for a thoroughly Christian account of truth and justification. From a trinitarian position, he maintains that the Christian way of identifying God ought to have unrestricted primacy in the process of justifying belief and suggests a trinitarian construal of the concept of truth. While the proposals differ with respect to particular details, they are agreed on the centrality of the Trinity for Christian construals of truth and the knowledge of God. Marshall's work is particularly suggestive in his delineation of an approach to truth that arises from the identification of God as triune and the particular primacy of Jesus as the one in whom all things "hold together" according to the will of the Father.[72] The Spirit comes into view as "the one who empowers us to recognize the epistemic ultimacy of Jesus Christ" and as the one who teaches us how "to order all of our beliefs around the narratives which identify the Father's crucified and risen Son."[73] Thus, the distinctive epistemic role of the Son is inseparable from those of the Father and the Spirit. Marshall's work produces an account that develops distinctively Christian understandings of the coherence and pragmatic approaches to truth and justification in a trinitarian context in which truth is viewed as christologically coherent according to the will of the Father and pneumatologically effective through the ongoing work of the Spirit.

The ongoing work of the Spirit is manifest in the appropriation of the biblical narrative in order to speak to the church for the purpose of creating a socially constructed "world" that finds its coherence in Jesus Christ in accordance with and in anticipation of the "real" world as it is willed to be by the Father. However, the world as God wills it to be is not a present reality but rather lies in the eschatological future. Thus, while acknowledging that there is indeed a certain objective actuality to the world, it is important to recognize that this objectivity is not that of a static actuality existing outside of and co-temporally with socially and linguistically constructed realities. It is not what some may call "the world as it is." Instead, the biblical narratives set forth the objectivity of the world as God wills it. Hence, Jesus taught his disciples to pray, "Your will be done on earth as it is in heaven"

72. Bruce D. Marshall, *Trinity and Truth* (Cambridge: Cambridge University Press, 2000), 108–40.
73. Ibid., 181.

(Matt. 6:10). The "real" world is the future, eschatological world that God will establish in the new creation. Because this future reality is God's determined will for creation, as that which cannot be shaken (Heb. 12:26–28), it is far more real, objective, and actual than the present world, which is even now passing away (1 Cor. 7:31). In this way, the biblical narratives point to what may be called "eschatological realism."

In relating this eschatological realism to the insights of social constructionists, we note that human beings, as bearers of the divine image, are called to participate in God's work of constructing a world in the present that reflects God's eschatological will for creation. This call has a strongly linguistic dimension because of the role of language in the task of world construction. Through the constructive power of language, the Christian community anticipates the divine eschatological world that stands at the climax of the biblical narrative in which all creation finds its connectedness in Jesus Christ (Col. 1:17), who is the Word (John 1:1) and the ordering principle of the cosmos. Hence, Christian theology may be construed as Christocentric in its communitarian focus and Christotelic in its eschatological orientation. This eschatological future is anticipated in the present through the work of the Spirit, who leads the church into truth (1 John 2:27). From this perspective, the Christian community affirms truth, under the guidance of the Spirit, through the construction of a linguistic world that finds its coherence in Christ in accordance with the will of the Father. This community also participates in the Spirit-guided process of justification that is ultimately realized only in the eschatological completion of the Spirit's epistemic ministry. Such an approach, arising out of particularly Christian theological commitments, affirms the participation and the responsibility of the Christian community in a process of justification that is vigorous and robust, as well as nonfoundational and contextual, while securing the epistemic primacy of God as the one who establishes truth and works out its justification.

From this perspective, Lesslie Newbigin concludes that the convictional confidence that is proper to a Christian "is not the confidence of one who claims possession of demonstrable and indubitable knowledge. It is the confidence of one who had heard and answered the call that comes from God through whom and for whom all things are made: 'Follow me.'"[74] The purpose of theology is to assist the church in the establishment of Christ-centered missional communities that promote the unity of the church and the pursuit of truth in order to foster this

---

74. Lesslie Newbigin, *Proper Confidence: Faith, Doubt, and Certainty in Christian Discipleship* (Grand Rapids: Eerdmans, 1995), 105.

confidence for the sake of the gospel and the hope that it offers to a broken world. In this way, theology bears faithful witness to its subject and participates in the divine mission of reconciliation and redemption through the grace of the Lord Jesus Christ, the love of God, and the fellowship of the Holy Spirit.

Index